Brassey's **AIR COMBAT** Reader

D0964025

Brassey's **AIR COMBAT** Reader

Edited by

Walter J. Boyne

and

Philip Handleman

Potomac Books, Inc.
WASHINGTON, D.C.

First The History of War edition published in 2005

Copyright © 1999 by Potomac Books, Inc.

Published in the United States by Potomac Books, Inc.
(formerly Brassey's, Inc.). All rights reserved. No part of this book
may be reproduced by any form or by any means—electronic,
electrostatic, magnetic tape, mechanical, photocopying, recording,
or otherwise—without permission in writing from the publisher.

Library of Congress Cataloging-in-Publication Data

Brassey's air combat reader / edited by Walter J. Boyne and
Philip Handleman.—1st ed.
p.   cm.
Includes index.

1. Air warfare.   2. Military biography.
I. Boyne, Walter J., 1929–   .   II. Handleman, Philip.
UG630.B627   1999
358.4′3—dc21   99-13246
CIP

ISBN 1-57488-752-1 (paperback)

Designed by Pen & Palette Unlimited

First Edition

10 9 8 7 6 5 4 3

Credits

To military flight crews in the hope
that their skies will remain forever
at peace

Contents

Introduction

Looking back on his early military career, especially his assignments with the 4th Hussars campaigning across India's frontier and with the 21st Lancers charging the Dervishes at Omdurman, Winston Churchill lamented the demise of war as he had known it as a young man in the late nineteenth century. He proclaimed that those were the days of "spectacular conflicts" possessed of "majestic splendor" where "everything was visible to the naked eye."

For him, the finely outfitted horsemen of a cavalry division maneuvering at the trot evoked "a thrill and charm" and, when at a gallop, "joyous excitement." But Sir Winston lived to see the character of battle transformed forever, from being, in his words, "cruel and magnificent" to being "cruel and squalid." Recognizing the new face of war, the profound and irreversible impact of emerging technologies, the old warrior himself referred disparagingly to "chemists in spectacles and chauffeurs pulling the levers of aeroplanes or machine guns."

The airplane, a wholly new technology born at the dawn of the twentieth century, changed the methodology of warfare more meaningfully than any other emergent mechanized forms, for, at once, the third dimension was added to the battlefield. Fighting among nations would never again be defined merely in terms of movements to and fro.

The iterations of the ungainly wood-and-fabric flying contraption produced by the pair of ingenious Dayton bicycle makers sparked an industry that relatively quickly developed the airplane into a feared instrument of war. From tentative beginnings, the combat aircraft has progressively evolved to the point where today it bears little resemblance to its forebears: jet engines, advanced polymers, and guided missiles have replaced propellers, tin, and rifle bullets, respectively. Yet, an undeniable constant accompanying airplanes and their pilots through the century has been a popular fascination.

Notwithstanding the perceptive comments of the late British prime minister, as the idealized view of war has been properly deflated over the years (all the more so in this age of instant communications), combat aviation has somehow retained, if not enhanced, its dashing image. War, of course, is the supreme form of competition, and within this broad arena is the highly intricate specialty of air combat, arguably the ultimate among the specialties. Few qualify for duty in the sky. Participants in air combat have been marked by their notable exclusivity, which, in turn, has contributed to the allure.

Moreover, the warplane, its purposeful shape enabling commensurate performance, displayed at air shows and exalted in pulp magazines, has long captured the public's imagination. Then, too, air combat has a beguiling sterility, for it is fought at a distance, the victims not discernible as flesh and bones but, at best, as specks in an onrushing sea. Legends, stories handed down of aces clashing in the din of a raging aerial engagement and of attack pilots boring down unfazed through a gauntlet thick with hostile fire, have played a role in cultivating the mystique.

To be sure, this collection contains its share of from-the-cockpit accounts of air combat. Those who have been there, controls in hand, confronting a determined foe, describe the sound of the passing wind, the smell of hot oil splashing against the windscreen, and the feel of the unsettled air as their winged contrivances cavort in life-or-death gyrations. This is an irreplaceable perspective, paramount to understanding the reality lived by heroic flyers.

But this anthology would be remiss if it did not also contain other vantage points. There are, for example, accounts dispassionately chronicling air battles and commentaries professionally explaining air combat tactics. The selections in the first four sections are drawn from World War I, World War II, the Korean War, and the Vietnam War. Then there are sections on Middle East conflicts and the Persian Gulf War. The concluding section takes a look at the art and science of air warfare.

In this latter section, an effort is made to touch on theories of air combat, where military thinkers and air warfare strategists have been and where they might be headed. Although no compilation of air warfare materials can be exhaustive, or even approach coverage of all the great air battles, this anthology provides a healthy smattering, a beginning for the serious student of air warfare. These selections, penetrating though many of them might be, are not offered as gospel but as prologue, a spark to light further investigation of an enormous, rich, and expanding body of work.

Winning the air battle hinges on many factors, but none as crucial as the motivation of the pilot. It is not enough to be well trained and well equipped. Often the tide of battle shifts by the weight of the warrior's will. Mercenaries are a poor substitute for patriots. Belief in one's cause transcends lesser forms of motivation and is the preferred driver for men at war. History is replete with instances of handfuls of ragtag partisans holding at bay much larger forces of professional soldiers.

The vastly outnumbered Hebrews at Masada, the plateau fortress besieged by Roman legions, continually repulsed their attackers until, in 73 A.D., their position was compromised and death or enslavement became certain. Rather than be subjected to such a dismal fate, the remaining defenders took their own lives. This example of commitment in the extreme is revisited by every newly minted pilot in the modern Israeli air force who pledges that his countrymen will not be forced to face such options in future wars, that "Masada shall not fall again."

Like their beleaguered ancestors, Israeli pilots have confronted overwhelming odds. Their answer has been to fly each sortie as though the destiny of their country depends upon it. They believe that without victory in the air battle, their freedom—their lives—would fall into jeopardy. It is not enough for them to be flyers; they must be warriors. Because the threat is omnipresent, the fervor among Israeli pilots is constant.

History's greatest air battles were won by pilots imbued with this kind of motivation, men who were just as much warrior as flyer. The Fighter Command pilots of the British Royal Air Force in the summer of 1940 knew that their dogfights in the sky above their cherished homeland would decide whether democracy or tyranny would prevail. In what became known as the Battle of Britain, this relatively tiny band of intrepid aviators, referred to affectionately as "the few," frequently scrambled from their ready shacks into the cockpits of waiting Spitfires and Hurricanes, hastening their ascent into a treacherous sky. Each victory over an intruding Messerschmitt meant one less menacing shadow over home and liberty.

In June 1942, the naval aviators at the Battle of Midway demonstrated similar resolve, the haunting image of fallen comrades at Pearl Harbor fresh in their memories. Skimming over the open sea, flak everywhere, enemy fighters swooping down in swarms, the American torpedo squadrons, unescorted and equipped in some cases with scandalously obsolete aircraft, pressed on nevertheless. These selfless young flight crews were decimated in a merciless hail of gunfire. But their sacrifice preoccupied the Japanese fleet and enabled equally dedicated airmen in Dauntless dive-bombers to successfully strafe the enemy aircraft carriers. The incalculable courage manifested at Midway resulted in a reversal of the fortunes of the Pacific War, and quite possibly the entire war.

The indomitable spirit of these heroic flyers follows in the tradition of the three hundred Spartans defending their homeland against invading Persian hordes at the pass of Thermopylae in 430 B.C. When one of the defenders, Dienices, was informed that the magnitude of the attack by enemy archers would block out the sun with a thick shower of arrows, he replied, "So much the better: we shall fight in the shade."

This is not to say that the combatants in every conflict are driven by a purity of motive. Greed, prejudice, and megalomania have accounted for a not inconsequential share of strife among nations. Yet, those who would exercise dominion have almost always failed in the long run if for no other reason than that the human spirit seems imbued with an irrepressible passion to be free.

Most pilots are not philosophers, but Antoine de Saint-Exupéry, the incomparably eloquent pilot-author, expressed what is probably the consensus view: "Why should we hate one another? We all live in the same cause, are borne through life on the same planet, form the crew of the same ship. Civilizations may, indeed, compete to bring forth new syntheses, but it is monstrous that they should devour one another." Later, while flying in combat to free his native France from German occupation, he noted, "When a fort is to be taken by storm some men necessarily are in the front rank. Almost always these men die. But the front rank must die if the fort is to be captured."

When a shooting war starts and bullets fired in anger whistle past, one's ideology, though perhaps still persuasive, takes a kind of back seat, a secondary position in the psyche, as a survivalist instinct rises to precedence. With someone on the other side trying to kill you, regardless of the platitudes enunciated by the politicians back home as justification for the battle or of your deeply held belief in the cause, you fire back in the first instance to save yourself.

Air-to-air combat engagements usually last for a few exceptionally intense seconds, so it is doubtful that the pilots are contemplating abstruse hypotheses in these fiercely contested moments. It is more likely that during the heat of battle the warrior in the sky, like the gunslinger of the Old West, is concentrating all of his energies, thoughts, and bodily functions on getting off a shot to eliminate the opponent, squelching the possibility of return fire. Conviction in the underlying purpose serves to sustain the warrior between skirmishes, girding his endurance.

War, carrying with it the awful prospect of sudden and ignominious consignment to oblivion, has a way of creating a bond among men unlike any other phenomenon. Whether serving together in a foxhole or a fighter squadron, comrades in arms share a commonality of interest, a mutual desire to survive the combat and return home. Indeed, it is said that in war men are really fighting for their buddies. It is no coincidence that the briefing auditoriums at air bases and the ready rooms on aircraft carriers ordinarily are abuzz with a buoyancy, a playfulness, a heartiness—the signs of camaraderie.

Loyalty among troops is the cement that forms a cohesive combat unit. Every link along the chain of command must remain true because character is the indispensable key to leadership. It was important, for example, that the second lieutenants ordered on interminably long B-17 bomber missions in Europe knew that their theater commander, Curtis LeMay, would, when possible, be there with them in the lead of their formations. Nothing could be more debilitating than for the pilots flying into harm's way to lose faith in each other and their leaders.

The preferred characteristics of the combat pilot have not changed much since the earliest days of air warfare. Like all good pilots, the air warrior must be first and foremost honest with himself. This means that he knows and understands the limitations of himself and his equipment. He recognizes that his operational envelope is all the more unforgiving because in combat the automatic hammer of the laws of physics are supplemented by the roving hammer of inhospitable adversaries.

The war fighter, to adopt a term popular among today's military strategists, must also have the warrior's heart. Although, it is hoped no one yearns for war, once the fighting begins it will generally end only with a countereffort at least equally as vigorous. Referring to fighter pilots, an authority no less than Manfred von Richthofen, the Red Baron himself, emphatically declared, "When they see an opponent they must attack and shoot him down. Anything else is rubbish. . . . It is only in the fight that the battle is won."

Traditional attributes remain valuable. Keen eyesight, good hand-eye coordination, perfected airmanship skills, extensive training, lots of experience, situational awareness, and a mission-dedicated aircraft help to accomplish the objective. But in the new era of the digital battle space an array of added factors has become important to achieving victory.

It is now not only possible but desirable to obtain a God's-eye view of the battle space. Commanders can know in real time what is happening in the field, on the sea, and in the air, and act accordingly. Without being tapped into this stream of information, the opponent is at a distinct disadvantage. Armed with such vital data as the positions and movements of enemy aircraft, and having stealth coupled with the ability to electronically jam, the potential exists to strike the enemy with his barely even knowing that missiles are en route. Possessing digital control of the battle space, as was more or less demonstrated in the Persian Gulf War, can have devastating consequences for the opposing air force. Although it would be premature to predict the end of one-on-one air combat, opportunities appear to be diminishing for the dogfighting of previous air wars.

Given the highly complex environment into which combat pilots are thrust today, it is legitimate to wonder if the premium placed on certain fabled and tacitly accepted pilot behavior is worthy, let alone relevant, anymore. For example, returning to base drunk the night before a mission and using the aircraft's oxygen system to resuscitate oneself on the way to the target might have broken tension and gained acceptance among the fellows in the old days. But it is a stretch to expect pilots flying modern fighters, with the concomitant demands from programming onboard computers to sustaining up to nine Gs in combat maneuvering, to effectively zoom through contested and increasingly lethal airspace if suffering from a hangover. Indeed, they would presumably want assurance that the air combat controller vectoring them from the airborne command and control aircraft is stone sober. Likewise for the boomer replenishing their critically low fuel supply after the engagement.

Combat flying has been characterized as a macho business. Certainly the self-confident swagger of combat pilots will remain with us, but the fact is that, when given the chance to fly military aircraft during World War II, women performed admirably—American women as instructor, test, and ferry pilots, and Soviet women as members of fighter squadrons. Since 1977, American women, once again, have been quietly and effectively flying military aircraft on noncombat missions. With their role officially expanded in recent times to include combat flying, it will be interesting to see over time how they perform. In today's squadrons perhaps the premium deserves to be placed on brains.

Computers are at the center of modern war. A lone hacker, adept in the world of cyberspace, can wreak havoc on computer-dependent military forces. An entire expeditionary composite air wing might find itself grounded because of a few miscreant taps on a computer keypad. Encryption codes must be secured from interception and contamination. It is imperative that computer software be accorded sacrosanct status.

Other growing threats requiring a specialized form of vigilance are the proliferation of nuclear devices and the willingness of at least one mischievous ruler to use chemical and biological weapons. At a minimum, this requires air and ground crews to prepare for operations in "hot zones." Cumbersome and climatically uncomfortable protective suits, purified breathing systems, cleanup kits, and vaccination programs are part of the precautions.

There is a troubling new lethality in today's battle space. Just about every component moves faster, whether a bullet or an encrypted piece of data, and weapons pack a more devastating punch. One can hardly find a safe corner in the battle space. Even when enemy skies are swept clean, as happened in the Persian Gulf War, shoulder-launched missiles still pose a serious threat. On the offensive side, a new generation of relatively inexpensive and precision-guided stealthy cruise missiles is about to be born. This development has ominous implications, as such missiles, unlike the primitive Scuds of the Persian Gulf War, can be deployed in massive quantity, can be targeted against prime military sites, can escape easy detection, and can carry a variety of deadly warheads.

The most advanced next-generation fighter, the Lockheed Martin F-22 Raptor, will be flying in this hostile environment. To survive and to accomplish its mission, it is outfitted with new or improved technologies. An inherent stealthiness will cloak it from enemy sensors. At the same time, its advanced integrated avionics will permit it to locate, identify, track, and fire at the opponent. All the while the latest intelligence data will be fed into onboard computers via satellite and other downlinks. The vast streams of information will be automatically sifted through, analyzed, and presented to the pilot in the most user-friendly color-graphic format, fused together with relevant archival information from the onboard database.

The Raptor is the first production fighter to have supercruise capability, meaning that it can cruise supersonically without employing its afterburners and burning valuable fuel. It will be able to get to or break from the air battle faster than the opponent, and in a relatively fuel efficient manner. Moreover, if all the wizardry fails, it will be a most formidable dogfighter, for, among other things, its nozzles are thrust vectoring. The aircraft is capable of sustaining controlled flight in the poststall regime. Also, if any one major system is somehow disabled by enemy fire, the F-22 will still be able to fly the mission as the onboard computers will compensate, redistributing the loads accordingly. When attacking a ground target, the versatile aircraft will not have to get near it or the surrounding ground defenses because a new family of precision guided standoff weapons will be carried.

As prosecution of the air war becomes increasingly complicated, the fighters and bombers will be players on a crowded three-dimensional chessboard. Navigation coordinates, communications, and intelligence will emanate from or be relayed by ever-present satellites orbiting in the far reaches of space. Uninhabited aerial vehicles (UAVs) will draw enemy fire as decoys and thereby expose enemy positions. More sophisticated UAVs will loiter in hostile skies, sending back useful reconnaissance data. Patrolling airborne laser systems, linked to a network of infrared detection satellites, will be on the lookout for certain missile threats.

Possessing the technological advantage, while not guaranteeing success, stacks the odds in one's favor. Having newer, more effective weaponry, and employing the tactics that fit, give an edge in battle. More than a few times the outcome of a fight was determined by which side was ahead technologically. At the Battle of Hastings in 1066 A.D., King Harold's swordsmen and spearmen were no match for William the Conqueror's archers and crossbowmen. Like the knights of old, the pilots of today are likelier to win if their weapons and tactics are better.

The ongoing debate over quantity versus quality takes on a heightened germaneness in the current climate of budget cutting among the

Western industrial powers. There is no simple answer to whether an air force is better off with a thousand low-tech, inexpensive fighters or a handful of ultra-high-tech, very costly fighters. So much depends on the missions to be performed. Some air forces play a limited role, whereas the U.S. Air Force is engaged in a policy of global reach. It must spread its finite resources across a spectrum of missions—air and space dominance, close air support, air interdiction, strategic bombing, reconnaissance, airlift, and others—and excel in each.

Of course, the ideal is to have a dedicated aircraft for each type of mission, but the reality is that this just is not feasible. Instead, common airframes are being developed to serve a multiplicity of roles. Nowhere is this more conspicuous than in the Joint Strike Fighter program, where the same airframe is being applied to the requirements for the next multirole fighter for the Air Force, Navy, and Marines in the United States and for the Royal Navy in Britain. In general, the American military is taking a compromise approach. A small number of very sophisticated aircraft are being acquired for what is termed the "high end" of the mix and a somewhat larger number of less-expensive aircraft are being purchased for the so-called "low end" of the mix.

Concerned with the substantial reduction in the number of aircraft in the operational inventory over recent years, especially long-range heavy bombers, the U.S. Air Force is counting on precision munitions. In the past, it might have required hundreds of bombers dropping thousands of bombs to hit a target. By contrast, the smart bombs of today might be able to knock out several high-priority targets in a single pass by one aircraft.

Bigness alone is not necessarily a virtue in war. David was able to prevail over Goliath largely because of a technologically derived mobility advantage. The Bible states that Goliath was laden with a brass helmet, a coat of mail, brass leg and shoulder armor, a sword, and a heavy spear. David refused similar protective gear and a sword. Instead, he carried only five stones and a slingshot. This was a weapon with which he was familiar, and it afforded him an unmatched nimbleness and the initial volley.

There are many lessons here: strike first and hard, fight as you train, and always maintain flexibility. In air warfare this might translate into outmaneuvering the opponent, promptly disabling his essential command and control centers, and reallocating resources as the unfolding battle warrants. With the all-important goal of air superiority achieved, air assets can then be focused on systematically demolishing the enemy's remaining fighting power.

The subjects discussed in this brief essay and much more are explored in greater depth in the pages that follow. It is hoped that these compelling excerpts will shed light on the domain of combat aviation. Perhaps they will also foster an understanding—or better, an appreciation—of those who have participated courageously in the crucible of air warfare. Grab your helmet and goggles; it is going to be an exciting flight!

Philip Handleman

WORLD WAR I

1

The Machine Gun Takes Wings (1915)

from **THE YEARS OF THE SKY KINGS**
by Arch Whitehouse

As the stark frightfulness of trench warfare gradually enveloped the once-chivalrous realm of World War I flying, the race escalated for more lethal airborne firepower. If somehow the machine gun could be fixed to the front of the aircraft, firing forward so that the pilot could shoot off rounds as he was aligned with an enemy plane, it would, so some thought, relieve the tedious requirement of maneuvering a rear-seat observer/gunner into firing position. The key was to devise a mechanism by which bullets could rapidly fire through the fleeting gaps in the arc of a whirring propeller.

In April 1914, the French aircraft designer Raymond Saulnier developed a synchronizer, but the uneven manufacture of ammunition at that time caused erratic timing of machine gun firings. Therefore, Saulnier applied the simple solution of metal deflection plates on the propeller blades. This way the wooden propeller blades could withstand the stray bullets fired out of sequence. The need for technical refinements, coupled with adverse weather, delayed deployment of Saulnier's invention until a year later.

To give this new weapon system a real-world test, Saulnier enlisted the cooperation of French pilot Roland Garros, who, prior to the war, had been an employee of Saulnier's company. Garros had learned to fly under the tutelage of famed Brazilian aviator/aircraft builder Alberto Santos-Dumont. The year before the outbreak of hostilities, Garros achieved celebrity by being the first to fly across the Mediterranean Sea. When war came, Garros soon was flying for a French unit.

On the fateful day in 1915 described by Arch Whitehouse, himself a veteran of World War I air combat, the primitive forward-firing machine gun was first used with deadly result. A new era in air-to-air fighting was born. This mounting of a synchronizer with deflection plates onto a Morane-Saulnier Type L Parasol monoplane (described in this excerpt as a Morane Bullet) represented the emergence of a truly new kind of airplane—the fighter. Also, a cardinal rule of air-to-air combat—establish oneself on the tail of the opponent—was conceived. As for Garros, he eventually escaped from his German captors after making a forced landing behind enemy lines only to be fatally shot down later in the war.

In one of the ironies of war, the French lost any advantage they might have had with their innovative weapon system as Anthony Fokker, the brilliant airman and aircraft designer, modeled a new and improved system after the captured one. Employing the German Parabellum machine gun, Fokker obtained better utility with his synchronizer. He mounted the gun to his Eindecker, a relatively maneuverable monoplane, which made for a fearsome combination. In time, the British and the French responded with competing systems that used advanced gears in the synchronizers.

Perhaps because aviation was in its infancy at the start of World War I, four generations of combat aircraft were developed in the course of the war. The pace of aeronautical development was arguably matched only during the subsequent world war. Speed and altitude performance, maneuverability, and weapons systems were constantly enhanced—if not revolutionized. Depending upon how wisely the new technologies were employed, the military advantage shifted back and forth to one side or the other.

P.H.

THE MORNING OF APRIL 1, 1915, brought in the dawn of a new day in military history. A new weapon and a new breed of man were conceived. The day also provided a most tragic April Fool joke.

In spite of the calendar the day was cold and raw. In the barnyards of the French countryside steam rose from the manure piles. The Soissons rustics clumped about in heavy *sabots* and blew on their work-gnarled knuckles. A biting southeast wind off the Graian Alps knifed through woolen jerkins and froze men to the marrow.

A dished-wheeled monoplane scurried down a deserted meadow take-off track and hissed into the sky. A typical or routine flight, but it was to become one of the most memorable in history. Few realized it at the time, of course—least of all the pilot. Inventors have little idea of the real significance of their creations or what they have wrought.

This was a rickety, underpowered monoplane with a savage temperament. It snarled through the hydra nostrils of an 80-hp Le Rhone rotary engine, a primitive airplane of spruce, linen, piano wire, and some cockpit stiffening originally intended for the sides of orange crates. The Morane Bullet was already an outmoded type and had been stowed away in a spare-parts hangar awaiting final disposal when it was resurrected for this grim experiment. It was too treacherous for newly trained men to fly, too bedeviled for routine war scouting patrols.

The militant pilot had for years believed the airplane could be used as a fighting machine—not simply a platform for aerial observation. That is, it could if one apparently insolvable problem could be overcome. If one mechanical block could be bypassed. The man flying the Morane Bullet that morning was convinced he had solved it.

That same day two young German aeronauts, as they were then listed, took off aboard an Albatros two-seater with orders to check on French military activity behind Epernay. It was a routine patrol, one they had accepted and carried out a dozen times before.

The minute they crossed into Allied territory the French 75's, mounted as high-angle guns, opened up and dabbed white splotches of smoke all around them. The white smoke markers caught the eye of the French pilot in the masquerading Morane and he noted the German two-seater about 500 meters above him. He was glad he had no dead-weight observer with him. He spent the next ten minutes stalking and climbing up to the level of the observation machine.

The two Germans watched him with only nominal interest as they continued their reconnaissance work. When the Bullet curled to a position behind their tail and gained the last few feet of necessary height the German pilot simply presumed the Frenchman was out on an observation mission too. He had no observer waving a rifle or loading a machine gun. What was there to worry about? This mid-air activity had to be carried out by both sides. So long as the Morane Bullet didn't get in the way, he could have his share of the sky, and welcome.

And just so long as the Frenchman didn't start crabbing up sideways, it was only another observation patrol.

April Fool!

A few seconds later a burst of fifteen rounds of Hotchkiss machine gun fire tore through his shoulder blades. The burst had come straight from the Morane Bullet directly behind. Only Observer Fritz Dietrichs saw that the slugs were apparently coming through the sheen of the propeller—from a stripped-down gun mounted over the engine cowling.

Firing through the whirling blades of the propeller? How could that be?

Dietrichs never lived to find out. He knew nothing about piloting an Albatros and he went down, utterly helpless to aid himself. In his last breath he screamed his outrage that a French monoplane could shoot at him with a gun set behind the spinning blades of a wooden propeller! The Albatros plunged to its end with a dead man hunched over its controls.

But it was true. A Frenchman named Roland Garros had given the machine gun wings. His fantastic device gave birth to a new and most deadly weapon, providing the military forces with a lethal piece of armament. It made the airplane as important a war machine as the naval dreadnought. It turned a collection of rickety flying machines into an air service, and overnight the airplane became the platform for sky-high gunnery, not simply an airy-fairy vehicle of observation.

After Garros's first victory against an early Albatros, which has been described, he was in the air again on April 11 in his deadly Morane Bullet. This time he came upon two unsuspecting Aviatik two-seaters and again employed the same strategy of moving to their rear and making the most of the belief that he could offer no opposition from that angle. The first Aviatik went down under a hail of Hotchkiss lead; the second stood and fought, the German observer vainly trying to hold off Garros with a revolver! It was a game stand, but the effort was hopeless. The second Aviatik soon followed the first to a fiery finish.

The following afternoon while returning from a visit to another escadrille, Garros caught an L.V.G., also a two-seater, and battered it into the ground near Dunkirk. Again a German was trapped by the Morane Bullet's approach.

Two days later one of the newer Aviatiks, equipped with a Parabellum machine gun in the observer's rear seat, was spotted flying toward the French lines. The German pilot hurriedly dumped his bomb load to gain more maneuverability. The German observer's first burst caught the Morane Bullet's wing root and punctured Garros's reserve fuel tank. Trailing a long cloud of gasoline vapor, he disregarded the possibility of fire in the air and closed in.

The German observer died with five bullets in his chest. The next five of that first clip tore through the pilot's head and slammed through the instrument panel and ignited the fuel line. The Aviatik went down and burned to a cinder in a marsh.

On the morning of April 16 Garros was attacked by four Albatros two-seaters which were returning from a bombing raid. A number of rifle bullets penetrated his machine—one of them hit the engine cowling and fell back into his lap. The moment the Frenchman's fixed gun began to sparkle behind the sheen of the propeller, all four two-seater pilots remembered important engagements elsewhere.

However, one Albatros appeared to be slower than the others and soon lagged behind. Garros darted in fast to get within range. The others, noting their companions' danger, turned about and tried to head off the impudent Morane, but Garros was "on" and his bullet gradually tore away the left wing of the laggard Albatros and the unfortunate crew went down in a fuselage that rejected the other wing before they spun in.

Five victories in sixteen days! That was the initial harvest of Roland Garros's front-firing gun.

That night Garros was cited for the Legion of Honor and every newspaper in Europe carried the news of his five victories. The gay *boulevardiers* toasted the newest hero and cried: "Oh, that Garros! That Roland Garros! Five enemy machines he has destroyed. That Garros is an ace!"

The word "ace" was a popular catchword of the day in Paris. Any newsworthy person who had performed anything unusual was an "ace" to the Parisians. The latest winning cyclist racer was an "ace." The newest popular jockey was an "ace." It was natural then that the phrase should be applied to Roland Garros.

The enthusiasm was overheard by an American newspaperman who interpreted it to refer to any pilot who had downed five enemy planes. In his next dispatch back to New York he applied the word to the name of Roland Garros and it became the journalistic standard by which a fighter pilot in any air service was rated.

Later the Germans doubled the requirements and any airman who had scored ten victories was publicized as a *Kanone*. The British ignored the "ace" standard for over two years and until well into 1915 no official record of "enemy machines destroyed" was kept or compiled. They did not publish the names and the day-by-day scores of their aces, and it was only upon the occasion of the decoration of these heroes that the number of their victories was made public.

However, the term "ace" has lasted to this day.

So Roland Garros became the world's first ace as well as the man who revolutionized aerial warfare. He was invited to appear before the Directorate of Military Aeronautics to give his views on this new art of aerial combat. The date was set for April 25, but unfortunately Roland Garros was unable to keep the appointment.

On the afternoon of April 19, 1915, Garros took off to bomb the railroad sidings at Courtrai. Why he was given such a mission with his single-seater fighter is something of a mystery. Although he was now the world's premier air fighter, he apparently still carried out routine bombing raids.

That day the pilots of Escadrille M-S. 23 fully expected him to return with another addition to his score. But that was not to be. Garros flew all the way to Courtrai without encountering an enemy aircraft of any kind. He presumed he would be more fortunate on the way back. He cut his Le Rhone engine, went into an attack glide, swept over the freight yard, and dropped his bombs.

He had no idea what he hit or whether he had missed the target entirely. He was too concerned with getting the impact-fused bombs overboard without blowing himself to bits. When he went to switch on his rotary engine again, the Le Rhone refused to pick up. Nothing happened! The propeller simply windmilled in the slip stream. Garros knew immediately what was wrong and cursed himself for his imbecility. In the long sure glide for the Courtrai freight yard the spark plugs had oiled up. He had forgotten to "burn" them off with intermittent blipping of the ignition switch and so had no alternative but to stretch his glide until he found a suitable spot to land.

He came down near Ingelmunster, about 40 miles from the Dutch frontier. His first thought was to destroy his plane and the details of the propeller's protective collar, which metal device was the secret of his front-firing gun. He did his best to set fire to the Morane, but the wing fabric and the spruce framework were damp and refused to burn. How ironic! Had an enemy bullet flicked a spark off a metal fitting near a punctured gas tank, the whole machine would have gone up like a pan of gunpowder. On the ground, with no slip-stream draft, nothing that Garros could do would set up so much as a smoke smudge.

Soon a party of German soldiers turned up and Garros made one last desperate bid for liberty. Running across the field, he slid into a ditch for cover where the depression was full of muddy water, weeds, and half-frozen sedge. He stayed there until darkness fell and then clambered out with the idea of reaching the Dutch border, but by sheer bad luck he wandered straight into a group of soldiers who were out gathering firewood. The game was up.

The Germans had examined the undamaged Morane and were of course interested in the strange steel wedges bolted around the propeller-blade butts. Blued bullet markings soon disclosed the purpose of the deflection plates, and in a flash the secret of the gun that could fire bullets through the whirling blades of a propeller was revealed.

The Germans moved fast. The French *cocardes* were quickly daubed out and the Morane Bullet was flown to Berlin. A young Dutch engineer, Anthony Fokker, was called in to examine it.

2

A Buzz-Saw in the Air

from ONE MAN'S WAR: THE STORY OF THE LAFAYETTE ESCADRILLE
by Bert Hall and John J. Niles

Weston Birch "Bert" Hall was a self-confessed liar who gambled, told stories, and engaged in colossal adventures either in reality or in fiction. Nonetheless, he was a founding member of the Lafayette Escadrille, the legendary French squadron comprised of American volunteers, and a man prominent in one field or another of aviation until his death in 1948. Hall was a lovable rogue who had four confirmed victories and four confirmed wives, as well as a number of probables in both fields of endeavor.

It is hard to understand why a film has not been made of the improbably romantic life of Bert Hall, whose adventures, real or imagined, took him from the Balkan wars to the position of Chinese warlord, and from being a merchant seaman to an adviser on Shirley Temple movies. His role in founding the Escadrille Americaine, as it was called prior to being renamed for diplomatic reasons the Lafayette Escadrille, is irrefutable. The Lafayette Escadrille was of inestimable propaganda value to the Allies. Although never a truly formidable combat organization, it was an important factor in rallying American support away from Germany and to the Allied cause.

One Man's War is an expanded version of his earlier book, *En L'air,* and this excerpt is probably as accurate as anything Hall wrote. While this may sound like faint praise, it is not, for, liar or not, Hall had been where the action was, and his confirmed victories demonstrated considerable bravery and élan on his part. He might have exaggerated from time to time, but there is no doubt that he mixed it up in combat with the best of them.

For a nitpicker, Hall's account is marred by minor inaccuracies in spelling (for example, "Aviatic" and "Albatross"), but this was par for the course at the time. What is real is Hall's ability to convey the mechanics of air combat in a two-seater "curved-wing" Nieuport as he maneuvers to give his observer a chance to shoot. He also convincingly relates his delight in the new single-seat thirteen-meter (a reference to wing area) Nieuports, with their wing-mounted Lewis guns.

Hall's account contains a never-ending mix of possibly real and probably apocryphal stories, all worth telling. One is reminiscent of the story told of famed British ace Douglas Bader during World War II, when he tried to inveigle his captors into allowing him to fly a Messerschmitt. In it Hall recounts the tale of a gleaming new Albatros that not only lands, out of fuel, at Hall's airfield but also has an American-born observer on board!

One Man's War is characterized by swift changes in pace, and Hall is no sooner flying his Nieuport than he is directed to undertake, for the second time, a special mission. He had previously landed a "shifty-eyed" spy behind enemy lines in a two-seat "Morane-Saunier;" now he was to pick him up again. This time it was a trap, and only by careful flying could he give his "motor the gun and zoom up and as far out of the way as possible." In the process he collected a lot of bullet holes in the airplane, and one in himself.

There was an undeniable element of snobbery among some of the members of the Lafayette Escadrille, and some of Hall's posturing might have been an attempt to show that he was as good a man as any in the unit. Never quite accepted, but somehow affectionately regarded by most, Hall was what would today be called a "character."

Hall's final story in this selection is one that makes the entire book worth reading—whether it happened or not. In it Hall gives a very accurate description of flight in his Nieuport, and an account of a courageous (if fumble-fingered) enemy that set the stage for many films to come.

You might not always believe Bert Hall, but you cannot refrain from liking his style!

W.J.B.

In August, after we had been supplied with the improved curved-winged Nieuports, Lieutenant le Cocque and I shot down our first German in flames. It was about three o'clock in the afternoon, August 21, 1915. The air was perfect and the fighting was good. There were lots of running scraps, but nothing serious until this one Aviatic came in close for what seemed to be a show-down.

We had been doing a tour of observation and were returning at the time. Our gasoline supply was naturally low, but if anybody wanted to fight, we were ready. The pilot of that Aviatic was an experienced fellow. We flew around each other, waiting for a chance to open up, each hoping the other would make a fatal blunder, do a tiny bit of bad flying and that would be the end. Lieutenant le Cocque was ready at the guns and so was the German observer.

My idea of attack has always been from the top down, but as we were almost up to our possible ceiling, there was no chance to get above this fellow. Climbing in very high, thin air is not as easy as it is down near the earth where the air is thick.

Finally the German observer fired a burst. It cut through our fuselage about three feet behind the rear cockpit. I pulled off as quickly as possible and apparently while the Germans were congratulating themselves in having got in the first blow, I caught them unawares. In what seemed to be half a second, Lieutenant le Cocque fired a long burst, which did something to the engine, besides damaging the state of mind inside the German plane.

From an altitude of 4,000 meters down to within 200 meters of the ground we combated, saving our ammunition for the best possible opportunity. After our first burst, Lieutenant le Cocque and I had the advantage. The Germans were trying to disengage themselves as skillfully as possible. They wanted to get away without giving us an opening. Finally, at 200 meters, they made a break. I swung around sideways to give le Cocque the best firing position and he did the rest.

The German plane buckled in the middle, crumpled up and burst into flames. It fell about a kilometer from the city of Sommepy, right in the middle of the French front line trenches. This made confirmation an easy matter. As soon as the enemy plane started down, all the German land batteries opened up on us, and we had to do a swell job of dodging to get back with our skins.

During the combat we had received about ten bullet holes, but during the anti-aircraft and machine gun barrage from the ground, we received a hundred, and they weren't all small holes either—anti-aircraft bursts sometimes throw hunks as big as a small-sized head of cabbage.

But we had a confirmation—le Cocque and I did—and that was worth flying through a dozen anti-aircraft barrages.

Two days later, a rare thing happened. I had just returned from my morning patrol when a mechanic came running, out of breath, all excited. At the same moment, a message came in from headquarters; a German plane was spiraling down right over our landing field. We expected that he would either drop bombs or open up on the hangars with his machine guns. But then we observed that his propeller was not moving. We knew we had him cold once he landed. Several machine guns were trained on him and we waited. We knew that unless he changed his direction, any bombs he might drop would do no damage; they would only make a few holes in the countryside, and that countryside of ours had been shot at and had had holes made in it by experts, so we didn't worry much.

Finally, the Boche landed. The plane was a bright new Albatross, and a beauty; even newer and prettier than the one I had captured. The French soldiers who guarded the field rushed over in the direction of the plane with their guns ready to do business, but the Germans merely smiled and asked for the Commanding Officer.

Captain Bouche stepped forward, still wondering what was about to happen. The German pilot spoke perfect French. He explained that he was out of gasoline and thought that it would be a sporting thing if the Captain would supply enough to take their Albatros back to the German lines. They also proposed, in lieu of the fact that the Captain would not agree to the first proposition, that a French pilot and an observer take off and do battle with the German plane after it had been re-gassed. If the German plane came off first best, it would be allowed to go back to Germany untouched.

Our Captain smiled in his wonderfully gracious manner and said that it was impossible to entertain either proposition. He would like to do the sporting thing, but Headquarters wanted to examine the latest Albatross. So we took both of them prisoners and rolled the nice new machine back into our only empty hangar.

Now comes the best part of it. The observer had been quiet all the while. Finally, he spoke up.

"...so you're an American!" he said, addressing me. "Christ," I said, "how'd you know?"

"Why, goddamit, I could tell an American in hell. I know you. I remember having seen you at Palm Beach in 1908. You were driving a racing car then. I remember you well."

"You're right, boy," I said. "By God, you're right. What the hell are you doin' in the Boche army?"

"Oh, I don't know. You see, my father's German and my mother's American and I'm nothing. So when the war broke out, the old man ballyhooed me into enlisting in the Aviation Section. It's all over now as far as I'm concerned and I'm glad of it too. Understand, I'm not afraid to die, but, hell, I believe we're wrong."

The other officers looked on with wide-eyed amazement.

"It's damned nice of you Americans fighting for France though, and I can understand why you're doin' it too."

We fed them and sent them off to the concentration centers, but not before the half-breed German-American had told us quite a lot of valuable things about the Boche flying outfits, the "Jagstraffels," as he called them. I was sorry for that poor bum. But that's what he got for having a German father; a fellow ought to look out for such things. It complicates matters so much, particularly at war-time....

In the middle of September we got our first single-seater Nieuports—thirteen meter affairs, with Lewis machine guns on the top wing. Those Lewis guns were never one hundred percent successful, but on the single place ships, they gave the pilot a chance to fight his own fight. They were looked upon as the best thing up to that time, but the Vickers with the belt-fed ammunition supplanted them ultimately. The little thirteen meter Nieuports were great ships. I loved them, and to this day, if I could get one and be sure it was in good condition, I'd fly it for all the world to see. The Nieuport was not a plane for amateur pilots, but with a 110 horsepower le Rhone motor, it was as sweet a flying ship as anything in the air.

With the arrival of the new Nieuports, I made my second Special Mission—the one that nearly finished me off. We left the field as usual in the very early morning, flying a Morane. I didn't like the looks of the spy they had given me; he had shifty eyes. I distrusted him. But we flew away and landed without mishap on the grass-grown field near Rocroi. He had the usual box of pigeons, and on landing, he hopped out and scurried off into the woods. That part of it was according to Hoyle. But the return! They nearly knocked me off. The only thing that saved my life was the poor shooting of those German gunners.

It was another early morning flight in a Morane-Saunier. We had, as usual, received a message by carrier pigeon to pick up the spy, and as far as one could tell, everything was going off exactly right. Just as I was about to land, I took a tour of the field down very low, instead of slipping in with a cut switch and taking a chance of starting the motor again at the last moment. That tour of the field was what saved me, because it warmed up my motor and also took me to a slightly different position on the field. If I had landed in the spot I had used on my three previous attempts, it would have been fatal.

I have always believed that that spy was a *Counter-Espion* working for the Germans. Captain Bouche was later advised by headquarters that our spy had been captured and had given out the details of my return trip, perhaps in the hope that he would not be executed. All this matters very little to me. I can only remember what happened on the landing field at Rocroi. As I said before, I took a tour of the field and then came down for my landing. Suddenly from the woods ahead of me, there was a burst of machine gun fire. After that, they shot at me with everything in the German Army. If they had only waited until my machine rolled to a stop, I would have been easy meat for them. But as usual, the Germans, from the Generals and the Chiefs of Staff down to the lowest private, never know when they're winning. So they opened up on me a little bit too soon. In fact, I hadn't touched the ground yet.

All I did was to give my motor the gun and zoom up as far out of the way as possible. My wings looked like a sieve. I had a small wound in the thigh. And, mind you, all this happened in less than fifteen seconds, because as soon as I zoomed, they had to change the angle of their machine gun fire to almost 180 degrees. This meant that they would have to turn around and wait until I had passed over them, and then fire at me from the rear.

Of course, I got away, but there was some cold perspiration on my brow, and a good many mouthfuls of profanity on my lips. If I ever see that spy again and have a shootin' iron handy, it's goin' to be Kingdom Come. I'll perforate that baby's hide and make him like it. His figure'll look much like my wings did when I landed back at la Cheppe.

The Captain said, "Well, where's the spy?"

I shook my head. The Captain looked back in the rear cockpit. I pointed to the perforated wings. The Captain understood. He was a war-wise fellow, that Captain of ours, and we liked him a lot for it too.

That was my last Special Mission.

Three days later, I witnessed what I consider to be one of the most extraordinary aviation accidents of the war, and as I was the only one there beside the German (who is now dead), you-all will have to take my word for it.

I had been flying inland, say about ten to twelve kilometers inside the German lines between Rheims and Machault. A German plane passed me. It was a new type. They were very fast and excellent climbers. The motor on my little thirteen-meter Nieuport was not working too well that afternoon and for that reason, I could never quite get up to my enemy's altitude. He was always above me, and apparently unwilling to stop and fight it out. I followed him all over the heavens at the height of about 4,500 meters, which is somewhere near 14,000 feet. I would pull my nose up occasionally and take a few random shots at the Boche, but he didn't mind. He just kept on leading me around, using up my gasoline and wearing out my patience.

Finally, I discovered that we were heading off in the direction of Epernay. I also realized that my enemy was preparing to do something in the way of attack, and it was a very strange attack too. He used hand grenades. It was the first and only time I ever encountered such an attack in the air. He would pull the fuse, swing the grenade down at me, and of course, miss by a wide margin.

The situation began to be funny and continued to be funny until a most unusual thing happened—the thing that to me was one of the most extraordinary accidents I'd ever seen.

After the German had thrown four or five grenades, he reduced his altitude a bit. I thought that at last we would fight, but I was mistaken. I saw that he was pulling the fuse on another grenade. He was still high enough above me to prevent me attacking him, so I could only stand around and wait for developments.

He drew back his arm and let the grenade fly. I have never been able to tell whether his coat got caught in some part of the plane or in his effort to throw harder than before, he reached up too high and thereby struck the grenade against the top wing. At least, I do know that the grenade fell back into his own cockpit. Now remember, the fuse had been pulled on that grenade and in five or six seconds it would explode, no matter where it was.

The German pilot immediately let go of his controls. His ship lost altitude rapidly. I followed, and in that moment, I could have shot him to pieces if I had wanted to. But the German pilot was not worrying about me; he was scrambling around on the floor of his cockpit looking for the infernal machine he had intended for my special benefit. It seemed to last hours—tense situations like that always do.

Suddenly I realized that the German had taken hold of his controls again. He righted his ship in one movement. We were then flying along beside each other, so closely that I could see everything he was doing. He had, by this time, given up the idea of recovering the lost grenade and I had given up the idea of shooting him full of holes until something happened one way or the other. All this took less than five seconds, because things happen in a hurry in the air.

At what seemed to be the last possible moment, he raised up in his cockpit and bringing his right arm up to his helmeted head, he saluted me in the best approved German manner. And almost the same instant there was an explosion.

The back portion of the fuselage of the German plane was disconnected from the fore part. For a very brief space of time, everything stood still, and then the German and the fore part of the plane tipped over and dived 14,000 feet, motor full open, at the ground.

The remains landed with a bang not far from the village of Prunay, on the grassy banks of the Marne Aisne Canal. The tail surfaces and the rear sections of the fuselage floated off and were lost in the blue depths beneath me.

I didn't put in for a confirmation. The anti-aircraft batteries no doubt claimed the poor fellow, although they didn't shoot a single shot. He was a game devil, that German, and I'm sorry he didn't give up the grenade idea and fight it out with me. I might have let him go; or who knows, he might have bumped me off. Wouldn't have mattered much—one pilot more or less.

It was a great lesson to me—never monkey with a buzz-saw in the air. And a hand grenade is the nearest thing to a buzz-saw I can think of.

3

Downing My First Hun

from FIGHTING THE FLYING CIRCUS
by Edward V. Rickenbacker

At a time when questions of character in leaders seems to dominate the media, it is refreshing to read an account by "Captain
Eddie" Rickenbacker. His book clearly reveals the strong character
of a man who rose from poverty to power, becoming the United
States's first "ace of aces" en route.

Fighting the Flying Circus is saved from being dated, as so
many World War I books on aviation are, because Rickenbacker was
assisted in the task of writing by Lawrence La Tourette Driggs.
Driggs was a popular author of the time, having written books like
Arnold Adair, American Ace and others. The collaboration permitted Rickenbacker to write in the first person and allowed him to
demonstrate the clarity of vision that came to characterize his business career as head of Eastern Airlines.

Rickenbacker was born in 1890 and thus mature—not to be
confused with over-the-hill—when he entered the Army Air
Service in 1917. Had he not been mature, he would have had more
difficulty enduring the condescension he encountered from
"bluer-bloods" who had preceded him and perhaps resented his
fame as a race car driver. He doesn't mention this, but does relate
his disappointment in his own performance as a pilot at the front,
undergoing a long period of mistakes before finally achieving his
first victory.

In his book, Rickenbacker demonstrated the refreshing attitude of the American pilots who were entering combat in what would prove to be the final year of the war. As yet untested, these new pilots looked forward to battle, confident in their skills and their equipment. This was due in part, no doubt, to the leavening of veterans like James Norman Hall (of later *Mutiny on the Bounty* fame) and Raoul Lufbery. But it was also due to the new arrivals' knowledge that they were but the leading edge of a vast contingent of airmen and aircraft that would arrive in the coming months.

Rickenbacker's account conveys the immediacy of battle during 1918. When he and Hall are scrambled after an intruding "Hun," they take off, and within five minutes are crossing their own balloons, just two miles behind the front. In his usual disarming style, Rickenbacker reveals his inexperience and embarrassment in yet another previctory miscue. After frantic signaling, he committed the ultimate wingman's error by leaving Hall's wing to make an attack on what turned out to be a French observation plane. The veteran Hall understood and waited for Rickenbacker to return, passing his time by stunting for the benefit of enemy antiaircraft guns—the famous "Archie," as antiaircraft fire was called during World War I.

Both Rickenbacker's technical and tactical talents are revealed in passing as he compares the diving qualities of the Pfalz (which aficionados of the period know to be good) with that of the Nieuport 28 he was flying. He notes the "droll habit" of the Nieuport of shredding the fabric of its upper wing in a dive, a phenomenon he would soon encounter himself—and survive. He anticipates the "Boche's" maneuvers, positions himself on the Pfalz's tail, and shoots it down without being "subjected to a single shot."

On landing, he and Hall are delighted to find the victory immediately confirmed, and are even happier when they are mentioned in French dispatches and are subsequently decorated.

Yet the heart of the book and the man can be found in the closing portions of the book. Rickenbacker never publicly complained of the less-than-friendly welcome he had received in his unit. He reveals his hurt unconsciously in this excerpt, by speaking so warmly of the congratulations that were now showered upon him, making him a part of a brotherhood that he characterizes in this way: "No closer fraternity exists in the world than that of the airfighters in this great war."

Rickenbacker went on to lead that fraternity in an exemplary way, not only in combat but through a depression, a second world

war, and in competition in the airline industry. I had the good fortune to meet him when he was on a book tour in 1968 with his
autobiography, *Rickenbacker*. He was then seventy-eight, but after
he signed the book, he stood up, ramrod straight. Ignoring the
long line, he spent a good five minutes talking to my four-year-old
son, Bill, on the importance of character. It was a subject Captain
Eddie knew well.

W.J.B.

It WILL BE NOTICED that my preparation for combat fighting in the air
was a gradual one. As I look back on it now, it seems that I had the rare
good fortune to experience almost every variety of danger that can beset
the war pilot before I ever fired a shot at an enemy from an aeroplane.

This good fortune is rare, it appears to me. Many a better man than
myself has leaped into his stride and begun accumulating victories from
his very first flight over the lines. It was a brilliant start for him and his
successes brought him instant renown. But he had been living on the
cream at the start and was unused to the skim-milk of aviation. One day
the cream gave out and the first dose of skim-milk terminated his career.

So despite the weeks and weeks of disappointment that attended my
early fighting career, I appreciated even then the enormous benefit that
I would reap later from these experiences. I can now most solemnly
affirm that had I won my first victory during my first trips over the lines
I believe I would never have survived a dozen combats. Every disappointment that came to me brought with it an enduring lesson that
repaid me eventually tenfold. If any one of my antagonists had been
through the same school of disappointments that had so annoyed me it
is probable that he, instead of me, would now be telling his friends back
home about his series of victories over the enemy.

April in France is much like April anywhere else. Rains and cloudy
weather appear suddenly out of a clear sky and flying becomes out of the
question or very precarious at best. On the 29th of April, 1918, we rose
at six o'clock and stuck our heads out of doors as usual for a hasty sur-
vey of a dismal sky. For the past three or four days it had rained steadily.
No patrols had gone out from our aerodrome. If they had gone they
would not have found any enemy aircraft about, for none had been
sighted from the lines along our sector.

About noon the sun suddenly broke through and our hopes began to rise. I was slated for a patrol that afternoon and from three o'clock on I waited about the hangars watching the steadily clearing sky. Captain Hall and I were to stand on alert until six o'clock that night at the aerodrome. Precisely at five o'clock Captain Hall received a telephone call from the French headquarters at Beaumont stating that an enemy two-seater machine had just crossed our lines and was flying south over their heads.

Captain Hall and I had been walking about the field with our flying clothes on and our machines were standing side by side with their noses pointing into the wind. Within the minute we had jumped into our seats and our mechanics were twirling the propellers. Just then the telephone sergeant came running out to us and told Captain Hall to hold his flight until the Major was ready. He was to accompany us and would be on the field in two minutes.

While the sergeant was delivering the message I was scanning the northern heavens and there I suddenly picked up a tiny speck against the clouds above the Forêt de la Reine, which I was convinced must be the enemy plane we were after. The Major was not yet in sight. Our motors were smoothly turning over and everything was ready.

Pointing out the distant speck to Jimmy Hall, I begged him to give the word to go before we lost sight of our easy victim. If we waited for the Major we might be too late.

To my great joy Captain Hall acquiesced and immediately ordered the boys to pull away the blocks from our wheels. His motor roared as he opened up his throttle and in a twinkling both our machines were running rapidly over the surface of the field. Almost side by side we arose and climbing swiftly, soared away in a straight line after our distant Boche.

In five minutes we were above our observation balloon line which stretches along some two miles or so behind the front. I was on Jimmy's right wing and off to my right in the direction of Pont-à-Mousson I could still distinguish our unsuspecting quarry. Try as I might I could not induce the Captain to turn in that direction, though I dipped my wings, darted away from him and tried in every way to attract his attention to the target which was so conspicuous to me. He stupidly continued on straight north.

I determined to sever relations with him and take on the Boche alone, since he evidently was generous enough to give me a clear field.

Accordingly I swerved swiftly away from Captain Hall and within five minutes overhauled the enemy and adroitly maneuvered myself into an ideal position just under his sheltering tail. It was a large three-seater machine and a brace of guns poked their noses out to the rear over my head. With fingers closing on my triggers I prepared for a dash upwards and quickly pulled back my stick. Up I zoomed until my sights began to travel along the length of the fuselage overhead. Suddenly they rested on a curiously familiar looking device. It was the French circular cocard painted brightly under each wing! Up to this time I had not even thought of looking for its nationality, so certain had I been that this must be the Boche machine that had been sighted by the French headquarters.

Completely disgusted with myself, I viraged abruptly away from my latest blunder, finding some little satisfaction in witnessing the startled surprise of the three Frenchmen aboard the craft, who had not become aware of my proximity until they saw me flash past them. At any rate I had stalked them successfully and might have easily downed them if they had been Boches. But as it was, it would be a trifle difficult to face Jimmy Hall again and explain to him why I had left him alone to get myself five miles away under the tail of a perfectly harmless ally three-seater. I looked about to discover Jimmy's whereabouts.

There he was cavorting about amidst a thick barrage of black shell-bursts across the German lines. He was half-way to St. Mihiel and a mile or two inside Hun territory. Evidently he was waiting for me to discover my mistake and then overtake him, for he was having a delightful time with the Archy gunners, doing loops, barrels, side-slips and spins imme-diately over their heads to show them his contempt for them, while he waited for his comrade. Finally he came out of the Archy area with a long graceful dive and swinging up alongside my machine he wiggled his wings as though he were laughing at me and then suddenly he set a course back towards Pont-à-Mousson.

Whether or not he knew all along that a German craft was in that region I could not tell. But when he began to change his direction and curve up into the sun I followed close behind him knowing that there was a good reason for this maneuver. I looked earnestly about me in every direction.

Yes! There was a scout coming towards us from north of Pont-à-Mousson. It was at about our altitude. I knew it was a Hun the moment I saw it, for it had the familiar lines of their new Pfalz. Moreover, my confidence in James Norman Hall was such that I knew he couldn't make a mistake. And he was still climbing into the sun, carefully keeping his position between its glare and the oncoming fighting plane. I clung as closely to Hall as I could. The Hun was steadily approaching us, unconscious of his danger, for we were full in the sun.

With the first downward dive of Jimmy's machine I was by his side. We had at least a thousand feet advantage over the enemy and we were two to one numerically. He might outdive our machines, for the Pfalz is a famous diver, while our faster climbing Nieuports had a droll little habit of shedding their fabric when plunged too furiously through the air. The Boche hadn't a chance to outfly us. His only salvation would be in a dive towards his own lines.

These thoughts passed through my mind in a flash and I instantly determined upon my tactics. While Hall went in for his attack I would keep my altitude and get a position the other side of the Pfalz, to cut off his retreat.

No sooner had I altered my line of flight than the German pilot saw me leave the sun's rays. Hall was already half-way to him when he stuck up his nose and began furiously climbing to the upper ceiling. I let him pass me and found myself on the other side just as Hall began firing. I doubt if the Boche had seen Hall's Nieuport at all.

Surprised by discovering this new antagonist, Hall, ahead of him, the Pfalz immediately abandoned all idea of a battle and banking around to the right started for home, just as I had expected him to do. In a trice I was on his tail. Down, down we sped with throttles both full open. Hall was coming on somewhere in my rear. The Boche had no heart for evolutions or maneuvers. He was running like a scared rabbit, as I had run from Campbell. I was gaining upon him every instant and had my sights trained dead upon his seat before I fired my first shot.

At 150 yards I pressed my triggers. The tracer bullets cut a streak of living fire into the rear of the Pfalz tail. Raising the nose of my aeroplane slightly the fiery streak lifted itself like the stream of water pouring from a garden hose. Gradually it settled into the pilot's seat. The swerving of the Pfalz course indicated that its rudder no longer was held by a directing hand. At 2,000 feet above the enemy's lines I pulled up my headlong dive and watched the enemy machine continuing on its course. Curving slightly to the left the Pfalz circled a little to the south and the next minute crashed onto the ground just at the edge of the woods a mile inside their own lines. I had brought down my first enemy aeroplane and had not been subjected to a single shot!

Hall was immediately beside me. He was evidently as pleased as I was over our success, for he danced his machine about in incredible maneuvers. And then I realized that old friend Archy was back on the job. We were not two miles away from the German anti-aircraft batteries and they put a furious bombardment of shrapnel all about us. I was quite ready to call it a day and go home, but Captain Hall deliberately returned to the barrage and entered it with me at his heels. Machine-guns and rifle fire from the trenches greeted us and I do not mind admitting that I got out quickly the way I came in without any unnecessary delay, but Hall continued to do stunts over their heads for ten minutes, surpassing all the acrobatics that the enraged Boches had ever seen even over their own peaceful aerodromes.

Jimmy exhausted his spirits at about the time the Huns had exhausted all their available ammunition and we started blithely for home. Swooping down to our field side by side, we made a quick landing and taxied our victorious machines up to the hangars. Then jumping out we ran to each other, extending glad hands for our first exchange of congratulations. And then we noticed that the squadron pilots and mechanics were streaming across the aerodrome towards us from all directions. They had heard the news while we were still dodging shrapnel and were hastening out to welcome our return. The French had telephoned in a confirmation of my first victory, before I had had time to reach home. Not a single bullet hole had punctured any part of my machine.

There is a peculiar gratification in receiving congratulations from one's squadron for a victory in the air. It is worth more to a pilot than the applause of the whole outside world. It means that one has won the confidence of men who share the misgivings, the aspirations, the trials and the dangers of aeroplane fighting. And with each victory comes a renewal and re-cementing of ties that bind together these brothers-in-arms. No closer fraternity exists in the world than that of the air-fighters in this great war. And I have yet to find one single individual who has attained conspicuous success in bringing down enemy aeroplanes who can be said to be spoiled either by his successes or by the generous congratulations of his comrades. If he were capable of being spoiled he would not have had the character to have won continuous victories, for the smallest amount of vanity is fatal in aeroplane fighting.

Self-distrust rather is the quality to which many a pilot owes his protracted existence.

It was with a very humble gratitude then that I received the warm congratulations of Lufbery, whom I had always revered for his seventeen victories—of Doug Campbell and Alan Winslow who had brought down the first machines that were credited to the American Squadrons, and of many others of 94 Squadron who had seen far more service in the battle areas than had I. I was glad to be at last included in the proud roll of victors of this squadron. These pals of mine were to see old 94 lead all American Squadrons in the number of successes over the Huns.

The following day I was notified that General Gerard, the Commanding Officer of the Sixth French Army, had offered to decorate Captain Hall and myself in the name of the French Government for our victory of the day before. We were then operating in conjunction with this branch of the French Army. The Croix de Guerre with palm was to be accorded each of us, provided such an order met the approval of our own government. But at that time officers in the American Army could not accept decorations from a foreign government, so the ceremony of presentation was denied us. Both Captain Hall and myself had been included, as such was the French rule where two pilots participated in a victory.

The truth was that in the tense excitement of this first victory, I was quite blind to the fact that I was shooting deadly bullets at another aviator; and if I had been by myself, there is no doubt in my own mind but that I should have made a blunder again in some particular which would have reversed the situation. Captain Hall's presence, if not his actual bullets, had won the victory and had given me that wonderful feeling of self-confidence which made it possible for me subsequently to return to battle without him and handle similar situations successfully.

4

Dave Ingalls, the Naval Ace

from THE FIRST YALE UNIT: A STORY OF NAVAL AVIATION 1916–1919
by Ralph D. Paine

In his best-selling history of the Kennedy and Johnson years, *The Best and the Brightest,* Pulitzer Prize–winning journalist David Halberstam opened with a description of an old man who personified more than anyone else of his generation the life of achievement and virtue implied in the book's title. He was a patrician by marriage, a prominent Wall Street banker, a distinguished public servant, an extraordinary individual so accomplished and so well connected, yet so purposely anonymous, that Halberstam called him "the very embodiment of the Establishment." When young John F. Kennedy, as the newly elected president, sought to fill his cabinet with men of position and stature, he turned to this old man and offered him his choice of the top jobs at State, Defense, or Treasury. Citing ill health, the old man graciously declined.

Robert A. Lovett's values were forged in the classrooms and on the playing fields at Yale in the early twentieth century. Yale, like the rest of the Ivy League at the time, was the province of the privileged class, an exclusive preserve for the sons of "old money" families. In those days, acceptance to Yale was a manifestation of one's pedigree, although many of the men who were sent there brought impressive intellect and maturity, qualities that had been honed ahead of time at the best eastern prep schools.

If a counterweight existed to balance the aristocratic leanings of this collection of blue-blooded youth, it was a deeply held sense of noblesse oblige. When dispatches from the trenches reached the serene New Haven, Connecticut campus, describing World War I battles in horrifying detail, some students became enraged over what they perceived as a demonic force sweeping away the cherished institutions of Western civilization. Empowered by the idealism of their youth, these Yalies, Bob Lovett among them, determined to establish a naval flying unit to halt the iniquitous enemy.

Spearheading the formation of Yale's inaugural naval flying unit, which came to be known appropriately enough as the First Yale Unit, was Trubee Davison, a leader in the student body. His father was a banking partner of none other than John Pierpont Morgan, one of the most influential men of the era, so the necessary arrangements for deployment of the unit to the war-torn skies of France would be easily smoothed over. Certain of the unit's members, like Davison, came from America's wealthiest families, their names synonymous with banking, retailing, and other important industries. The most affluent parents donated the costs of their sons' initial flight training in wooden seaplanes on the swank coast of Palm Beach, Florida.

Of course, the background of privilege did not soften the harshness of battle. In this excerpt, David Ingalls, the first U.S. Navy ace, describes firsthand the vagaries of World War I air combat in a letter to his parents. While in cooperative service with the British Royal Flying Corps, predecessor to the Royal Air Force, Ingalls participates in strafing runs on an enemy airfield, encountering flak from antiaircraft artillery emplacements, called Archies. Hurriedly climbing into the cover of fortuitously located clouds, he escapes the ground fire. Then his engine, having been stressed by extreme maneuvering, begins to sputter, reflecting the notorious unreliability of the era's aircraft power plants. This is followed by a pursuit, in which Ingalls's wingman joins, against an unsuspecting German two-seater that crashes and explodes. It was a long way from the peaceful Yale campus, and a full day for the naval aviator.

By and large, the historically obscure pilots of the First Yale Unit who survived the hazards of the front went on to outstanding careers in business or government or both. Their contributions in war and afterward were generally paid scant attention, but then that is how the men of the First Yale Unit were—driven by conviction, not the hollow reward of fame.

P.H.

For almost a week the members of the squadron had been sitting around waiting, apparently in vain, for a good day when we and several other squadrons were to bomb a certain aerodrome. For the first few days everyone rather welcomed the dud weather which had just come on, as a low bombing raid means coming down to within fifty feet or so to the earth, some twenty or thirty miles over the lines, which fact is rather disturbing to even the calmest and coolest pilots, but after a time we became restless and impatient to get the job done with.

So that it was rather a relief when the C.O., who had just been conversing with two of the flight commanders that had been testing a couple of machines in spite of the low clouds, entered the mess and announced that luncheon was to be served in half a hour, eleven-thirty, and we were to bomb the aerodrome. Only one squadron, as the weather was fine for a few machines to slip over the lines, was to drop through a break in the clouds, do their dirty work and get back safely in those clouds.

Upon hearing this, a few of the pilots, just out of the schools, hurried out to go over their machines, while the rest, well aware that all a pilot could do in the hangars was to get in the mechanic's way, gathered around the maps and discussed the different routes. A few minutes later the C.O. called a meeting and bringing forth larger maps and photographs, decided upon the leader, and fixed a particular target—a hangar hut or workshop—for each pilot, likewise detailing a man to shoot up the two or three machine-gun emplacements to be seen on the photos. Previous low raids had been done in a more haphazard manner, and this time we wanted to 'bring home the bacon' as Shakespeare did not say.

By the time each man knew his objective and place in the formation, lunch was served, all but a few heads acting in a rather hurried and nervous fashion. Luncheon over, we adjourned to our respective flight hangars, to don a helmet and gloves, and some to stuff a tooth-brush or small pistol in a pocket; at the same time everyone left behind all papers, letters, etc., which might be of value to the enemy in case one was captured.

Then I walked out to my machine. All R.F.C. mechanics are remarkably fine and efficient men, so I had complete confidence in mine, which is a comforting thing to have, and questioned him about a few faults in the machine, which I had told him about after the last flight. Of course he had attended to everything and was now occupied in cleaning the wind screen and brushing the seat. We got on board and the motors were started.

When their engines were warmed up and tested, the pilots took-off, flight by flight, the first three falling in behind the leader's flight. The leader climbed rapidly through a clear space in the clouds out to sea, where one and all tested the two guns with which the machines are armed. He then headed up the coast some ten miles out to sea, about 4,000 feet just above the clouds which were at about 3,000 feet.

The trip up to a spot opposite our objective seemed unusually long, as there was nothing to do but sit and wait. Finally, however, he turned towards shore, and I who was leading a flight which was to bomb a number of workshops which were slightly to one side of the aerodrome, drew up parallel to the leader. Fortunately the clouds were thick over the coast and no Archies came up. As we crossed the leader dived down, followed closely by all, through a break. As we appeared to their view the Archies started and it was mighty close, as the Huns had heard us and also had the range of the clouds, at our altitude. But not even the Hun Archies can hit a squadron of machines diving almost vertically down, and in a few seconds we were too low for them, tearing along at about 200 feet toward the junction of a canal and a railroad near our aerodrome—a landmark previously noted.

As we approached the aerodrome we slowed up and came down to about 100 feet; if lower one would be injured by the exploding of one's own bombs underneath. The hangars and huts were wonderfully placed for us, all in two lines wide enough to make a miss for almost any one an impossibility.

Getting a fine aim at my shop, I pulled the lever loosing the four twenty-five pounds carried, and looked up just in time to see one flight almost over us let go their bombs evidently at a perfectly smooth field beyond. I hoicked around so as not to be hit by the crazy beggars, and looked back to hear a continuous 'wonk wonk wonk'—practically the same sound an Archie makes when it bursts near one—to see a great number of direct hits on targets, and other explosions all around, except for the bombs of the flight which dotted the afore-mentioned field with beautifully spaced little holes.

Turning back, I dove, firing at two lorries standing near the shops, and, as I again hoicked away, I became aware of the sharp 'pat-pat' of several machine-gun emplacements firing from the ground. Being almost over one machine-gun emplacement, I looked in, but it was empty. Someone else was firing at the other machine-gun emplacement, while all the other machines, but two, climbing rapidly into the clouds, were diving and zooming around the aerodrome shooting like wild men. Why no one is hit by a pal is something I cannot understand.

I looked around for something to shoot. There were no men about nor any machines in the field, so I tried to puncture several huts. With these speeded-up guns one can fire an incredible amount in a slight dive from say 150 to 250 feet and it is very satisfying to see the tracers going into the roofs in a long line, an occasional one ricochetting off as it hits something at an obtuse angle. This time I could notice tracers coming from at least three machine guns but couldn't see where from.

By this time most of the machines were leaving, as there was really nothing worthwhile left to shoot up, so I flew over once more, and tried to locate correctly all the hits and two fires which were burning fiercely. At the far end of the field, as I was headed on a farm house, I located two of the machine-gun emplacements which were shooting at me, their tracers coming pretty close in spite of the maneuvering I was doing to escape them. I didn't see them in time to fire and as when I left I could see no other planes, I started after them, looking at several farm houses about the doors of which the whole family, Belgians of course, were heartily enjoying the spectacle.

Reaching 1,000 feet in no time I was taken note of by some Archie batteries, and so began turning, zooming and climbing to get to the clouds as quickly as possible. Those clouds looked mighty like a home to me. But now I got a shock, my engine almost cutting out, hitting at the most on three cylinders. I started on a gentle glide, looked at the gauges and switches, and tried running on the gravity tank, but no luck. So I looked around for a smooth field from an altitude of about 500 feet, and in the midst of Archie bursts. Then cheerio, the doggone engine grew better, though not best, and I encored my journey to the clouds, reaching them just before going over the coast, and disappeared therein. When I came out again into the clear sky I saw only one machine near, the others had almost disappeared in the direction of France. But this one turned back and I recognized one of my own flight. We waved happily, and set out at an easy pace for home, till I saw six Huns overland coming our way, but they never saw us and they turned off to one side. At which we both breathed easier.

By this time we were opposite Ostend, and again I saw a Hun, seemingly a two-seater climbing out of the clouds, probably thinking to get the last man ahead of us. S. and I put the helm over and edged in behind him, hoping he would [go] further out to sea. This he did, and thinking that he'd have to turn getting back, I opened up and started after him. At last he saw us, turned and dove back for Ostend, but we gained on him and soon opened fire at 400 yards. His observer was evidently new at the game, or killed by one of our shots, for I saw no tracers coming back. We continued to dive and shoot, he finally reaching the clouds. I was only 150 yards behind now, so followed, coming out of the clouds almost over Ostend piers, luckily right behind the Hun. One good burst and he caught fire, so I hoicked off swerving, to dodge the land M.G.S. [machine gun station] from the shore. A last look showed him crashing into the water by the beach, and S. joined me above the clouds. He had seen the Hun burst into flames and crash through a break and we went home rejoicing.

A minute later the Commanding Officer, who on seeing the Hun and scrap, had turned back, joined us and waved. A few minutes later we climbed out of our machines and hurried into the Records Office to report. Here we learned that two fellows had been wounded, one slightly, the other had three shots in his arm and leg, but all machines had returned. After the tension, everyone was feeling in great form, kidding one another and confirming the damage done. The reports and the official photos, taken next day, proved the raid to be one of the best done so far.

WORLD WAR II

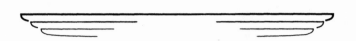

5

Man Does Not Die

from **FLIGHT TO ARRAS**
by Antoine de Saint-Exupéry

The lyrical rambling combination of a hazardous combat mission, reflections upon his childhood, and exposition of his philosophy of life and death impart an unusual significance to Antoine de Saint-Exupéry's *Flight to Arras.*

Despite the legends of Georges Guynemer and the achievements of Pierre Closterman, Saint-Exupéry remains unquestionably France's most popular aviation figure, combining as he does the romance of flying in the golden age, a mysterious death in combat, and an extensive literary heritage.

The reason for his popularity is found in this selection, in which his deep feelings about the immorality of warfare are placed aside in the conduct of a futile reconnaissance mission for an already defeated France. He reports: "There is no longer an army, there is no liaison, no matériel, and there are no reserves." But he flies on, and in the end, knows that it is only duty, a strange and meaningless word in the circumstances, that spurs him on.

Saint-Exupéry was a writer who flew rather than a pilot who wrote. We now know that he was not always as proficient as he might have been at his secondary profession, but his passion for democracy and for France was enough to motivate him to seek combat at an age when he could easily have sat out the war.

The poignant emotional quality of *Flight to Arras* is rendered in two modes. One is in his reflections on life and death; the other is in his eloquent description of a hazardous combat mission.

On any flight, there are moments of quiet when you are tasked simply to fly out a heading en route to your target. As Saint-Exupéry flies on in his beautiful twin-tail, twin-engine Potez 637, he responds to the call of his navigator, Dutertre, for course corrections, checks on his gunner—and lets his mind go back to Paula, his Tyrolian governess, his "memory of a memory." Then, while he is flying at 2,300 feet, a hail of antiaircraft fire brackets him and he kicks the rudder bar to jink the aircraft. In the midst of the battle, he "talks" to Paula, and says about being in combat: "All my memories, all my needs, all my loves are now available. My childhood, lost in darkness like a root, is at my disposal."

His navigator calls "Captain, Captain, I've never seen anything like it" as the flak roars. "Each burst of a machine gun or a rapid-fire cannon shot forth hundreds of these phosphorescent bullets that followed one another like beads of a rosary. A thousand elastic rosaries strung themselves out toward the plane, drawing themselves out to the breaking point, and burst at our height. When, missing us, the string went off at a tangent, its speed was dizzying. The bullets were transformed into lightning. And I flew drowned in a crop of trajectories formed into lightning."

Saint-Exupéry presses on, seeing the flak not as guns firing but as swords of light; he is not frightened but dazzled by the luxury that envelops him even as he runs the gauntlet of antiaircraft fire. His Potez is hit again and again, each "fragment of shell sank into the hull of the plane like a claw into living flesh."

The goal of the mission is to get to Arras, assess what the situation is there, and return with the information. Saint-Exupéry expects to die in the process, and in the process he learns that he does not fear death. He concludes: "Man does not die. Man imagines that it is death that he fears; but what he fears is the unforeseen, the explosion. What man fears is himself, not death."

Saint-Exupéry certainly did not fear death; he fought to return to combat, finally doing so flying a Lockheed P-38. There is irony in the fact that he sacrificed his life on a routine mission, probably the victim of a Focke Wulf Fw 190, at a time when the war was certain to be won. In a sense, he and his fallen compatriots did not die, since their quest for a life of freedom remains the essential component of the human spirit. Even now Saint-Exupéry's humane voice resonates powerfully, serving as a reminder that there is nobility among us.

W.J.B.

WHICH DOES NOT PREVENT this from being a funny war—aside from the spiritual reality that made it necessary. A funny war! I was never ashamed of this label. Hardly had we declared war when, being in no state to take the offensive, we began to look forward to our annihilation. Here it is.

We set up our haycocks against their tanks; and the haycocks turned out useless for defence. This day, as I fly to Arras, the annihilation has been consummated. There is no longer an army, there is no liaison, no matériel, and there are no reserves.

Nevertheless I carry on as solemnly as if this were war. I dive towards the German army at five hundred miles an hour. Why? I know! To frighten the Germans. To make them evacuate France. For since the intelligence I may bring back will be useless, this sortie can have no other purpose.

A funny war!

As a matter of fact, I am boasting. I have lost a great deal of altitude. Controls and throttles have thawed out. I have stepped down my speed to no more than three hundred and thirty miles an hour. A pity. I shall frighten the German army much less.

After all, it is we ourselves who call this a funny war. Why not? I should imagine that no one would deny us the right to call it that if we please, since it is we who are sacrificing ourselves, not those others who think our epithet immoral. Surely I have the right to joke about my death if joking about it gives me pleasure. And Dutertre has that right. I have the right to play with paradoxes. Why is it that those villages are still in flames? Why is it that that population has poured pell-mell out on the pavements? Why is it that we rush with inflexible determination towards an unmistakable slaughter-house?

I have every right to my joke; for in this moment I am fully conscious of what I am doing. I accept death. It is not danger that I accept. It is not combat that I accept. It is death. I have learnt a great truth. War is not the acceptance of danger. It is not the acceptance of combat. For the combatant, it is at certain moments the pure and simple acceptance of death.

And while men in the outside world were wondering, "Why is it that more Frenchmen are not being killed?" I was wondering, as I watched our crews go off to their death, "What are we giving ourselves to? Who is still paying this bill?"

For we were dying. For one hundred and fifty thousand Frenchmen were already dead in a single fortnight. Those dead do not exemplify an extraordinary resistance. I am not singing the praises of an extraordinary resistance. Such a resistance was impossible. But there were clusters of infantrymen still giving up their lives in undefendable farmhouses. There were aviation crews still melting like wax flung into a fire.

Look once again at Group 2-33. Will you explain to me why, as I fly to Arras, we of Group 2-33 still agree to die? For the esteem of the world? But esteem implies the existence of a judge. And I have the impression that none of us will grant whoever it may be the right to sit in judgment. To us who imagine that we are defending a cause which is fundamentally the common cause, the cause of Poland, of Holland, of Belgium, of Norway; to us who hold this view, the role of arbiter seems much too comfortable. It is we who sit in judgment upon the arbiter. I invite you to try to explain to us who take off with a "Very good, sir," having one chance in three to get back when the sortie is an easy one; I invite you to try to explain to a certain pilot out of another group, half of whose neck and jaw were shot away so that he is forced to renounce the love of woman for life, is frustrated in a fundamental right of man, frustrated as totally as if he were behind prison walls, surrounded inescapably by his virtue and preserved totally by his disfigurement, iso- lated completely by his ugliness—I invite you to explain to him that spectators are sitting in judgment upon him. Toreadors live for the bull- fight crowd: we are not toreadors. If you said to another of my friends, to Hochedé, "you've got to go up because the crowd have their eye on you," Hochedé would answer: "There must be some mistake: it is I, Hochedé, who have my eye on the crowd."

For after all, why do we go on fighting? For democracy? If we die for democracy then we must be one of the democracies. Let the rest fight with us, if that is the case. But the most powerful of them, the only democracy that could save us, chooses to bide its time. Very good. That is its right. But by so doing, that democracy signifies that we are fighting for ourselves alone. And we go on fighting despite the assurance that we have lost the war. Why, then, do we go on dying? Out of despair? But there is no despair. You know nothing at all about defeat if you think there is room in it for despair.

There is a verity that is higher than the pronouncements of the intelligence. There is a thing which pierces and governs us and which cannot be grasped by the intelligence. A tree has no language. We are a tree. There are truths which are evident, though not to be put into words. I do not die in order to obstruct the path of the invasion, for there is no shelter upon which I can fall back with those I love. I do not die to preserve my honor, since I deny that my honor is at stake, and I challenge the jurisdiction of my judge. Nor do I die out of desperation.

And yet Dutertre, looking at his map, having pin-pointed the position of Arras somewhere round the one hundred and seventy-fifth degree of the compass, is about to say to me—I can feel it:

"175°, Captain."

And I shall accept.

"172°."

"Right! 172°."

Call it one seventy-two. Epitaph: "Maintained his course accurately on 172°." How long will this crazy challenge go on? I am flying now at two thousand three hundred feet beneath a ceiling of heavy clouds. If I were to rise a mere hundred feet Dutertre would be blind. Thus we are forced to remain visible to anti-aircraft batteries and play the part of an archer's target for the Germans. Two thousand feet is a forbidden altitude. Your machine serves as a mark for the whole plain. You drain the cannonade of a whole army. You are within range of every calibre. You dwell an eternity in the field of fire of each successive weapon. You are not shot at with cannon but beaten with a stick. It is as if a thousand sticks were used to bring down a single walnut.

I had given a bit of thought to this problem. There is no question of a parachute. When the stricken plane dives to the ground the opening of the escape hatch takes more seconds than the dive of the plane allows. Opening the hatch involves seven turns of a crank that sticks. Besides, at full speed the hatch warps and refuses to slide.

That's that. The medicine had to be swallowed some day. I always knew it. Meanwhile, the formula is not complicated: stick to 172°. I was wrong to grow older. Pity. I was so happy as a child. I say so; but is it true? For already in that dim hall I was moving on this same course, 172°. Because of my uncles.

Now is the time when childhood seems sweet. Not only childhood, but the whole of my past life. I see it in perspective as if it were a landscape.

And it seems to me that I myself am unalterable. I have always felt what I now feel. Doubtless my joys and sadness changed object from time to time. But the feelings were always the same. I have been happy and unhappy. I have been punished and forgiven. I have worked well and badly. That depended on the days.

What is my earliest memory? I had a Tyrolian governess whose name was Paula. But she is not even a memory: she is the memory of a memory. Paula was already no more than a legend when at the age of five I sat marooned in the dim hall. Year after year my mother would say to us round the New Year, "There is a letter from Paula." That made all the children happy. But why were we happy? None of us remembered Paula. She had gone back long before to her Tyrol. To her Tyrolian house. A house, we imagined, deep in snow and looking like the toy chalet on a Tyrolian barometer. And Paula, on sunny days, would come forth to stand in the doorway of that house like the mechanical doll over the Tyrolian barometer.

"Is Paula pretty?"

"Beautiful."

"Is it sunny in the Tyrol?"

"Always."

It was always fine weather in the Tyrol. The Tyrolian barometer sent Paula farther forward out of her doorway and on to her snow-covered lawn. Later, when I was able to write, I would be set to writing letters to Paula. They always began: "My dear Paula, I am very glad to be writing to you." The letters were a little like my prayers, for I did not know Paula.

"One seventy-four."

"Right! One seventy-four."

Call it one seventy-four. Must change that epitaph.

Strange, how of a sudden life has collected in a heap. I have packed up my memories. They will never be of use to me again. Nor to anyone else. I remember a great love. My mother would say to us: "Paula sends kisses to you all." And my mother would kiss us all for Paula.

"Does Paula know I am bigger?"

"Naturally."

Paula knew everything.

"Captain, they are beginning to fire."

Paula, they are firing at me! I glanced at the altimeter: two thousand one hundred and fifty feet. Clouds at two thousand three hundred. Well. Nothing to be done about it. What astonishes me is that beneath my cloudbank the world is not black, as I had thought it would be. It is blue. Marvelously blue. Twilight has come, and all the plain is blue. Here and there I see rain falling. Rain-blue.

"One sixty-eight."

"Right! One sixty-eight."

Call it one sixty-eight. Interesting, that the road to eternity should be zigzag. And so peaceful! The earth here looks like an orchard. A moment ago it seemed to me skeletal, inhumanly desiccated. But I am flying low in a sort of intimacy with it. There are trees, some standing isolated, others in clusters. You meet them. And green fields. And houses with red tile roofs and people out of doors. And lovely blue showers pouring all round them. The kind of weather in which Paula must have hustled us rapidly indoors.

"One seventy-five."

My epitaph has lost a good deal of its laconic dignity: "Maintained his course on 172°, 174°, 168°, 175°...." I shall seem a very versatile fellow. What's that? Engine coughing? Growing cold. I shut the ventilators of the hood. Good. Time to change over to the reserve tanks. I pull the lever. Have I forgotten anything? I glance at the oil gauge. Everything shipshape.

"Beginning to get a bit nasty, Captain."

Hear that, Paula? Beginning to get nasty. And yet I cannot help being astonished by the blue of the evening. It is so extraordinary. The color is so deep. And those fruit trees, plum trees, perhaps, flowing by. I am part of the countryside now. Gone are the museum cases. I am a marauder who has jumped over the wall. I am running through the wet alfalfa, stealing plums. This is a funny war, Paula. A war nostalgic and beautifully blue. I got lost somehow, and strayed into this strange country in my old age.... O, no, I am not frightened. It's a little melancholy, that's all.

"Zigzag, Captain!"

Here is a new game, Paula. You kick the rudder bar with your right foot and then your left, and the anti-aircraft battery can't touch you. When I fell down I used to bruise myself and raise swellings. I am sure you used to cure me with compresses of arnica. I am going to need arnica awfully, I think. But still, you know this evening air is marvelously blue!

Forward of my plane I saw suddenly three lance-strokes aimed at my machine. Three long brilliant vertical twigs. The paths of tracer-bullets fired from a small-calibre gun. They were golden. Suddenly in the blue of the evening I had seen the spurting glow a three-branched candlestick.

"Captain! Firing very fast to port. Hard down!"

I kicked my rudder.

"Getting worse!"

Worse?

Getting worse; but I am seated at the heart of the world. All my memories, all my needs, all loves are now available to me. My childhood, lost in darkness like a root, is at my disposal. My life here begins with the nostalgia of a memory. Yes, it is getting worse; but I feel none of those things I thought I should feel when facing the claws of these shooting stars.

I am in a country that moves my heart. Day is dying. On the left I see great slabs of light among the showers. They are like panes in a cathedral window. Almost within reach, I can all but handle the good things of the earth. There are those plum trees with their plums. There is that earth-smelling earth. It must be wonderful to tramp over damp earth. You know, Paula, I am going gently forward, swaying to right and left like a loaded hay wain. You think an aeroplane moves fast; and indeed it does, if you think of it. But if you forget the machine, if you simply look on, why, you are merely taking a stroll in the country.

"Arras!"

Yes. Very far ahead. But Arras is not a town. Arras thus far is no more than a red plume against a blue background of night. Against a background of storm. For unmistakably, forward on the left, an awful squall is collecting. Twilight alone would not explain this half-light. It wants blocks of clouds to filter a glow so somber.

The flame of Arras is bigger now. You wouldn't call it the flame of a conflagration. A conflagration spreads like a chancre surrounded by no more than a narrow fringe of living flesh. That red plume permanently alight is the gleam of a lamp that might be smoking a bit. It is a flame without flicker, sure to last, well fed with oil. I can feel it moulded and kneaded out of a compact substance, something almost solid that the wind stirs from time to time and bends as it bends a tree. That's it: a tree. Arras is caught up in the mesh of roots of this tree. And all the pith of Arras, all the substance of Arras, all the treasures of Arras leap, now become sap, to nourish this tree.

I can see that occasionally top-heavy flame lose its equilibrium to right or left, belch forth an even blacker cloud of smoke, and then collect itself again. But I am still unable to make out the town.

The whole war is summed up in that glow. Dutertre says that it is getting worse. Perched up forward, he can see better than I can. Nevertheless, I am astonished by a sort of indulgence shown us: this venomous plain shoots forth few stars.

Yes, but....

You remember, Paula, that in the fairy-tales of our childhood there was always a knight who passed through frightful experiences before reaching the enchanted castle. He scaled glaciers, leapt across abysses, outwitted villains. And in the end the castle rose before him out of a blue plain gentler beneath the galloping hoofs than a green lawn. Already he thought himself victorious. Ah, Paula, you can't fool an old fairy-tale reader! The worst of his trials was still before him—the ogre, the dragon, the guardian of the castle.

Like that knight, I ride in the blue of the evening towards my castle of flame. And not for the first time. You had already left us when we began to play games. You missed the game called Aklin the Knight. We had invented it ourselves, for we sneered at games that other children could play. This one was played out of doors in stormy weather when, after the first flashes of lightning, we could tell from the rising smell of the earth and the sudden quivering of the leaves that the cloud was about to burst. There was a moment when the thickness in the boughs turned into a lightly soughing moss. That was the signal. Nothing could hold us back.

We would run as fast as we could from the deep end of the park towards the house, flying breathlessly across the lawns. The first drops of that rain were always scattered and heavy. The child first touched by them was beaten. Then the next. Then the third. Then the rest. He who survived longest was acknowledged the darling of the gods, the invulnerable. Until the next storm came he had the right to call himself Aklin the Knight. It was only a matter of seconds, and the result was each time a hecatomb of children.

I fly my plane, playing at being Aklin the Knight. I am running slowly and out of breath towards my castle of flame.

"Captain! Captain! I've never seen anything like it!"

Nor have I.

Where now is my vulnerability? Unknown to myself, I had been hoping. . . .

———————————————

Despite my lack of altitude, I had been hoping. Despite the tank parks, despite the flame over Arras. Desperately, I had been hoping. I had escaped into a memory of early childhood in order to recapture the sense of sovereign protection. For man there is no protection. Once you are a man you are left to yourself. But who can avail against a little boy whose hand is firmly clasped in hand of an all-powerful Paula? Paula, I have used thy shade as a shield.

I have used every trick in my bag. When Dutertre said to me, "It's getting worse," I used even that threat as a source of hope. We were at war: necessarily, then, there had to be evidence of war. The evidence was no more than a few streaks of light. "Is this your terrible danger of death over Arras? Don't make me laugh!"

The man condemned had imagined that the executioner would look like a pallid robot. Arrives a quite ordinary decent-appearing fellow who is able to sneeze, even to smile. The man condemned clings to that smile as to a promise of reprieve. The promise is a wraith. The headsman sneezes—and the head falls nevertheless. But who can reject hope?

I myself could not but be deceived by the smile I saw—since this whole world was snug, and verdant, since the wet slate and tile shone so cordially, since from minute to minute nothing changed nor promised to change. Since we three, Dutertre, the gunner, and I, were men walking

across fields, sauntering idly home without so much as the need to raise
our collars, so little was it raining. Since here at the heart of the German
zone nothing stood forth that was really worth telling about, whence it
must follow that farther on the war need not of necessity be different to
this. Since it seemed that the enemy had scattered and melted into the
wide and rural plain, standing perhaps at the rate of one soldier to a
house, one soldier to a tree, one of whom, remembering now and then
the war, would fire. The order had been drummed into the fellows ears:
"Fire on all enemy planes." But he had been day-dreaming, and the
order had been dimmed by the dream. He let fly his three rounds without much expectation of results. Thus at dusk I used to shoot ducks that
meant very little to me if the evening invited my soul. I would fire while
talking about something else. It hardly disturbed the ducks.

It is so easy to spin fine tales to oneself. The enemy takes aim, but
without firm purpose; and he misses me. Others in turn let us pass.
Those who might trip us up are perhaps at this moment inhaling with
pleasure the smell of the night, or lighting cigarettes, or finishing a funny
story—and they let us pass. Still others in the village where they are bil-
leted, are perhaps dipping their tin cups into the soup. A roar rises and
dies away. Friend or enemy? There isn't time for them to find out: their
eyes are on the cup now filling—they let us pass. And I, whistling a tune
and my hands in my pockets, do my best to walk as casually as I can
through this garden forbidden to trespassers where every guard, counting on the next guard, lets us pass.

How vulnerable I was! Yet it seemed to me that my very vulnerability
was a trap, a means of cajoling them: "Why fire? Your friends are sure to
bring me down a little farther on." And they would shrug their shoulders: "Go break your neck somewhere else." They were leaving the
chore to the next battery—because they were anxious not to miss their
turn at the soup, were finishing their funny story, or were simply enjoying the evening breeze. I was taking advantage of their negligence, and
I was saved by the seeming coincidence that all of them at once appeared
to be weary of war. And why not? Already I was thinking vaguely that
from soldier to soldier, squad to squad, village to village, I should get
through this sortie. After all, what were we but a passing plane in the
evening sky? Not enough to make a man raise his eyes.

Of course I hoped to get back. But I could feel at the same time that
something was in the air. You are sentenced: a penalty hangs over you;

but the gaol in which you are locked up continues silent. You cling to that silence. Every second that drops is like the one that went before. There is no reason why the second about to drop should change the world. Such a task is too heavy for a single second. Each second that follows safeguards your silence. Already this silence seems perpetual.

But the step of him who must come sounds in the corridor.

Something in this countryside suddenly exploded. So a log that seemed burnt out crackles suddenly and shoots forth its sparks. How did it happen that the whole plain started up at the same moment? When spring comes, all the trees at once drop their seed. Why this sudden springtime of arms? Why this luminous flood rising towards us and, of a sudden, universal?

My first feeling was that I had been careless. I had ruined everything. A wink, a single gesture is enough to topple you from the tight-rope. A mountain climber coughs, and he releases an avalanche. Once he has released the avalanche, all is over.

We had been swaying heavily through this blue swamp already drowned in night. We had stirred up this silent slime; and now, in tens of thousands, it was sending towards us its golden bubbles. A nation of jugglers had burst into dance. A nation of jugglers was dribbling its projectiles in tens of thousands in our direction. Because they came straight at us, at first they appeared to be motionless. Like colored balls which jugglers seem not so much to fling into the air as to release upwards, they rose in a lingering ascension. I could see those tears of light flowing towards me through a silence as of oil. That silence in which jugglers perform.

Each burst of a machine gun or a rapid-fire cannon shot forth hundreds of these phosphorescent bullets that followed one another like the beads of a rosary. A thousand elastic rosaries strung themselves out to the breaking point, and burst at our height. When missing us, the string went off at a tangent, its speed was dizzying. The bullets were transformed into lightning. And I flew drowned in a crop of trajectories as golden as stalks of wheat. I flew at the center of a thicket of lance strokes. I flew threatened by a vast and dizzying flutter of knitting needles. All the plain was now bound to me, woven and wound round me, a coruscating web of golden wire.

I leant towards the earth and saw those storied levels of luminous bubbles rising with the tardy movement of veils of fog. I saw as I stated the slow vortex of seed, swirling like the husks of threshed grain. And when I raised my head I saw on the horizon those stacks of lances. Guns firing? Not at all! I am attacked by cold steel. These are swords of light. I feel... certainly not danger! Dazzled I am by the luxury that envelops me.

What's that!

I was jolted nearly a foot out of my seat. The plane has been rammed hard; I thought. It has burst, been ground to bits.... But it hasn't; it hasn't.... I can still feel it responsive to controls. This was but the first blow of a deluge of blows. Yet there was no sign of explosion below. The smoke of the heavy guns had probably blended into the dark ground.

I raised my head and started. What I saw was without appeal.

I had been looking on at a carnival of light. The ceiling had risen little by little and I had been unaware of an intervening space between the clouds and me. I had been zigzagging along a line of flight dotted by ground batteries. Their tracer bullets had been spraying the air with wheat-colored shafts of light. I had forgotten that at the top of their flight the shells of those batteries must burst. And now, raising my head, I saw around and before me those rivets of smoke and steel driven into the sky in the pattern of towering pyramids.

I was quite aware that those rivets were no sooner driven than all danger went out of them, that each of those puffs possessed the power of life and death only for a fraction of a second. But so sudden and simultaneous was their appearance that the image flashed into my mind of conspirators intent upon my death. Abruptly their purpose was revealed to me, and I felt on the nape of my neck the weight of an inescapable reprobation.

Muffled as those explosions reached me, their sound covered by the roar of my engines, I had the illusion of an extraordinary silence. Those vast packets of smoke and steel moving soundlessly upward and behind me with the lingering flow of icebergs, persuaded me that, seen in their perspective, I must be virtually motionless. I was motionless in the dock before an immense assizes. The judges were deliberating my fate, and there was nothing I could plead. Once again the timelessness of suspense seized me. I thought,—I was still able to think—"They are aiming too high," and I looked up in time to see straight overhead, swinging away from me as if with reluctance, a swarm of black flakes that glided like eagles. Those eagles had given me up. I was not to be their prey. But even so, what hope was there for me?

The batteries that continued to miss me continued also to adjust their aim. New walls of smoke and steel continued to be built up round me as I flew. The ground-fire was not seeking me out, it was closing me in.

"Dutertre! How much more of this is there?"

"Stick it out three minutes, Captain. Looks bad, though."

"Think we'll get through?"

"Not on your life!"

There never was such muck as this murky smoke, this mess as grimy as a heap of filthy rags. The plain was blue. Immensely blue. Deep-sea blue.

What was a man's life worth between this blue plain and this foul sky? Ten seconds, perhaps; or twenty. The shock of the exploding shells set all the sky shuddering. When a shell burst very near the explosion rumbled along the plane like a rock dropping through a chute. And when for a moment the roar stopped, the plane rang with a sound that was almost musical. Like a sigh, almost; and the sigh told us that the plane had been missed. Those bursts were like the thunder: the closer they came, the simpler they were. A rumble meant distance, a clean *bang!* meant that we had been squarely hit by a shell fragment. The tiger does not do a messy job on the ox it brings down. The tiger sets its claws into the ox without skidding. It takes possession of the ox. Each square hit by a fragment of shell sank into the hull of the plane like a claw into living flesh.

"Anybody hurt?"

"Not I!"

"Gunner! You all right?"

"O.K., sir!"

Somehow those explosions, though I find I must mention them, did not really count. They drummed upon the hull of the plane as upon a drum. They pierced my fuel tanks. They might as easily have drummed upon our bellies, pierced them instead. What is the belly but a kind of drum? But who cares what happens to his body? Extraordinary, how little the body matters.

There are things that we might learn about our bodies in the course of everyday living if we were not blind to patent evidence. It takes this rain of upsurging streamers of light, this assault by an army of lances, this assizes set up for the last judgment, to teach us those things.

I used to wonder as I was dressing for a sortie what a man's last moments were like. And each time, life would give the lie to the ghosts I evoked. Here I was, now, naked and running the gauntlet, unable so much as to guard my head by arm or shoulder from the crazy blows raining down upon me. I had always assumed that the ordeal, when it came, would be an ordeal that concerned my flesh. My flesh alone, I assumed, would be subjected to the ordeal. It was unavoidable that in thinking of these things I should adopt the point of view of my body. Like all men, I had given it a good deal of time. I had dressed it, bathed it, fed it, quenched its thirst. I had identified myself with this domesticated animal. I had taken it to the tailor, the surgeon, the barber. I had been unhappy with it, cried out in pain with it, loved with it. I had said of it "This is me." And now of a sudden my illusion vanished. What was my body to me? A kind of flunkey in my service. Let but my anger wax hot, my love grow exalted, my hatred collect in me, and that boasted solidarity between me and my body was gone.

Your son is in a burning house. Nobody can hold you back. You may burn up; but do you think of that? You are ready to bequeath the rags of your body to any man who will take them. You discover that what you set so much store by is trash. You would sell your hand, if need be, to give a hand to a friend. It is in your act that you exist, not in your body. Your act is yourself and there is no other you. Your body belongs to you: it is not you: Are you about to strike an enemy? No threat of bodily harm can hold you back. You? It is the death of your enemy that is you. You? It is the rescue of your child that is you. In that moment you exchange yourself against something else; and you have no feeling that you lost by the exchange. Your members? Tools. A tool snaps in your hand: how important is that tool? You exchange yourself against the death of your enemy, the rescue of your child, the recovery of your patient, the perfection of your theorem. Here is a pilot of my Group wounded and dying. A true citation in general orders would read: "Called out to his observer, 'They've got me! Beat it! And for God's sake don't lose those notes!'" What matters is the notes, the child, the patient, the theorem. Your true significance becomes dazzlingly evident.

Your true name is duty, hatred, love, child, theorem. There is no other you than this.

The flames of the house, of the diving plane, strip away the flesh; but they strip away the worship of the flesh too. Man ceases to be concerned with himself: he recognizes of a sudden what he forms part of. If he should die, he would not be cutting himself off from his kind, but making himself one with them. He would not be losing himself, but finding himself. This that I affirm is not the wishful thinking of a moralist. It is an everyday fact. It is a commonplace truth. But a fact and a truth hidden under the veneer of our everyday illusion. Dressing and fretting over the fate that might befall my body, it was impossible for me to see that I was fretting over something absurd. But in the instant when you are giving up your body, you learn to your amazement—all men always learn to their amazement—how little store you set by your body. It would be foolish to deny that during all those years of my life when nothing insistent was prompting me, when the meaning of my existence was not at stake, it was impossible for me to conceive that anything might be half so important as my body. But here in this plane I say to my body (in effect), "I don't care a button what becomes of you. I have been expelled out of you. There is no hope of your surviving this, and yet I lack for nothing. I reject all that I have been up to this very instant. For in the past it was not I who thought, not I who felt: it was you, my body. One way and another, I have dragged you through life to this point; and here I discover that you are of no importance."

Already at the age of fifteen I might have learnt this lesson. I had a younger brother who lay dying. One morning towards four o'clock his nurse woke me and said that he was asking for me.

"Is he in pain?" I asked.

The nurse said nothing, and I dressed as fast as I could.

When I came into his room he said to me in a matter-of-fact voice, "I wanted to see you before I died. I am going to die." And with that he stiffened and winced and could not go on. Lying in pain, he waved his hand as if saying "No!" I did not understand. I thought it was death he was rejecting. The pain passed, and he spoke again. "Don't worry," he said. "I'm all right. I can't help it. It's my body." His body was already foreign territory, something not himself.

He was very serious, this younger brother who was to die in twenty minutes. He had called me in because he felt a pressing need to hand on

part of himself to me. "I want to make my will," he said; and he blushed
with pride and embarrassment to be talking like a grown man. Had he
been a builder of towers he would have bequeathed to me the finishing
of his tower. Had he been a father, I should have inherited the education
of his children. A reconnaissance pilot, he would have passed on to me
the intelligence he had gleaned. But he was a child, and what he confided
to my care was a toy steam engine, a bicycle, and a rifle.

Man does not die. Man imagines that it is death he fears; but what he
fears is the unforeseen, the explosion. What man fears is himself, not
death. There is no death when you meet death. When the body sinks
into death, the essence of man is revealed. Man is a knot, a web, a mesh
into which relationships are tied. Only those relationships matter. The
body is an old crock that nobody will miss. I have never known a man
to think of himself when dying. Never.

6

Bader's Bailout

from **REACH FOR THE SKY**
by Paul Brickhill

Douglas Bader was the finest example of indomitable Englishman. He had crashed doing low-level aerobatics in a Bristol Bulldog fighter in 1931, losing his right leg above the knee and his left below. It was a devastating blow that might have felled another man, but not Douglas Bader. He fought his way back into the cockpit to become one of the most celebrated RAF fighter pilots of World War II. In honor of his courage, which seemed to characterize not only the RAF but also the British people, Bader was selected to lead the 1945 Battle of Britain flypast.

I had the pleasure of meeting Bader on two occasions, both when he was my guest at the National Air and Space Museum. He was an absolutely charming dinner companion with an endless fund of stories, a few of which were quite naughty. He was also immensely courageous, trying to ignore the inconvenience and the pain caused by his artificial legs.

Bader was insistent on seeing everything in the museum, and we walked the long halls together. Refusing to admit that he was tired, he would, every hundred feet or so, find an object of such immense interest that we would be required to stop and discuss it at length—until he had caught his breath again. But his great courage was best shown in his courtesy. If he was seated, and approached by a woman, no matter how young or old, he would, with a curious little rocking motion, literally hurl himself to his feet. The act must have been physically exhausting, for it depended entirely on mustering his upper-body strength in a convulsive leap, but he would repeat it every time.

Paul Brickhill captures the essence of the man and his times in this brilliant excerpt from *Reach for the Sky,* in which Bader is characterized as "bomb-proof, bullet-proof and fire-proof."

Fiercely competitive, Bader had flown more missions than almost anyone else in Fighter Command, leading his men by his own hard fighting example. At the time of his last combat mission, he was credited with twenty and a half officially confirmed victories. By his own, probably accurate, count, he had seven more.

But Bader was more than an ace; he was a brilliant wing commander who tempered his fiery leadership with demonstrations of low-level aerobatics over the airfield and with humor. His combat reports were meticulous in their accounting of victories and probables, yet he always managed to add a line or two about the enemy aircraft he "frightened," a trait that Group Headquarters found not to be amusing at all.

Bader was also a fine judge of talent. He had selected Denis Crowley-Milling, "Cocky" Dundas, Stan Turner, and Johnny Johnson as comers, and all became highly decorated wing commanders. Johnson also became the top-scoring ace of the RAF during World War II, with thirty-eight victories.

Author Brickhill is as expert in conveying Bader's sometimes difficult, always colorful personality as he is the swift, sudden drama of the whirling dogfights between Spitfires and Messerschmitts. During the Battle of Britain they had been conducted over home territory, and the RAF had established a solid superiority. By the summer of 1941, things had changed. The RAF was ranging over enemy territory, and the victory ratio shifted to the Luftwaffe's favor with two kills for every loss.

Yet, just as in World War I, the RAF persisted with its offensive tactics. So it was that on August 9 Bader found himself in a malfunctioning Spitfire, engaging with the Messerschmitts of JG 26 over the French coast.

Brickhill is at his finest as he describes Bader's headlong attack, his probable victory over one Messerschmitt, and his shattering collision with another. Bader fell in a tailless Spitfire from 24,000 feet, trapped in the cockpit, his right "tin leg" caught as if in a bear trap. The gyrations of the tailless Spitfire battered Bader into unconsciousness until he was somehow thrown free, leaving his prostheses in the cockpit.

For most men the war would have ended right there, but Bader was made of stronger stuff. Brickhill records faithfully how the admiring Germans treated Bader well, giving him adequate medical treatment and repairing his mechanical leg, which they had retrieved from the wreckage of his Spitfire. Yet Bader would show them no mercy; within days he was plotting, then attempting, an escape. It would be the first of many such attempts. During his long confinement, Bader's unfailing insolence to his German captors would rally his fellow prisoners of war, raising their morale. If ever a man deserved to lead a Battle of Britain flyby, it was Wing Commander Douglas Bader, as Brickhill's narrative makes very clear.

W.J.B.

Now the Messerschmitts were ever more numerous and bolder, every day savaging the flanks. More and more often Bader broke the wing to go for them, and for frantic minutes the sky was full of snarling, twisting, spitting aeroplanes. Several of the wing scored "kills" and three Spitfires did not come back.

The Messerschmitts—quite rightly—never stayed long to mix it with the more manœuvreable Spitfires as they could never hold their own in a round-about tail chase. Despite British propaganda, the 109's were slightly faster and their proper tactics were to dive, shoot and break off. Sometimes they pulled up again and sometimes they half-rolled on to their backs and dived steeply out of the fight in the reverse direction. Any Spitfire on its own after a fight was under standing orders to join up with the nearest friendly fighters so there would be at least two in line abreast to watch each other's tail. It was jungle law up there and the devil took the odd man out.

Coming back over the Channel one day, Dundas was startled to see Bader, flying alongside, flip back his cockpit top, unclip his oxygen mask, stuff his stub pipe in his mouth, strike a match (apparently holding the stick between his good knee and tin knee), light up and sit there like Pop-Eye puffing wisps of smoke that the slipstream snatched away. Dundas longed to light a cigarette himself, but desire was tempered by realisation that no normal man lit a naked flame in a Spitfire cockpit. Bader looked across, caught Dundas's wide eyes, beamed and made a rude gesture.

After that he always puffed his pipe in the cockpit on the way back, and pilots flying alongside used to sheer off, half in joke, half in earnest, in case Spitfire D.B. blew up. But it never did, adding to the growing and inspiring myth that Bader was bomb-proof, bullet-proof and fire-proof.

With virtually daily trips now, he christened the wing "The Bee-Line Bus Service. The Prompt and Regular Service. Return Tickets Only." That tickled everyone's fancy, and some of the pilots painted it on the side of their cowlings. It felt good to be one of the Tangmere Wing. Almost every night he took a few of his boys (and sometimes their girl friends) back to the Bay House, where Thelma and Jill made sandwiches and they sat yarning and quaffing beer.

Any new pilots he nursed carefully, yarning to them about tactics, air discipline (e.g., strict radio silence at the right times) and putting them in the middle of the pack for their first few trips. Once in mid-Channel on the way out a new boy in 145 called: "Hallo, Red Leader. Yellow Two calling. I can't turn my oxygen on."

A brooding silence followed.

The voice plaintively again: "Hallo, Red Leader. Can you hear me? I can't turn on my oxygen."

Then Turner's Canadian voice, ferociously sarcastic:

"What the hell do you want me to do? Get out and turn it on for you? *Go home!*"

No one made that mistake again.

On 2nd July they went to Lille, and Bader dived 616 on fifteen 109's. He fired at one from almost dead behind, and as its hood flew off and the pilot jumped, another 109 plunged past and collected a burst. Smoke and oil spurted and he went down vertically. Bader left him and pulled up, obeying the dictum that it is suicide to follow an enemy down. Coming back over the Channel, he dived on another enemy, and as he started firing the 109 rolled on its back like lightning and streaked back into France. Bader was getting fed up with 109's diving out of a fight like that (though he respected the correctness of their tactics), and when he got back to claim one destroyed and one probable, he added as a flippant afterthought: "and the third one I claim as frightened."

He hoped for a bite from Intelligence at Group but they maintained a dignified silence. Instead he got a phone call from Leigh-Mallory, who said: "Douglas, I hear you got another 109 today."

"Yes, sir."

"Well," Leigh-Mallory went on in his deceptively pompous voice, "you've got something else too—a bar to your D.S.O."

Down at dispersals next day when he was congratulated, Bader said awkwardly: "All this blasted chest cabbage doesn't matter a damn. It's what the wing does that really counts." He meant it, too, and the pilots were surprised at the self-consciousness that lay under the boisterous exterior.

Coming away from Lille a couple of days later, little schools of Messerschmitts began pecking at them again. Bader fired at three but they half-rolled and dived away. Two more dashed in and Bader shot one in the stomach from 100 yards. Explosive bullets must have slugged into the tank behind the cockpit because it blew a fiery jet like a blow-torch and fell out of the sky, dragging a plume of black smoke.

Remembering the three that got away, he claimed one destroyed and "three frightened,"and this time got a bite from Group. A puzzled message arrived asking what he meant and he sent a signal back explaining. Group answered stiffly that they were not amused (though everyone else thought it was a "good giggle").

It takes an odd genius to handle a wing in the lightning of battle where it is so easy to become confused or excited or tempted by a decoy. There was a day a 109 flew in front and just below them, and Bader called: "That—looks too obvious. Look up-sun, everyone, and see if you can see anything." No one could and at last Bader said: "Come on, Cocky. Let's take a pot. The rest stay up."

As he led Dundas down, the 109 half-rolled and dived, presumably transmitting, because seconds later his friends came out of the sun. Holden's squadron intercepted some and the rest came down on 616, which swung back into them. Turner's men plunged from above and the fight was on. Separated and set on by four 109's, Dundas fought them alone for five minutes, twisting and gyrating, unable to shake them off, until finally he took the last chance . . . stick hard back and hard rudder to flick into a spin. He let her go for 12,000 feet, came out at 5,000, dived for the coast, dodged several 109's, flashed over an airfield, squirted at a 109 coming in to land, and was chased by others for miles, seeing glowing little balls darting past his wingtip as they fired. Not till mid-Channel did he shake them off and landed with empty tanks, a dry mouth and sweaty brow.

Bader hailed him: "You stupid goat, Cocky. Serves you damn well right. Teach you to get stuck out on your own."

A day or two later after a brisk "shambles," Bader found himself isolated and called Holden:

"Hallo, Ken. I'm on my own. Can you join me?"

"O.K., D.B. What's your position?"

"About fifteen miles north of Big Wood."

"Good show. I'm in the same area at 25,000 feet. What are your angels?"

"8,000."

In his broadcast Yorkshire, Holden said: "Eee, we'll be a bit conspicuous down there."

He heard Bader's domineering rasp:

"To hell with that. You come on down here."

A pregnant silence, and then Holden:

"Nay...you coom oop here."

Dreadful words came over the R/T, but Holden, grinning behind his mask, was already on his way down, and they came home together.

After a while, to the regret of the Beauty Chorus, Woodhall disconnected the loud-speaker in the Ops Room, feeling that some of the battle comments were too ripe even for the most sophisticated W.A.A.F.s. ("They laugh, you know," he said, "but dammit I get so embarrassed.") Bader was not exactly the least of the R/T offenders, but whenever his buccaneering presence lurched into the Ops Room there was a lot of primping, giggling and rolling of eyes.

On 9th July, near Mazingarbe, he sent a 109 down streaming glycol and black smoke, and noted the flash on the ground where it presumably exploded. Another 109 lunged at him, and he turned quickly and got in a burst as it broke off. His combat report said:

"A glycol stream started. I did not follow him down and claimed a damaged. Several others were frightened and I claim one badly frightened, who did the quickest half-roll and dive I've ever seen when I fired at him."

No further bite from Group about the "frightened." They only allowed victories when the enemy was seen by witnesses in flames, or seen to crash, or the crew baled out.

Over Chocques next day he dived 616 on twenty Messerschmitts. More 109's swung in from one side and ran into Holden's squadron, then Turner's men came plunging down and the welkin shook to the roaring, swelling thunder of the dogfight. Bader sent one down shedding bits and pieces, pulled up behind another and fired into its belly. Under its cockpit burst a flash of flame, and suddenly the whole aeroplane blossomed with red fire as the tanks blew up and it fell like a torch. July was turning out a wonderful month. In eight days he had four destroyed, two probables and two damaged, but it only whetted his appetite.

For two days the weather was bad and he took Holden to a nearby links for golf, arranging first that if it cleared over France and a "show" was "on," they would fire Véry lights from the airfield. Holden would then run to the car parked by the first tee, drive across the course, pick up Bader and have them both back at the airfield in ten minutes. Bader spent most of his time on the links watching for a Véry light, on edge in case something happened and he missed it. He had led the wing on every sweep so far and obviously intended to keep on doing so. But he had little time to relax at golf; even when the wing was not flying, they were on stand-by or readiness in flying kit from dawn to dusk, waiting for a "show" or waiting in case the Luftwaffe attacked England again. There were no days off for the nerves to relax.

For Bader there was paper work, too, in his office, but he gave it little courtesy. Holden was with him one day when a flight-sergeant came in and dumped a pile of files in his "in" tray. Bader growled: "What the hell's this, flight sergeant?"

"Files for your attention, sir."

"I'll give 'em attention all right." He picked them up and threw the lot in his waste-paper basket.

He had time to write to a small boy, however. Norman Rowley, aged seven, had had both legs amputated after being run over by a bus in a Yorkshire mining village, and Bader wrote to tell him he would be all right and could be a pilot if he tried hard. (It helped the boy more than anything. He was proud to be Bader's friend.)

In some ways Bader overdid the personal leadership, leaving no one trained to follow him. He could not always lead the wing, and it was obvious what a gap his going would leave. But that did not seem in the realm of reality, and people were recognising now that he had more genius for fighter leadership than anyone else alive.

When there were no sweeps (rarely) he still liked to throw his Spitfire round the sky. His solid frame and square jaw would block Holden's doorway.

"Ken! Aerobatics!"

"O.K., sir. I'll be with you in a minute."

"What's the matter, you clot?" (rasping). "Don't you want to come?"

"Yes, sir, but I've got to finish this readiness roster."

"Damn that! You come with me!"

For the next hour Holden, Turner and Burton (press-ganged in the same way) would be careering round the sky following Bader in formation loops, rolls, stall-turns and the rest of the repertoire. It was forbidden to do them over the aerodrome but Bader as often as not ignored that. Coming out of a formation loop one day, he saw other Spitfires doing the same thing over the airfield and snapped into his R/T: "Dogsbody calling. Stop messing about over the airfield."

Later, after he had reprimanded the offenders, Holden observed: "That was a bit tough, sir. Hardly fair to bawl 'em out when you do the same thing yourself."

With a deep laugh Bader said: "Ah, I can do what I like."

But that was only cheerful bombast, not meant at all seriously. What he usually told aerobatic offenders was: "Don't do it. I lost my legs doing it and more experienced chaps than you have killed themselves doing it. If you're going to be killed let it be an enemy bullet, not bad flying. I know—you're thinking you've seen me do it. Well, when you're wing commanders you can do it too. Until then stick to the regulation height."

Aerobatics after battle was the worst offence. He had never forgotten a World War I picture in a hangar at Cranwell, "The Last Loop," showing a tail breaking off at the top of a loop after battle damage. He himself never in his life did one of the so-called "victory rolls" and threatened to "crucify" anyone else who did, adding: "Next time I'll have you posted."

In all important things he was meticulous. One heard muted criticism that he was too much of a "one-man-band," but all dynamic leaders get that. At least, ninety percent of the feeling was devoted adulation. Even at dusk when they came off readiness, Bader had seldom had enough and kept pestering Tom Pike, C.O. of the night-fighter squadron, to take him up in a Beaufighter chasing night bombers, his excuse being: "I'd love to see one of these things come down in flames. It'd look so much better at night." But Pike could never take him because there was no room in the aircraft.

On 12th July, over Hazebrouck, Bader took 616 down on fifteen 109's, shot at one and saw a flash on its cockpit as he swept past, then fired head-on at another and saw pieces fly off as it swerved under him. A few seconds later he shot at a third, which spurted black smoke and glycol and wrenched into a violent drive. Then he chased a fourth through a cloud and fired from right behind. An orange, blow-torch flame squirted behind its cockpit and it fell blazing all over. One destroyed and three damaged, but he only put one asterisk in his log-book, no longer bothering to record "damaged."

A couple of days later, coming back with Dundas and Johnson, he streaked after a lone 109 below. Seeing him coming, the 109 dived and then climbed, and Bader, trying to cut him off, pulled up so sharply that he blacked out, hunched in the cockpit like an old man carrying a great weight, seeing nothing till he eased the stick forward and the grey film lifted. Then he still saw nothing—the 109 had vanished.

Back at Tangmere, when he landed Dundas and Johnson came charging over and Dundas said: "By God, sir, that was good shooting."

"What the hell are you talking about?" Bader grunted suspiciously, wary of sarcasm.

"Well," Dundas said, "you must have been 400 yards when that Hun baled out."

"What!" (incredulously). "I never even fired."

None of them had fired. The patches were still over gun-ports in the wings. Yet the German *had* baled out. Bader lurched over to get a combat report form and wrote it down quickly: "Claimed—one Me. 109 destroyed. Frightened. Confirmed. Seen by two pilots."

Group maintained a stony silence, in marked contrast to the mirth at Tangmere.

Bad weather set in again and the pilots had time off to relax in surrounding towns. Bader always went with a group round him, demanding the presence of Holden, Turner, Dundas, Johnson, Crowley-Milling and others, even when they did not want to go. He hated being alone and liked to be the genial centre of a little Court Circle, ignoring their feelings in that respect. Not that they usually minded; being under the influence of his personality.

There was an evening dancing with Thelma at Sherry's in Brighton when the other dancers recognised him and queued up for his autograph. He loved it and no one minded that either, because he did not try to hide it but was like a small boy having a whale of a good time. In those moments the loss of his legs must have meant nothing at all.

Everyone felt Bader was invincible, and that this power shielded those who flew with him. Thelma now literally *knew* that the enemy would never get him. Every time he came back from a sweep he swooped low over the Bay House to let her know he was safely back, but she had come to regard this more as an affectionate salute than a reassurance.

Some of the Messerschmitts had shrewdly taken to setting about the Beehive as it came home over the French coast when the fighters were short of petrol. It was suggested that a fresh wing should go out to meet the homing Beehive, and over the Channel on 19th July the Tangmere Wing came down like wolves on an unsuspecting pack of 109's. Bader's first burst sent a 109 spinning down in a sea of flame. His second shot pieces off another, and as the Messerschmitts split up in alarm his bullets flashed on the fuselage of a third. In seconds the fight was over, half a dozen Messerschmitts were going down and the rest hurrying back into France.

On 23rd July, when the weather prevented any sweep, he took Billy Burton on a "rhubarb," and near Dunkirk saw a Spitfire hurtling out of France, chased by a 109. He squirted into the Messerschmitt's belly and it cart-wheeled into the sea with a great splash.

Bader had done more sweeps now than anyone else in Fighter Command and still jealously insisted on leading the wing on every raid, urged by the inner devil, driving himself to the limit and driving others to keep pace.

In seven days he did ten sweeps—enough to knock out the strongest man, still more for one who had to get around on two artificial legs. Now he was the last of the original wing leaders still operating—the rest were either dead or screened for a rest.

Peter Macdonald arrived at Tangmere on posting, and was disturbed to note that the skin round Bader's deep-set eyes was dark with fatigue. He and Woodhall began telling him that he must take a rest but Bader refused tersely. At last, at the end of July, Leigh-Mallory said to him:

"You'd better have a spell off operations, Douglas. You can't go on like this indefinitely."

"Not yet, sir," Bader said. "I'm quite fit and I'd rather carry on, sir."

He was so mulish that the A.O.C. at last grudgingly said: "Well, I'll let you go till September. Then you're coming off."

Thelma was increasingly worried about him but he would not listen to her, either. The *Daily Mirror* columnist Cassandra wrote that Bader had done enough, was too valuable to lose and should be taken off operations. He read it angrily.

He was not fighting on to build up a personal string of kills, though he was fifth on the list of top-scoring R.A.F. pilots. By this time in 1941 he had 20½ enemy aircraft confirmed destroyed but, like other leading fighter pilots, his actual score was probably greater. In his logbook he had nearly thirty asterisks—the ones he himself was fairly sure he had got, though he never displayed them. Malan and Tuck had nearly thirty official victories each but Bader was not jealous, though he would have loved to have caught them. The wing was the thing and the battle an intoxicant that answered his search for a purpose and fulfillment.

No luck early in August. On the 4th he noted in his logbook: "High escort. Dull." Next day to Lille power station tersely: "Damn good bombing. Blow 'em to hell."

On 8th August Peter Macdonald cornered him in the mess: "I'm going to insist you take a few days off," he said. "I'm taking you and Thelma up to Scotland for a week and you can relax with some golf at St. Andrews."

After an argument, Bader said: "I'll think about it," and that evening Macdonald forced the issue by ringing St. Andrews and booking rooms for the three of them from the 11th. That, he thought, would settle it.

Next day everything went wrong from the start.

First there was a tangle on take-off and the top-cover squadron went astray. Climbing over the Channel, the others could see no sign of it, and Bader would not break radio silence to call them. Then, half-way across, his air-speed indicator broke, the needle sliding back to an inscrutable zero, which meant trouble timing his rendezvous with the Beehive over Lille, and after that a difficult landing at Tangmere, not knowing in the critical approach how near the aeroplane was to a stall. Time to worry about that later: more urgent things loomed. It looked a good day for a fight, patches of layer cloud at about 4,000 feet but a clear vaulting sky above with a high sun to veil the venom of attack. He climbed the squadrons to 28/30,000 feet so that they, not the Germans, would have the height and the sun.

The job that day was to go for German fighters where they found them, and they found them as they crossed the French coast, just south of Le Touquet—dead ahead and about 2,000 feet below a dozen Messerschmitts were climbing the same way, spread in "finger fours" abreast (which they seemed to have copied lately). None of them seemed to be looking behind. They were sitters.

Bader said tersely into his mask: "Dogsbody attacking. Plenty for all. Take 'em as they come. Ken, stay up and cover us," and plunged down at the leading four, Dundas, Johnson and West beside him and the rest hounding behind. The Germans still climbed placidly ahead, and steeply in the dive he knew it was the perfect "bounce." Picking the second from the left, he closed startlingly fast; the 109 seemed to slam slantwise at him and, trying to lift the nose to aim, he knew suddenly he had badly misjudged. Too fast! No time! He was going to ram, and in the last moment brutally jerked stick and rudder so that the Spitfire careened and flashed past into the depth below, seeing nothing of the carnage among the enemy as the other Spitfires fired and pulled back up.

Angrily he flattened again about 24,000 feet, travelling fast, watching alertly behind and finding he was alone. Better climb up fast again to join the rest: deadly to be alone in this dangerous sky. He was suddenly surprised to see six more Messerschmitts ahead, splayed abreast in three parallel pairs line astern, noses pointing the other way. More sitters! He knew he should pull up and leave them; repeatedly he'd drummed it into his pilots never to try things on their own. But the temptation! They looked irresistible. A glance behind again. All clear. Greed swept discretion aside and he sneaked up behind the middle pair. None of them noticed. From a hundred yards he squirted at the trailing one and a thin blade of flame licked out behind it. Abruptly a flame flared like a huge match being struck and the aeroplane fell on one wing and dropped on fire all over. The other Germans flew placidly on. They must have been blind.

He aimed at the leader 150 yards in front and gave him a three-second burst. Bits flew off it and then it gushed volumes of white smoke as its nose dropped. The two fighters on the left were turning towards him, and crazily elated as though he had just pulled off a smash and grab raid, he wheeled violently right to break off, seeing the two on that side still flying ahead and that he would pass between them. In sheer bravado he held course to do so.

Something hit him. He felt the impact but the mind was curiously numb and could not assess it. No noise but something was holding his aeroplane by the tail, pulling it out of his hands and slewing it round. It lurched suddenly and then was pointing straight down, the cockpit floating with dust that had come up from the bottom. He pulled back on the stick but it fell inertly into his stomach like a broken neck. The aeroplane was diving in a steep spiral and confusedly he looked behind to see if anything were following.

First he was surprised, and then terrifyingly shocked to see that the whole of the Spitfire behind the cockpit was missing: fuselage, tail, fin— all gone. Sheered off, he thought vaguely. The second 109 must have run into him and sliced it off with its propeller.

He knew it had happened but hoped desperately and foolishly that he was wrong. Only the little radio mast stuck up just behind his head. A corner of his brain saw that the altimeter was unwinding fast from 24,000 feet.

Thoughts crowded in. How stupid to be nice and warm in the closed cockpit and have to start getting out. The floundering mind sought a grip and sharply a gush of panic spurted.

"Christ! Get out!"

"Wait! No oxygen up here!"

Get out! Get out!

Won't be able to soon! Must be doing over 400 already.

He tore his helmet and mask off and yanked the little rubber ball over his head—the hood ripped away and screaming noise battered at him. Out came the harness pin and he gripped the cockpit rim to lever himself up, wondering if he could get out without thrust from the helpless legs. He struggled madly to get his head above the windscreen and suddenly felt he was being sucked out as the tearing wind caught him.

Top half out. He was out! No, something had him by the leg holding him. (The rigid foot of the right leg hooked fast in some vise in the cockpit.) Then the nightmare took his exposed body and beat him and screamed and roared in his ears as the broken fighter dragging him by the leg plunged down and spun and battered him and the wind clawed at his flesh and the cringing sightless eyeballs. It went on and on into confusion, on and on, timeless, witless and helpless, with a little core of thought deep under the blind head fighting for life in the wilderness. It said he had a hand gripping the D-ring of the parachute and mustn't take it off, must grip it because the wind wouldn't let him get it back again, and he mustn't pull it or the wind would split his parachute because they must be doing 500 miles an hour. On and on . . . till the steel and leather snapped.

He was floating, in peace. The noise and buffeting had stopped. Floating upwards? He thought it is so quiet I must have a rest. I would like to go to sleep.

In a flash the brain cleared and he knew and pulled the D-ring, hearing a crack as the parachute opened. Then he was actually floating. High above the sky was still blue, and right at his feet lay a veil of cloud. He sank into it. That was the cloud at 4,000 feet. Cutting it fine! In seconds he dropped easily under it and saw the earth, green and dappled, where the sun struck through. Something flapped in his face and he saw it was his right trouser leg, split along the seam. High in the split gleamed indecently the white skin of his stump.

The right leg had gone.

How lucky, he thought, to lose one's legs and have detachable ones. Otherwise he would have died a few seconds ago. He looked, but saw no burning wreck below—probably not enough left to burn.

Lucky, too, not to be landing on the rigid metal leg like a post that would have split his loins. Odd it should happen like that. How convenient. But only half a leg was left to land on—he did not think of that.

He heard engine noises and turned in the harness. A Messerschmitt was flying straight at him, but the pilot did not shoot. He turned and roared by fifty yards away.

Grass and cornfields were lifting gently to meet him, stocks of corn and fences. A vivid picture, not quite static, moving. Two peasants in blue smocks leaned against a gate looking up and he felt absurdly self-conscious. A woman carrying a pail in each hand stopped in a lane and stared up, frozen like a still. He thought—I must look comic with only one leg.

The earth that was so remote suddenly rose fiercely. Hell! I'm landing on a gate! He fiddled with the shrouds to spill air and slip sideways and, still fumbling, hit, feeling nothing except vaguely some ribs buckle when a knee hit his chest as consciousness snapped.

Three German soldiers in grey uniforms were bending over him, taking off his harness and Mae West. No one spoke that he remembered. They picked him up and carried him to a car in a lane, feeling nothing, neither pain nor thought, only a dazed quiescence. The car moved off and he saw fields through the windows but did not think of anything. After timeless miles there were houses and the car rumbled over the pavé, through the arch of a gateway to a grey stone building. The Germans lifted him out and carried him through a door up some steps and along a corridor... he smelt the familiar hospital smell... into a bare, aseptic room, and then they were laying him on a padded casualty table. Old memories stirred. A thinnish man in a white coat and rimless glasses walked up and looked down at him. A girl in nurse's uniform hovered behind.

The doctor frowned at the empty trouser leg, pulled the torn cloth aside and stared in amazement, then looked at Bader's face and at the wings and medal ribbons on his tunic. Puzzled he said: "You have lost your leg."

Bader spoke for the first time since the enemy had hit him. "Yes, it came off as I was getting out of my aeroplane."

The doctor looked at the stump again, trying to equate a one-legged man with a fighter pilot. "Ach so!" he said obviously. "It is an old injury," and joked mildly. "You seem to have lost both your legs—your real one and your artificial one."

Bader thought: God, you haven't seen anything yet. He waited with a grim and passive curiosity for the real joke.

"You have cut your throat," the doctor said. He put his hand up and was surprised to feel a large gash under his chin, sticky with blood. It did not hurt.

The doctor peered at it, then stuck his fingers between the teeth and felt round the floor of the mouth. Light-headed, Bader felt a sudden horror that the cut might have gone right through. For some absurd reason that mattered terribly. But apparently it was all right.

"I must sew this up," the doctor murmured. He jabbed a syringe near the gash and the area went numb. No one spoke while he stitched the lips of the gash.

"Now we must have your trousers off and see your leg," he said.

Bader thought: This is going to be good, and raised his rump a little as the doctor unbuttoned the trousers and eased them down over the hips. The doctor froze, staring transfixed at the leather and metal that encased the stump of the left leg. There was a silence.

At last he noisily sucked in a breath, and said "Ach!" He looked once more at Bader, back at the two stumps and again at Bader, and said in a voice of sober discovery: "We have heard about you."

Bader grunted vaguely.

"Are you all right?" asked the doctor.

"Fine," he said tiredly. "Whereabouts are we?"

"This is a hospital," said the doctor. "St. Omer."

St. Omer!

"That's funny," Bader said. "My father is buried here somewhere."

The doctor must have thought his mind was wandering. Two grey-uniformed orderlies came and picked him up, carried him up two flights of stairs into a narrow room and dumped him like a sack of potatoes, though not roughly, on a white hospital bed. They took his clothes and left leg off, wrapped him in a sort of white nightshirt, pulled the bed-clothes over him, stood the left leg, still clipped to the broken waistband, against the wall, and left him there.

He lay motionless, aching all over, feeling as though he had been through a mangle, his head singing like a kettle. Every time he stirred a piercing pain stabbed into the ribs under his heart, cutting like a knife. Reaction drained him and he knew only utter exhaustion and hurting all over the body, so that for a while he did not think of England or the wing or of captivity, nor even of Thelma.

A nurse came and held his head while she ladled some spoonfuls of soup into his mouth. She went. His mind slowly cleared and a thought came into focus: "I hope the boys saw me bale out and tell Thelma."

Dusk gathered slowly in the room and he dozed fitfully. Some time later he woke in darkness wondering where he was. Then he knew and sank into misery, black, deep and full of awareness. He remembered he was to go dancing with Thelma that night and longed to see her, feeling lonely and helpless without legs among enemies. There was the golf, too, at St. Andrews. For the first time in his life he looked back over his shoulder, rejecting the present and trying to hold on to the past, but the clock would not go back and the night moved slowly on.

No one had seen him go down. He had vanished after the first dive and did not answer when they called him. In the air they had been chilled by the absence of the familiar rasping banter. Back at Tangmere there was stunned disbelief when he did not return. They watched the sky and the clock until they knew he could have no petrol left, and a gloomy hush seemed to fall over the place.

Pike said to Woodhall: "You'd better tell his wife," and Woodhall stalled, saying: "No, give him time. He may have landed somewhere else with his R/T u/s [radio transmitter]. He'll turn up."

But John Hunt, a shy young Intelligence officer, thought Thelma had been told and drove over to cheer her up with a horoscope that a local woman had cast of Douglas, saying that he was in for a dreary time but had a magnificent career after that. He thought it would help her to think that Douglas might he a prisoner.

She was in a deck-chair in the sun, and only when she said "Hallo, John. Come for tea?" he realised that she did not know. Somehow, in an agony of embarrassment, he talked of irrelevant things, trying to find an unbrutal way of breaking it when a car drew up and Woodhall got out and walked straight up to them. Without preamble he said: "I'm afraid I've got some bad news for you, Thelma. Douglas did not come back from the morning sortie."

Thelma stood dumbly.

Woodhall went on: "We should get some news soon. I shouldn't worry too much. He's indestructible . . . probably a prisoner."

Too numb to ask what had happened, she stood very pale and said: "Thank you, Woody." Woodhall was saying something else and after a while she became aware that he had gone and that her sister Jill was there. Hunt thrust a piece of paper into her hand and said: "This might be a comfort, Thelma. Read it later." Then he was gone. Jill was saying: "Darling, you *know* he'll pop up again. They can't get him." But Thelma had believed he was invincible and now the whole illusion had burst. She would not cry. A fortnight ago a young wife had cried for days when her husband in the wing had been shot down and Thelma stubbornly would not repeat the exhibition. As always with strong emotions, she covered them up.

Later Dundas came with flowers in one hand and a bottle of sherry in the other. He had been out twice alone that afternoon over the Channel as far as France looking for Bader's yellow rubber dinghy till Woodhall had ordered him back. He looked tired and felt guilty because he had not seen Douglas go down. He and Jill got Thelma to take a little sherry but she brought it up again. Stokoe, Douglas's batman, brought in some soup with tears rolling down his face.

Later, in bed when they left her, the tears came and she lay awake all night thinking: If they got Douglas, what chance have the other boys got? They haven't any chance. A thought rose and obsessed her all night: How can I warn them? How can I make them understand they will all be killed now?

In the morning the reporters came.

Dawn brought new strength to Bader. In the light he saw many things more clearly; knew where he was and what it meant and accepted it unwistfully. First things first and to hell with the rest. He must get legs and must get word to Thelma.

The door opened and in came two young Luftwaffe pilots, dark young men in tight short tunics pinned with badges, shapely breeches and black riding boots.

"Hallo," brightly said the leader, who was Count von Someone-or-other. "How are you?" His English was good.

"All right, thanks."

Bader was fairly monosyllabic but the Germans chatted amiably. Would he like some books? They'd just come over from St. Omer airfield to yarn as one pilot to another. Spitfires were jolly good aeroplanes.

"Yes," Bader said. "So are yours."

After a while the Count said politely: "I understand you have no legs?" He was looking at the fore-shortened form under the bedclothes.

"That's right."

They asked what it was like flying without legs. An elderly administrative officer came in and listened, looked at the left leg leaning against the wall and observed heavily: "Of course it would never be allowed in Germany."

Later they left and the next visitor was a baldheaded Luftwaffe engineering officer, who asked more boring questions about legs. Bader cut him short: "Look, can you radio England and ask them to send me another leg?" He did not know how they would do it, but if they did Thelma would know he was alive.

The German thought it a good idea.

"And while you're about it," Bader followed up, "could you send someone to look at the wreckage of my aeroplane. The other leg might still be in it."

The German promised to do what he could.

A nurse brought in a basin of water. She was German and not talkative, making signs that he was to wash himself. He did so, moving painfully, and when he got to his legs was shocked to find a great dark swelling high up on his right stump. It looked as big as a cricket ball and was terribly sore. For ten years since the agony at Greenlands Hospital he had flinched at the thought of anything going wrong with his stumps, and now it loomed large and ugly in his mind.

Later, yesterday's doctor came in, looking precise behind the rimless glasses. Bader showed him the swelling, and the doctor looked grave and prodded it. After a while he said hesitantly: "We will have to cut this."

Bader burst out, "By God, you don't," panicky at the thought of an experimental knife. They argued violently about it till the doctor grudgingly agreed to leave it for a while.

A dark, plump girl came in, put a tray on his bed, smiled and went out. He realised he was hungry till he tasted the bowl of potato water soup, two thin slices of black bread smeared with margarine and the cup of tepid ersatz coffee. It left a sour taste in his mouth.

Later it was the doctor again, with orderlies. "We are going to put you in another room," he said. "With friends."

Friends?

The orderlies carried him along a corridor into a larger room with five beds and dumped him on one of them. A fresh-faced young man in another bed said cheerfully in an American accent: "Hello, sir. Welcome. My name's Bill Hall. Eagle Squadron. We heard you were here." He had a cradle over one leg which was in traction, the foot pulled by a weight on a rope. His kneecap had been shot off. In the next bed was a Pole with a burnt face, and beyond him Willie, a young Londoner who had been shot through the mouth. All Spitfire pilots. They chatted cheerfully till well after dusk. Willie and the Pole had been trying to think up some way of escaping, but the Germans had taken their clothes and they had only the nightshirts, which made it rather hopeless.

Bader asked: "Isn't there any way out of here?"

"Yes," Willie answered a little bitterly. "Soon as you can stagger they whip you off to Germany." Apparently he and the Pole were due to go at any moment.

"If you had clothes," Bader persisted, "how would you get out?"

"Out the bloody window on a rope," Willie said. "The gates are always open and no guards on them." He jerked his head at the door of the room. "They put the guards outside that door."

"How would you get a rope?"

Willie said there were French girls working in the hospital who might smuggle one in.

Bader slipped off to sleep thinking grimly about that, but he slept well and in the morning did not feel so stiff and sore.

The plump girl came in early with more black bread and acorn coffee, and Bill Hall introduced her to Bader as Lucille, a local French girl. He tried to joke with her but she barely understood his schoolboy French, though she coloured nicely and smiled at him again. She did not say anything: a German guard stood in the doorway.

The doctor came in to see his stump but the swelling was visibly less, which was an enormous relief. In his blunt way Bader told the doctor that the food was "bloody awful," and the doctor bridled. Bader waved a piece of black bread in his face and they had a shouting match till the doctor stormed out. Lucille came back with lunch—more potato water and black bread.

Later a tall, smart Luftwaffe officer of about forty came in. He wore the red tabs of the Flak, clicked his heels, saluted Bader and said: "Herr Ving Commander, ve haf found your leg." Like a star making his entrance, a jackbooted soldier marched through the door and jerked magnificently to attention by the bed, holding one arm stiffly out. Hanging from it was the missing right leg, covered in mud, the broken piece of leather belt still hanging from it. Bader, delighted, said, "I say, thanks," then saw that the foot still ludicrously clad in sock and shoe stuck up almost parallel to the shin.

"Hell, it's been smashed."

"Not so badly as your aeroplane," said the officer. "Ve found it in the area of the other pieces."

The soldier took two smart paces forward, clicked to a halt again, and Bader took the leg. He unpeeled the sock and saw, as he feared, that the instep had been stove in.

"I say," he said, turning on the charm. "D'you think your chaps at the aerodrome could repair this for me?"

The officer pondered. "Perhaps," he said. "Ve vill take it and see." After a mutual exchange of compliments the officer clicked his heels, saluted, swung smartly and disappeared.

Next it was a new girl, fair-haired and with glasses, carrying a tray. She was Hélène, and everyone goggled to see that she carried real tea on the tray and some greyish-white bread. Apparently the shouting match had been worthwhile.

In the morning the swelling on the stump had deflated with amazing speed and that was a great relief.

Later the officer with the red tabs marched crisply in, saluted, and as he said "Herr Ving Commander, ve haf brought back your leg," the jack-booted stooge made another dramatic entrance behind and came to a crashing halt by the bed, not flicking an eyelid, holding out a rigid arm with the leg suspended from it: a transformed leg, cleaned and polished and with the foot pointing firmly where a foot should be. Bader took it and saw they had done an amazing job on it; the body belt was beautifully repaired with a new section of intricately-worked, good quality leather and all the little straps that went with it. The dent in the shin had been carefully hammered out, so that apart from a patch bare of paint it looked normal. A dent in the knee had been hammered out, and even the rubbers correctly set in the ankle so there was resilient movement in the foot.

"It is O.K.?" the officer asked anxiously.

Bader, impressed and rather touched, said: "It's really magnificent. It is very good of you to have done this. Will you please thank the men who did it very much indeed."

He strapped both legs on, eased off the bed, feeling unsteady for a moment, and went stumping round the room, a ludicrous figure in nightshirt with the shoe-clad metal legs underneath. Without a stump sock (lost in the parachute descent), the right leg felt strange, and it gave forth loud clanks and thumps as he swung it. The others looked on fascinated. Beaming with pleasure, the Germans finally left. Bader lurched over to the window and looked thoughtfully at the ground three floors and forty feet below. To the left of the grass courtyard he could see the open gates, unguarded.

They became aware of a drone that began to swell and fade and swell again. The Pole and Willie joined him at the window, and high above they saw the twisting, pale scribble of vapour trails against blue sky; obviously a sweep and some 109's were having a shambles over St. Omer. Tensely they watched but the battling aircraft were too high to see. Shortly a parachute floated down. A German, he hoped, and hoped there were more coming down without parachutes. He looked up at the contrails, at the parachute and down at the courtyard and the gates, his mind a fierce maelstrom.

A Luftwaffe Feldwebel came in and told Willie and the Pole to be ready to leave for Germany after lunch. He would bring their clothes later.

When he had gone Willie, depressed, said: "Once they get you behind the wire you haven't got much chance." Bader began worrying that it would be his turn next. He *must* stay in France as long as possible.

Lucille came in with soup and bread for lunch. The guard looked morosely in the doorway, and then turned back into the corridor. Bader whispered to the Pole: "Ask her if she can help me get out or put me in touch with friends outside."

In a low voice the Pole started talking to Lucille in fluent French. She darted a look at Douglas and whispered an answer to the Pole. They went on talking in fast, urgent whispers, each with an eye watching the door. Bader listened eagerly but the words were too fast. They heard the guard's boots clump in the corridor, and Lucille, with a quick, nervous smile at Douglas, went out.

The Pole came across and sat on his bed. "She says you're 'bien connu' and she admires you tremendously and will help if she can, but she can't get a rope because the Germans would guess how you got it. She doesn't know whether she can get clothes, but she has a day off next Sunday and will go to a village down the line called Aire, or something. She says there are 'agents Anglais' there."

English agents? It sounded too good. But she was going to try, and hope welled strongly. Sunday! This was only Wednesday. Hell, they mustn't take him. The uncertainty of fear gnawed. Better try and act weak from now on.

They took Willie and the Pole that afternoon. Now he had to rely on his schoolboy French.

In the morning Lucille came in with the usual bread and acorn coffee. The sentry lounged in the doorway. She put the tray on Bader's bed, leaning over so that her plump body hid him from the sentry. He grinned a cheerful "Bon jour" at her as she squeezed his hand and then the grin nearly slipped as he felt her pressing a piece of paper into his palm. He closed his fingers round it and slid the clenched fist under the bedclothes. It was very quick. She said nothing, but her mouth lifted in a pale smile as she went out of the room. The door closed behind the sentry.

7

The Ace

from FIGHTER PILOT: THE FIRST AMERICAN ACE OF WORLD WAR II
by William R. Dunn

In the late 1930s and the beginning of the 1940s, a large segment of the American populace adhered to an America-as-island philosophy. Europe and the Far East were becoming engulfed in a widening war that many in the United States wanted to avoid at all costs. A counterpoint to this emphatic isolationism was the participation of young American pilots—motivated variously by patriotism, adventure, or simple pecuniary reward—as volunteers in the expanding overseas imbroglio. They jumped into the fighting well before the United States declared war against the Axis powers.

Some, like Frank G. Tinker Jr., flew for the Loyalist side in the Spanish Civil War. There were men like David Lee "Tex" Hill, who joined Claire Chennault's famous Flying Tigers, operating in the Orient. And, though little known, eager American flyers, including William R. Dunn, composed three squadrons in the British Royal Air Force.

The brainchild of colorful American expatriate Charles Sweeny, the British fighter units with American aviators were dubbed Eagle Squadrons. These volunteer forces were seen as a way for willing and able airmen to assist a besieged Britain, which suffered from, among other things, a shortage of pilots. Also, having Americans in the thick of battle against Nazi Germany would advance the British propaganda war.

Because U.S. law discouraged Americans from serving in the militaries of foreign nations, Eagle Squadrons' recruiting was at first conducted clandestinely. But, in time, the process opened up with volunteers coming via Canada. Bill Dunn, the author of this excerpt, traveled an especially circuitous route to get into the cockpit of RAF fighters.

Crossing into Canada only three days after England declared war on Germany in September 1939, Dunn offered his services as a fledgling pilot with all of 160 flying hours. The Canadian recruiter, however, would not take him as a pilot. With the prospect of entering military aviation foreclosed at the moment, Dunn enlisted instead in the Seaforth Highlanders, a Scottish infantry regiment. Once shipped to England, Dunn applied for a transfer to flight duty, and, after some RAF flight training, he was assigned to the first of the American volunteer units, No. 71 Eagle Squadron.

On August 27, 1941, the action-filled day described in this excerpt, Dunn was awakened in the wee hours at North Weald, an RAF station on the outskirts of London. His mission was to escort Blenheim bombers on a morning raid of a steel factory at Lille. Flying the quintessential British fighter of the early war years, the Supermarine Spitfire, Dunn was on the lookout for Messerschmitt Bf 109s, the Luftwaffe's leading fighter type at the time.

In the day's harrowing air combat, Dunn became the first American ace of World War II, albeit more than three months before America's entry into the war and while flying for the RAF. Dunn, driven by a profound sense of idealism, believed deeply in the cause, and his conviction preceded the commitment of his country. Because of him and his fellow volunteers, victory over tyranny came a little sooner.

Eventually, Dunn was transferred to the U.S. Army Air Force and wound up commanding the Luchow air base in China. He stayed in the Air Force, where he had a full and distinguished career. Following stints in Vietnam and at the Aerospace Defense Command Headquarters, he retired in 1973 as a lieutenant colonel. The British air attaché in Washington made a special trip to the retirement ceremony in Colorado Springs to pay tribute for a grateful Britain. Dunn acknowledged the tribute with an RAF-type salute.

P.H.

The time was now 0815 hours. I am flying with my squadron at 18,000 feet near the French city of Lille. Our position in the formation, top cover, is to protect the nine Blenheim bombers from surprise top and rear attacks by enemy fighters. We had crossed the French coast near Cape Gris Nez at 15,000 feet, and then climbed to 18,000 on our course to Saint Omer and on toward the steel plant target at Lille. Our entire formation, nine bombers and thirty-six fighters, comprised Circus 86.

Far below me, through the scattered clouds, I see the bright flashes of German 88-mm antiaircraft guns firing at us from the seemingly peaceful green fields. The brownish-black shell bursts come quite close to us at times, though usually a little behind and below our formation. I can easily see the course we have flown by glancing behind my Spitfire at the long avenue of slowly diminishing dark smoke puffs. From the moment we had crossed the French coast the Huns had fired at us constantly.

Our squadron leader had ordered us to fly in a wide "vic" battle formation, to keep changing height, and to weave back and forth above the Blenheims. His voice came to me clearly through my R/T earphones as he delivered his orders to the section leaders.

"Parson leader here. Parson White Section keep together. Don't straggle White Two. Blue Section, you're too far out. Close up that gap."

I look over at the right side of the formation, A Flight's side, to see if White Two had received the instruction and is getting back into position. He has. It's like asking for it to straggle. One seldom sees what happens to stragglers. They just disappear. They're easy prey for enemy fighters to bounce and shoot down. As ordered, our Blue Section altered course to close the gap in our top cover formation.

Again Paddy's crisp voice comes to me over the R/T: "Parson Squadron, heads up! Red flak. Watch out for 109s."

Behind us I see several red antiaircraft smoke puffs. Not dangerous looking stuff, but it means that enemy fighters are up and being vectored towards us by a combination of these red visual markers and radio communications. The brownish-black flak is still being fired at us, and intermingled with these dark bursts are the bright red puffs. Every time I see these red bursts I get a kind of tingling sensation running up and down my spine. I know that within the next ten minutes my life may end. It just doesn't seem possible that in this bright beautiful sun-filled summer sky there are men waiting to kill me—or for me to kill them. I wonder if the Hun pilots have these same feelings. I suppose they do.

I reach up to the instrument panel and switch on my reflector gunsight. Its circle and dot glow a faint orange color on the glass plate before my eyes. I double check the gunsight's span setting (32 feet) and the range setting (250 yards). Then I check the fuel contents gauge. Yes, plenty of petrol. Enough for another hour, even at high boost. Next I set my compass ring on the reciprocal of my present course heading—the return direction to England. This latter simple precaution eliminates the initial orientation problem after the confusion of an air battle. Last, I turn the gun button on the control column to "fire." I am now ready to fight.

I continue weaving across the back of the formation, watching to the rear and above, peering out of my aircraft's hood, first to one side and then the other. Far below me I see the aircraft of the two close escort squadrons surrounding the nine bombers. Their Spitfires look small and black and deadly.

"Hello Parson leader. Blue One here. Three 109s, seven o'clock high!" My head snaps around toward the left rear and I search the sky until I see three little light-colored specks—enemy aircraft—flying about 4,000 feet above us. They are flying the same course as we are. Although they are some distance behind us, they are evidently waiting to jump some straggler.

Now, suddenly, startling, like a whip crack, white streaks shoot past my starboard wing. I yank the control column hard to the left and back as I jam the throttle full open, whirling around in a steep climbing turn. I switch my R/T transmitter to "send" and, while trying to control my inward excitement, say in a slow, even voice, "Parson Squadron. Blue Three. Snappers, six o'clock high!" My job as top weaver is done. I've warned my squadron and the other Circus 86 aircraft. Maybe a bit late for the first attacking enemy fighters—but I've alerted them against those Me.109s that follow.

Below me there is no longer a formation of our eleven top cover fighter aircraft. The individual sections of my squadron have split away, breaking up the wide "vic." They're all mixed up in groups of twos, threes and fours. Each little group is twisting and turning as the air battle's individual combats develop. The attacking Huns have come straight down on us, hoping to break through the escort and get to the bombers. It was the leader of the first section of four 109s that had taken a quick squirt at me as he dove past.

Over on the right side of the formation I see a long trail of white smoke. One of our Spitfires is in a fast, steep dive with glycol streaming out behind it. He has been hit in the radiator or engine coolant system and is making for the French coast and home with his damaged aircraft. Hope he makes it before his engine seizes. Getting shot up in the first few seconds of an attack sometimes happens; somebody must be unlucky and get clobbered first.

Another section of four Huns comes hurtling down to join in the scrap. The bluish-white bellies of their aircraft flash in the morning sun. I can clearly see the black crosses, bordered with white, painted on their stubby, square-tipped wings. All the Messerschmitts' noses are painted a bright yellow. We know this German unit—we've met in battle before— as the "Abbeville Kids." Most of the Hun kites are Me.109Es, with a few of the newer type Me.109Fs.

A Spitfire from A Flight—Flight Lieutenant George Brown, I think— climbs up to engage the four newcomers. I watch his eight machine guns send a long burst of .303s into the belly of the third 109. The enemy aircraft's fuselage is blown in half just in front of the tail section. Then the port wing explodes and rips off as the ammunition tray for the 20-mm cannon in it is hit. Another second and the Messerschmitt's hood jettisons off. Out comes the enemy pilot from his cockpit. I momentarily watch his body falling through the air until his parachute snaps open far below the fight. How he was able to get out of that 109 alive, I'll never know. The lucky SOB.

On the far side of the scrap there is a large flash—just a flash and that's all. Someone has been blown to bits. I can't tell whether it was a Spitfire or a 109. Fragments, all that remains of the aircraft and its pilot, rain down from the sky.

The fight is now about twenty or thirty seconds old. Things happen very fast in air combat. To the onlookers, or rather the uplookers, our fights last for only a few minutes, but to us, the fighter pilots, they sometimes seem an eternity.

So far in this engagement I have only been attacked by the first enemy section. I look around for a 109 that will give me a good target. In the previous months I had shot down four enemy aircraft. Now I needed one more victory to earn the coveted title of fighter ace. Just above the scrap I see two Me.109Fs that are evidently waiting for a shot-up Spitfire or Blenheim to drop out of the fight and try to get home. Then they'll dive down and finish it off—easy meat.

I climb fast behind and above the two Huns. I'm about 1,500 feet above them now, and I have the sun at my back. I give my engine full throttle and dive on the rearmost enemy aircraft. The German leader of the two sees me coming and quickly half-rolls onto his back, diving away from me. The second 109, my target, does a climbing turn to the left. I close the range to about 150 yards, line the Hun up in my gunsight, then I press the gun-firing button. My aircraft shudders as I hear the sharp chatter of its eight machine guns. Acrid fumes of burned gunpowder fill my cockpit and sting my nostrils. I like this odor. It seems to stiffen my spine, tighten my muscles, make my blood race. It makes my scalp tingle, and I want to laugh.

I see the grayish-white tracer streaks from my guns converge on the Messerschmitt's tail section. The elevators and rudder disintegrate under the impact of the explosive DeWild bullets. Pieces fly off the enemy's fuselage. The range is now down to 50 yards. Black liquid—engine oil— spatters my windscreen and a dense, brownish colored smoke is flung back at me. My enemy is finished. Splash one, but good! I've got my fifth victory!

I lift my gloved thumb from the gun button and do a steep climbing turn, first to the right and then left, as I watch the German fall to the French fields below. His aircraft is burning furiously now. It doesn't leave a long fiery trail behind it. This one looks like the blue-white flame of a blowtorch. It seems odd that the Hun pilot didn't really try to get away from me. I guess he must have been a new boy. Well, what the hell, they all count.

The sections of my squadron are fighting at about 11,000 or 12,000 feet now. I am a couple thousand feet above them. I see the buildings and tall chimneys of the steel plant, the Blenheims' target, far below and on the outskirts of Lille. Sticks of bombs are now falling. Soon I can see the shock waves caused by their heavy explosions in the target area. All nine Blenheims are still with us, surrounded by the defending fighters of our close escort. Now, to get them safely home again.

From what I can see, the scrap below is breaking up into a number of running dogfights. Our Spitfires use a lot of petrol in a battle such as this one. The fuel left in our tanks will get us back to England, but it isn't enough to allow us to stay over enemy territory and fight much longer. Maybe another ten minutes or so.

My port wing jerks and skids my Spitfire to the right. Now there are several long rips in the metal skin and a jagged hole near its tip. I look back quickly and see my attacker coming at me from the left rear quarter, slightly higher, and closing fast. I think he is the leader of the pair I had first attacked.

There are perhaps three seconds left between life and death for me. The German's tracers, glowing like little balls of fire, flash past my cockpit. I yank back the throttle, give my prop full fine pitch, jam the flaps down, and violently skid my aircraft out of his gunsight. He is now closing too fast. I have greatly decreased my speed by changing prop pitch and by dumping flaps—luckily the flaps didn't blow off. He overshoots me, skimming not more than ten feet above my head.

The bluish-white belly of the 109F fills my windscreen. I can even see oil streaks and rivets on the underside of its fuselage, and above that the black cross insignia, unit markings, and a red rooster painted on the side of the cockpit. The Hun pilot is looking directly down at me. His expression tells me that he fully realizes (Gott in Himmel!) the mistake he has just made.

I fire. I can't miss. My guns chatter for no more than three or four seconds. I see the bullets smashing into the Hun aircraft's belly. Pieces fly off the 109. Then a wisp of gray smoke streams back from its engine, and then the whole aircraft is suddenly engulfed in a sheet of white-hot flame. It rolls over slowly onto its back and starts down at a high rate of speed. The tail section breaks off. I last see it, tumbling as it falls, far below me. Splash two! My face is wet with nervous sweat. I can hear myself gasping in my oxygen mask.

I see another 109 flying level some 500 feet below me and crossing my path from left to right—heading for home, I assume. The Hun pilot has now seen me. He starts taking violent evasive action as I make a diving turn toward his tail. I close to 75 yards. He suddenly pulls up into a steep climb. I fire a short burst into his back. He flicks over into a right turn and flies straight across my gunsight. No more than thirty yards separate our two aircraft. I fire again. He begins to smoke.

At this moment, in my rear-vision mirror, I see four Me.109s climbing up to intercept me. This is getting too hot for me. I jam the throttle through the gate, jerk the control column back into my stomach, and climb up and over them. The nearest one takes a squirt at my fast-moving Spitfire. His deflection is bad, luckily. The 20-mm cannon shells and machine gun bullets streak past me and then veer off my tail.

I roll my Spit onto its back, pull on the stick, and the reversed horizon comes up to meet me. I hear explosions and a banging like hail on my aircraft's fuselage. My port wing is hit again. I see splashing holes and rents send pieces flying off. A ball of fire flashes through the cockpit, smashing into my instrument panel. My right foot takes a heavy blow, bounces off the rudder pedal, and is numb. Two sharp blows bang into my right leg. My head snaps forward and my vision bursts in a blinding white flash. Then comes a soft, deep darkness. I can just faintly hear bits of broken glass and metal strike the cockpit floor.

Fear grips me with strong arms. It is finally happening to me, the one who wasn't going to die in this war. The one who had planned so many things to do when the war ended. The one who had seen so many aircraft shot down, but had always told himself, "It won't be you—you'll live through." I am being shot down and killed!

My neck and the back of my head ache horribly. My arms and legs seem to be floating lightly on air, yet I can feel their weight against my body. My hand on the control column becomes leaden. I want to let go of it, but I haven't the strength to loosen my fingers. It doesn't make any difference anyway. In a few seconds it will all be over. There will be a grinding crash, an explosion, and then nothing. I shall be smashed into fragments of bone and burned flesh.

Visions of my family and friends, those I'd loved in life, appear before my mind's eye. I can see them all smiling tenderly at me. I hear familiar voices murmuring softly, caressingly. They seem to give me a sense of being watched over and comforted during the passage of these last fleeting moments.

My swaying head strikes the side of the cockpit hood. It jars my vision. The deep darkness that covers my eyes lightens little by little. Dimly I see my instrument panel, broken and shattered.

I raise my head and look through the windscreen toward the swirling fields of earth charging madly upward to enfold me. Suddenly I become conscious of my two hands tugging back on the control column. The nose of my Spitfire is slowly lifting. The land below me stops whirling as earth and sky return to their rightful places. The horizon reappears. My brain tells me that I live! I laugh without sound. I still own life!

Strength has returned to my body. My pulse is beating violently. My skin feels cold and clammy, yet I know that I am perspiring profusely. I shiver. My brief interlude with death has ended.

I am again in level flight at 1,200 feet. I look behind and above me for attacking enemy aircraft. There are none. I am alone in this hostile sky, near the little town of Ambleteuse, and about five miles from the French coast. I point my Spit's nose toward England as I inspect its and my own damage.

There are large holes and rips in the port wing, though the aileron controls seem right enough. A shaft of light penetrates the left side of my cockpit. It must be the hole made by the 20-mm cannon shell that struck my instrument panel. Bits of broken glass from the smashed instruments and twisted scraps of metal lie scattered on the cockpit floor.

I look at my right flying boot. The whole toe of the boot is shot off and covered with blood. My top rudder pedal is also blood-spattered and bent out of shape. My right trouser leg, just below the knee, is drenched with blood and is dripping on the cockpit floor. My head and neck pain me terribly—but I am afraid to inspect myself further. I can feel a wet stickiness in my hair, seeping from under my leather flying helmet onto my neck and cheek. I turn on full oxygen and breathe deeply. I must not pass out now!

Ahead of me the waters of the English Channel gleam. My Spitfire's engine is running rough, surging. I have enough petrol to get me home. I gently weave, as assurance against further enemy attacks. The flight across the channel seems endless, until in the far distance I see Dover's white cliffs reaching out to greet me. My engine is losing power. I am now down to 800 feet. I switch on the R/T and squawk "May Day." In no more than a minute or so two Spitfires join me. The leader waggles his wings and directs me to follow him. The other Spit drops into a position behind me to protect my tail.

My escort leads me across the coastal cliffs to the little grass airfield at Hawkinge, near the town of Folkestone. I change the fuel mixture to "rich," set the propeller to "fine" pitch, select the undercarriage "down," and, as I turn to final approach, drop the flaps. One of the escorting Spitfire pilots signals that my landing gear is down. I have no indicator lights in the cockpit. Everything is smashed. I follow my escort's descent and air speed until the grass surface of the airfield is rushing under my wings. Gently I close the throttle, feel a slight sinking motion, then my wheels are rolling smoothly across the green turf.

I'm home! I'm safe! A feeling of complete relief from the last hour's extreme tension envelopes me. Thank you, dear God, thank you.

I see an ambulance parked at the edge of the airfield, so I taxi over to it and stop my aircraft's engine. A medical orderly points toward a fuel bowser and several other fighter aircraft parked near a dispersal hut, telling me that I must go over there to refuel and rearm. I tell him that I'm wounded and to help me get out of my kite. He looks at my bloody face and helmet, then at the bloody mess in the cockpit, vomits, and promptly slides off the wing.

A medical officer now arrives, quickly takes in the situation, and has me out of the cockpit and lying on the grass in the shade of my Spitfire's wing in a minute. I feel very weak now. My fingers close on the cool, crisp blades of grass. It's good to be back on earth again. Someone puts a lighted cigarette between my lips.

I hear cloth ripping—my trouser leg—two machine gun bullet holes in the right calf. My flying boot is cut off. The front of my right foot has been blown off by a 20-mm cannon shell. The medics carefully remove my leather helmet, just creased across the back of my head by a machine gun bullet. Lucky! Bloody lucky!

Two medical airmen help me onto a stretcher and carry me to the waiting ambulance. The Doc gives me an injection in my arm and says he's sending me to the Royal Victoria Hospital in Folkestone. So long XR-D. You were a good kite. Hope they can patch us both up.

As the ambulance starts to drive me away an intelligence officer scrambles in and sits down on the opposite stretcher. He asks my home station and squadron number. He'll let them know where I am. Then, briefly, I dictate my combat report as he writes in a little notebook. I have done my job today; now he must do his. He must inform No. 11 Group and Fighter Command Headquarters that today, 27 August 1941, we have fought and destroyed enemy aircraft, and that most of our aircraft and aircrews have returned safely, one way or another, from these combat operations.

The injection in my arm begins to take effect and I—the Ace—pass out.

8

English Channel Collision

from **EAGLES AT WAR**
by Walter J. Boyne

A retired U.S. Air Force colonel with more than 5,000 flight hours in his logbook, Walter J. Boyne, my longtime friend who serves as co-editor of this volume, has piloted the old piston-powered C-47 Gooney Bird, the sleek B-47 Stratojet, and the awesome B-52 Stratofortress, among other military aircraft. As pilot-in-command, while manipulating the controls of his airplane in combat zones, he knew the full weight of a military pilot's obligations.

The stark terror, the rush of adrenaline, and the survivalist instinct that are sparked by such experience have been real, not imagined, for Walt. Flying large, relatively slow aircraft simply compounded the life-or-death equation. The fact that the lives of crewmen onboard were also in the balance increased the stakes as well as the ever-present burden of responsibility. With the gift of a seasoned storyteller, he has taken his dramatic life's experience as an air force combat pilot and seamlessly applied it to some of history's best-known air battles—for example, the haphazard aerial attack on the German warships *Gneisenau, Scharnhorst,* and *Prinz Eugen* as they boldly attempted a mad dash through the English Channel in 1942.

In *Eagles at War,* Walt weaves his fictional characters into realistic scenarios, using historical figures where appropriate. Adolf Galland, the real-life Luftwaffe ace, is described preparing the fighter escort for the German warships. One of Galland's fighter pilots is Helmut Josten, a character created by Walt to convey the actual wartime experiences of those who flew in the Luftwaffe. Walt, the consummate aerospace historian, having served as director of the Smithsonian Institution's National Air and Space Museum, first sets the story of this unique air-sea chase in historical context. By the time the shooting starts, we know the players and their relative strengths and weaknesses.

The obsolete Fairey Swordfish is properly described as a relic from prewar days and as easy game for the Messerschmitt Bf 109s. The superior British Royal Air Force Spitfires become engaged in the air battle, but in minimal numbers. The advantage of technological prowess and the disadvantage of quantitative inferiority are clearly presented here. Equally compelling is the point that battle is frequently shrouded in a confusing fog in which the opposing sides, relying on the best that they can muster at the time, give their all in a nightmarish circus, with luck determining the result at least as often as logic.

As perhaps only one who has seen it up close can do, Walt powerfully describes the indiscriminate loathsomeness of war. Men who were one moment dueling to the death at the helm of war machines, infused with a bottomless self-confidence and an unswerving belief in their underlying cause, are transformed a moment later into beleaguered and forlorn castaways, clinging desperately, even to each other, for life itself. In this excerpt by one of the aviation community's most insightful participants, we are movingly reminded of war's grotesque nature and capricious ways.

P.H.

LE TOUQUET, FRANCE/FEBRUARY 10, 1942. Hitler, the frustrated architect, had made one characteristic contribution to the art: the reinforced concrete bunker. All over Europe, Todt Organization crews had despoiled the landscape with massive ugly structures sited half above and half below the ground, many of them taken from Hitler's own design sketches. They varied in size and function, but all were cloaked with certain dismal characteristics: the hum and grind of auxiliary power units, salts exuding from every tunnel wall, and the pervasive odor of a Parisian *pissoir*. The gloom was amplified by the dim yellow lighting pulsing to the fluctuations of the generators. The only decorations on the wall were the phantom impressions of the long-gone wooden forms that had contained the pour.

Colonel Galland, relishing his new role as General of the Fighter Arm, had assembled all of the leaders of fighter units in the West for "Operation Thunderbolt," a literal sink or swim operation for the still formidable remnants of the German surface fleet. Three of the proudest names in German military history adorned the ships bottled up in the harbor at Brest. The British bitterly wanted revenge against all three. The *Gneisenau* and the *Scharnhorst* had sunk the aircraft carrier HMS *Glorious* in 1940, while *Prinz Eugen* had escaped after aiding the *Bismarck* in sinking the *Hood*. The RAF had launched more than three hundred attacks against the ships; sooner or later they would sink them where they floated at Brest.

Josten knew no words would be wasted as Galland stepped to the podium, forcing himself to speak in slow, measured tones that compelled attention, his rich baritone reaching to every corner of the briefing room.

"The Fuehrer has directed that the battle cruisers *Gneisenau* and *Scharnhorst* and the heavy cruiser *Prinz Eugen,* with the necessary escorts, leave the harbor at Brest, and proceed"—he paused for emphasis"—*via the English Channel* to Wilhelmshaven, and then to ports in Norway."

There was a collective gasp. The British had permitted no enemy navy to force the channel since The Armada; they would certainly throw in everything they had in order to stop this effort.

"I understand your reaction, but the fact is there is no alternative. If we leave the ships in Brest, they will eventually be sunk by the RAF; if we take the other route, around Ireland and Scotland, we will be met and outgunned by the Home Fleet. If we sail the Channel"—he grinned broadly at the Navy men fuming near the podium—"the Luftwaffe can protect the Navy."

"The Fuehrer recognizes that this is a high-risk project, but has determined that the effort must be made. These ships will be vital for the defense of Norway, and to attack the convoys."

Some of the men were taking notes; others looked on in a stunned silence.

Galland swiftly laid out the plan—the ships would weigh anchor at night and steam at full speed through freshly swept minefields. Absolute radio silence was required. At noon the next day they would force their way through the narrowest part of the Channel, the Dover Strait.

"It is his view that the British reaction will be delayed long enough for us to effect a daylight passage of the narrowest part of the Channel. It is the most prudent time, even though we'll be vulnerable to air and sea attack, and even to shelling from the shore."

Galland went down an exhaustive list of requirements, detailing radio frequencies, takeoff times, and the absolute necessity for radio silence. He took a few questions, then began his conclusion.

"Gentlemen, this is one mission for which the only acceptable result is success. We must try to remain undetected for as long as possible, for as soon as the British learn we are at sea they will launch every available bomber and torpedo aircraft against us. These must be shot down at all costs."

He paused, conscious that he was beginning to speak too rapidly and that he must not lose the import of his final comment. He surveyed the room, letting his presence fill it.

"No matter what the reason—no ammunition, guns jammed, low fuel, whatever it might be—the Luftwaffe pilots who cannot shoot the hostile aircraft down will ram them."

There was another stunned silence among the Air Force men as their naval counterparts broke into broad smiles, realizing that the Luftwaffe had just accepted the ultimate responsibility for the success of the mission.

Driving back to base in his Horch cabriolet, Josten had time to digest the full meaning of Galland's briefing and to consider how it influenced his own position, already highly unusual. Galland had selected him as an airborne commander during the critical initial part of the operation. That sort of recognition would help him with his advocacy of the jet fighter. And he needed all the help he could get because time was so critical. If Russia were knocked out this year, the Me 262 could be developed at leisure. If Russia fought on, the jet would be absolutely necessary to ward off an invasion in the West, perhaps as early as next year. Then the 262 would be invaluable, perhaps even decisive.

THE ENGLISH CHANNEL/FEBRUARY 12, 1942. Galland's plan called for a minimum of sixteen fighters to be over the fleet at all times. For twenty minutes of each hour the relief aircraft overlapped, combining to form a force of thirty-two. The squadrons were to leapfrog along the French and Belgian coasts, landing to refuel at progressively more northern bases until the job was done.

At first the term "over the fleet" was a misnomer. To avoid the British radar for as long as possible, they flew below the mast height of the three capital ships that steamed north at full speed, their bows diving like eager dolphins into the slate-gray ocean, rising to toss back V-shaped spumes of green-white spray. On the day's first sortie, the miserable weather forced the ships to weave in and out of the gray-white frosting that heaped the surface of the sea like whipped cream on a Sacher torte. Josten maintained a constant watch for the destroyers and motor torpedo boats that bounded around the ships like dogs nipping at the heels of sheep.

By Josten's second sortie, the clouds began to lift, and he had a clear view of the extent of the fleet. The three big vessels were in line astern, with destroyers ranging ahead and on each side, and the German E boats scampering about, crisscrossing in a watery gymkhana.

The noise of the engine receded into the background of his consciousness, and there remained only the unremitting crackle of the receiver of the non-transmitting radios. Dolfo must have impressed them; the Luftwaffe was maintaining perfect radio discipline. All of Galland's preparations had been good, from the gradual increase in jamming to confuse British radar to the flurry of Luftwaffe sorties that had been flown in the past few weeks to disguise today's efforts.

The fleet had been at sea for fourteen hours, the last four in broad daylight. It was a February blessing that little more than four more hours of daylight remained. It seemed impossible that the British had not detected them by radar or by the innumerable aircraft with which they patrolled. Was it a trap?

He knew that the fabled white cliffs of Dover were only eighteen miles away; the ships were within the range of the guns there. And where were the bombers and the torpedo planes?

Josten banked sharply as a wall of water erupted in front of him; gunfire from the coast, well behind the stern of the last ship, *Prinz Eugen*. Very well, they had been sighted, and the code words "Open visor" came over the headsets, relieving them of radio silence and low altitude flight. The Messerschmitts quickly broke up into groups flying at one-, two-, and three-hundred meters height.

The bombers would not be far behind. The relief flight of Messerschmitts had just showed up; that meant Josten had ten more minutes on this sortie, then back for fuel and a cup of coffee.

Five minutes later he saw a German E boat swing sharply to engage five British motor torpedo boats approaching at high speed from the west. Where were the British aircraft?

The British were coming, in a balls-up rivaling the Charge of the Light Brigade for both bravery and stupidity. The mighty British Empire, forewarned of the possibility of the German sortie for weeks, had so disposed its forces that only six ancient Swordfish torpedo planes were available when, after incredible delay, the first attack was made.

The open cockpit Fairey Swordfish would have looked at home on the Western Front in 1918. Encumbered with a stiltlike fixed landing gear and laden with drag-inducing struts and wires, it was nicknamed "Stringbag," after the bags made of string netting that women carried when shopping. Designed in 1934, the three-placer—pilot, gunner, and radio man—could drop an eighteen-inch torpedo. Its crews bolstered their courage by bragging that Luftwaffe gunners could never hit it because their ranging devices were not designed to fire at a target that flew as slow as eighty-five miles per hour. And, they boasted, any lucky hits would pass right through the Swordfish's wood and fabric frame without damage. There was some minimal truth to both of these whistles in the dark.

The Stringbag had already done heroic work. Operating from HMS *Illustrious,* twenty-one Swordfish had crippled the Italian fleet at Taranto in November 1940. The following spring, Swordfish from the *Ark Royal* had launched torpedoes that jammed the *Bismarck*'s rudder and set her up for the heavy guns of the Home Fleet. But those attacks had been made without fighter opposition.

Lieutenant Commander Eugene Esmonde flew the lead Swordfish. He had just made a command decision, the last of his short life. The fighter escort had not arrived at the rendezvous point; the German fleet was getting away, beyond the Strait into the Narrow Sea. He elected to attack, knowing that the German fighters were waiting, and that few, if any, of the Swordfish would survive.

As the six Swordfish lumbered toward the target, a flight of ten Spitfires—less than a quarter of the promised escort—suddenly materialized and a brief glow of hope stirred Esmonde—there might be a chance after all.

The red fuel warning light was blinking as Josten saw a sheet of flak erupt from the destroyers on his left. All of them had been fitted with crude welded mounts for extra 20-mm automatic weapons, and the wall of smoke and flame they laid down looked impenetrable. To his amazement, six Swordfish stumbled through the curtain of fire in two flights of three, battered but on course to the main fleet. Banking to engage them he reefed back on the stick to avoid a forest of water spouts blossoming in front of him. The eleven-inch guns of the battle cruisers were firing shells right through his own line of flight to ensnare the Swordfish. He shrugged; he'd never know if one hit him.

The port lower wing of one Swordfish vanished, as if Neptune had reached up from the sea to clutch it. Its nose rose sharply, then bowed to the left before disappearing in a spray of water. Josten's own starboard wing scraped the wavetops he racked around to slow himself enough to pick up a head-on shot at a target. He pressed the trigger and saw his tracers passing behind his target as he whipped through the formation. He blinked as he did so, not believing his eyes. On the third Swordfish a madly brave gunner had crawled out of his seat and was straddling the fuselage like a horse, facing the rear, trying to beat out a fire in the fabric with his hands.

Josten throttled back, slowing down to drop some flaps; there were Spitfires about, but the top flight of Messerschmitts had already engaged them. His targets were the remaining Swordfish.

Other Messerschmitts were attacking, barracuda against bonito, getting into each other's way as the Fleet Air Arm planes lumbered forward. One of the Swordfish disappeared in a huge ball of flame—a shell must have exploded its torpedo: another simply stopped flying, to drop limply into the Channel like a dead fly in a glass of beer.

Josten gained on the formation slowly this time, aiming and firing with care. The wood and fabric of the trailing Swordfish sponged up his gunfire. Smiling grimly, he trod on the rudder pedals, walking his tracers back and forth across the cockpit until the guns went silent. Just as he ran out of ammunition, he saw the gunner throw his hands up and the pilot lurch forward on the stick. The big biplane tucked its nose into a wave and halted, swamped immediately to its aft cockpit by the building sea, then slipping without reluctance beneath the surface.

He had overflown the attackers again, reaching almost to the jaws of the *Scharnhorst*'s thundering main batteries when he threw his fighter in a steep bank to reverse his course. The amount of cannon fire roaring past him did not bear thinking about. There was only one Swordfish still flying, gamely headed directly toward the big battle cruiser, torpedo ready to be launched.

The fuel warning light was burning red steadily now. It didn't matter, for Josten knew he would never reach shore. He caught the Swordfish in his sights, the big three-bladed fixed-pitch propeller glistening in the mist, the enormous wings pushing the shell-freighted air aside like a child burrowing in the sand. He pressed the trigger, just in case, but nothing happened. The two airplanes closed. In a single fluid motion, Josten lifted his fighter over the huge upper wing of the torpedo plane, then dipped his port wing so that it sheared off the Swordfish's vertical fin. The Swordfish dropped straight into the sea, the Messerschmitt cartwheeling at its side. A geyser of water covered Josten's cockpit, turning the outside world rapidly from blue to gray to blue again as his tired fighter bobbed up and down before lurching to a halt. Jettisoning the canopy, he pulled his one-man life raft out just as the plane sank beneath him.

Battered, stomach and mouth engorged with the teeth-rattling chill of the seawater, Josten inflated the raft and struggled into it. He looked up to find the last Swordfish directly in front of him, engine sunk deep, water flowing over the cockpit rails. The gunner was dead in his harness, but another man, the radio operator probably, was dragging the unconscious pilot out of the cockpit. He had just freed him when the tailless Swordfish rolled over and plunged out of sight, as if glad to end its embarrassing agony.

Josten choked back nausea as he paddled toward the two British survivors. The radio man was treading water, holding the pilot up and trying to inflate his life jacket as the rolling sea bounced them. Josten knew that he could expect to survive no more than a few hours in his raft; the two enemy crew members would not last for twenty minutes as the chilly Channel sucked warmth from their bones.

A wave crested, dropping Josten's raft next to the British airmen. He reached out and grabbed the pilot's jacket, saying to the radio operator, "Hold on to the raft. I'll take care of him."

The radio man, too cold to be surprised by Josten's English, nodded gratefully. Josten managed to get the jacket inflated and then held his arms around the pilot's head, keeping it from bobbing forward into the water, the long blond hair slicked tight against his skull, veins showing big and blue beneath the translucent skin, deep blue eyes open with pupils fixed.

The radio operator's teeth chattered like a flak battery while his color drained to a gray-blue as, cell by cell, he gave in to the cold.

"Can't hold on, going to let go."

"Nonsense, there are dozens of E boats looking for us. Just hang on."

A decision was forming in Josten's mind as he scanned the water, praying that a German boat would spot them. The unconscious pilot was not going to make it. He could not afford to waste his strength on him. The radio man was a goner unless he somehow got out of the water. The raft was not supposed to be able to hold two people, especially in the swelling chop of the Channel, but he'd have to take the chance. He shook the radio man's arm, forcing his eyes open.

"I'm going to have to let your friend go. I can't hold on to him. When I do, you crawl aboard. You've got to help, I don't have the strength to bring you in myself."

The radio man looked mutely at his comrade and mumbled, "No, hold on to him."

Josten let the pilot go; he bobbed away, disappearing at once, then reappearing, his head lolling back now so that his accusing open eyes stared deep into Josten's soul, seeming to say, "I have died and you are going to live." It was a sight Josten would never forget.

"Do you have the strength to get in?"

The radio man shook his head.

Josten tried and failed to haul him in the raft.

He was still holding him, arms aching with the cold and fatigue, when an E boat came alongside thirty minutes later. Rough hands pulled him on board; the radio operator, dead for many minutes, slipped out of their hands to drift in search of his pilot.

Below deck they wrapped Josten in blankets and forced *muckefuck*—ersatz coffee—laced with schnapps down his throat. It acted like a depth charge to the seawater he'd swallowed; he vomited and at once felt better.

The E boat raced at top speed back to port, the water pounding the thin planks on which Josten lay. As warmth returned to his extremities, he had time to rethink the battle. It was incredible that the British had thrown antiques like the Swordfish against them. No matter how brave the pilots were, they couldn't overcome their disadvantage in equipment.

The true meaning of the battle dawned on him. It wouldn't make any difference how many airplanes Germany had, unless they were of superior performance. The jet fighter had to be built.

9

Tempsford—New Secrets, MacRobert's Reply, and Gelsenkirchen

from A THOUSAND SHALL FALL
by Murray Peden

Fighter pilots write the most memoirs; a bomber pilot, Murray Peden, has written one of the best. His autobiographical *A Thousand Shall Fall* is at once a testament to his bravery, his flying skills, his writing ability, and more than anything else, his compassionate humanity.

In one of these selections, Peden recalls how he was assigned what he thought was a "highly undesirable Joe-job"—carrying supplies to the French resistance—that became one of the most interesting and satisfying of his career.

Now when one thinks of working with the French resistance, the first image that springs to mind is of those strange-looking high-winged Army cooperation Westland Lysanders. The Lysanders were slow but admirably suited to short field landings and takeoffs from the rough French farms that served as landing strips. Peden was tasked to fly his Short Stirling, an admirable aircraft unduly handicapped by a design requirement that its wing be no longer than existing RAF hangar doors—that is, 100 feet. Its deficiency in wing area compromised its altitude capability, and it suffered grievous losses as a result.

About this mission, Peden says, "While the low flying carried with it, as always, the wonderful exhilaration of manifest speed, it exacted its own special brand of nervous strain as we peered ahead for power lines and other obstacles." Nervous strain indeed; Peden had to fly his four-engine bomber at a height of no more than 300 feet into enemy-occupied France and there locate a tiny field where his load of clandestine supplies could be dropped.

Then, in an unusual turn of events, Peden was assigned to No. 224 (BS) Squadron, a "Bomber Support" unit that was operating specially equipped Boeing B-17s. The B-17s were used to drop chaff, but more important, to jam essential VHF communications between the German night fighter controllers and the fighters themselves. Peden's description of a night raid into the heavily defended "Happy Valley," Germany's Ruhr, is a masterpiece of writing, understated even as it presents in the clearest terms the stark fear such a mission induced.

Halfway through the mission, a Messerschmitt Me 410 attacked Peden's B-17, knocking out his number-three engine and setting it on fire. Mustering all his skill, Peden managed to keep the B-17 airborne despite the windmilling propeller, which refused to feather, and a recurring engine fire. More night fighters attacked, and he forced the shaking B-17 into the standard corkscrew evasion maneuver. A Junkers Ju 88 stalked the cripple, trying to pick it off and pumping more shells into it.

Peden battled to keep the aircraft flying; as he struggled, he felt a tap on his shoulder. It was his German-speaking special wireless operator, who screamed, "The wireless operator's been hit. And I've been hit. And we all want to go home."

No one wanted to get home more than Peden, but the trip was nerve-wracking, what with the propeller on the number-three engine continually threatening to overspeed and the threat of fire burning through the wing spar. Back at his base, Peden managed an almost miraculous landing that was turned into further hazard by a collision on the ground with a Lancaster. All in all, quite a mission—and not quite routine, not even for Peden.

W.J.B.

TEMPSFORD—NEW SECRETS. There was nothing about the morning of November 9th to indicate that we would be facing anything in our flying other than the pattern to which we were becoming hardened—at least not until 11:00 AM. The Tannoy sounded at that point, ordering

F/O Peden to report forthwith to the Wing Commander. My conscience was reasonably clear, so, as I repaired at speed to his office, my overriding emotion was simple curiosity.

Without preamble McGlinn told me that be had selected my crew for temporary service "for a week or two" with No. 161 Squadron at Tempsford. Responding to my mystified look, responding negatively that is, he told me stonily that I would find out all about it when I got there; although he was good enough to show me roughly where the place was: 50 miles north—northwest of London, near Bedford. He also imparted the information that we were to pack our worldly belongings, take H Hal, and shake the dust of Chedburgh from our feet in two hours. Allowing for travelling time back down to the billets, that meant we actually had about 20 minutes to pack and arrange the usual ineffectual messages for the forwarding of laundry and mail. It sounded to me suspiciously like a buildup for a brush-off onto some highly undesirable Joe-job. (As usual, I was quite wrong, and in due course came to feel highly flattered at having been chosen.)

By three o'clock we had flown to Tempsford, unloaded our gear, and transported it to the Flights. The Adjutant wasted no time on me, giving me a quick speech over his shoulder as he left his office to do something more important, the gist of which was that I would be flying second dickey that night with Flight Lieutenant Dixon, that briefing was in half an hour, and that I had better look sharp as the King and Queen were coming to inspect the aircrew immediately after briefing. Oh yes, and just leave my trunk there, he would see that it was sent to the mess and that I got fixed up with a bed after I got back from wherever it was I was going to be sent. I parted from him with the vaguely resentful feeling that there must surely be some squadron in the RAF to which one could be posted and find upon arrival that he had time to squeeze in a fast visit to the toilet before being packed into an aeroplane and sent on operations.

Once at briefing the clouds of mystery began to lift. What 161 Squadron and 138 Squadron were doing quickly became apparent, and as it did, I understood why the Wingco had been so close-mouthed about it.

Tempsford was the main centre from which Special Air Service and Special Operations Executive were supplying the French resistance movement with arms and equipment. The Resistance was variously called the FFI (French Forces of the Interior), the Maquis, or simply the

Underground. The magnitude of the supply program was particularly impressive, and I began to understand why security at Tempsford was noticeably tighter than anything we had yet encountered.

The big operations board listed about 20 aircraft of assorted types, and opposite their identifying letters, the components of their cargoes. I noticed that in addition to a large number of canisters that we would carry in H Hal's bomb bay, we were also carrying, inside the aircraft, several crates of carrier pigeons and one or two other large cases which would have to be pushed out the big hatch in the Stirling's belly. I quizzed Flight Lieutenant Dixon.

"Oh, that'll likely be a printing press and a radio," he said.

I turned my eyes back to the board. In the extreme right-hand column, opposite the letters of three Halifaxes, I saw beside each the inscription "1 Joe."

"What's a Joe?" I said to Dixon.

He turned back toward me: "A spy usually. We don't often carry them, because a Stirling's not the best aircraft in the world to jump from. You won't see the Joes in here though. Wait until we go out to the aircraft and you'll see them brought out." He pointed at a lower line on the board.

"You see the Lysanders?"

I nodded.

"They go right in and land on the other side. That first one's taking a Joe in with him; and you'll notice he's picking up two more in France to bring back. Things must be getting pretty hot for them." He sat silent for a moment then spoke again: "The Lysander pilots get an automatic DFC if they pull off five trips successfully."

I sat there digesting that for a few minutes, finding it difficult to realize that I was now part of this glamorous cloak and dagger operation. Then I tried to imagine what it would be like flying a slow and vulnerable Lysander to some little hay meadow in France, landing there by moonlight, exchanging one or two inbound spies for a corresponding number of outbound agents, probably with the Germans not too far off their tails, and then bringing the overloaded and unarmed aircraft home again. I concluded that they were not cheapening the DFC by handing it out to someone who had completed five assignments of that type.

Briefing was considerably different at Tempsford, since the aircraft were all bound for different destinations, destinations which were referred to only by code name on the board. Each crew received individual briefing on its planned time of arrival and the recognition signal to be flashed by its "reception committee." While other crews were getting the particulars for their drops, Dixon kept feeding me little snippets of information about peculiarities of this new type of operation and about some of the personalities involved in the work.

The first name he mentioned was that of Group Captain P. C. Pickard, well known to most of us already as the pilot of F Freddie in the RAF documentary film "Target for Tonight." Pickard had won the second bar to his DSO as the Wing Commander of 161 Squadron, and was just beginning his career as a Mosquito pilot in one of the Mosquito Wings in No. 2 Group. (He was to lose his life only a few weeks later, February 18th, 1944, leading one of the most daring and successful operations of the war, the low level Mosquito attack on Amiens Prison, an operation mounted in an attempt to free several hundred members of the French resistance imprisoned there, many of them facing execution at the hands of the Germans. The walls of the prison were breached and well over 200 prisoners escaped and remained out of the Germans' hands; but Operation "Jericho" cost Pickard his life.)

Travelling in a comparable aura of glamour was the redoubtable French navigator Philippe Livry-Level, who had escaped from France and made his way to England to carry on the war with the RAF. By lying brazenly about his age, he had wangled his way into aircrew. Dixon pointed him out to me, a distinguished looking gentleman whom I had noticed earlier because of his older appearance. As I later learned, he was approximately 45 years of age—about double the age of most of the people he was flying with—a fact which by itself was a significant commentary on his martial spirit. The boys, said Dixon, used to ask Philippe jokingly after each trip whether he had managed to drop in on his wife, for if he was anywhere in the area after the drop, Philippe used to get his pilot to fly him to the little village just out of Caen where his wife and family still lived. The deep roar of the Halifax's four engines was the welcome message to Madame Level that Philippe was there circling the house in the moonlight, only a few hundred feet away, thinking about her and letting her know that all was well with him. On one occasion, when his plane had landed in France to drop off and pick up some Joes, he had left a parcel with the reception committee, who had casually delivered it to his wife a short time later. I liked that story and made up my mind to have a chat with Philippe at the first convenient opportunity.

The moment all the crews had been briefed, we hurried out, battle-dress blouses betraying by rectangular bulges the escape kits buried in the inside pockets, and lined up outside one of the hangars. The timing was faultless. We had been standing there only a few minutes—in earlier days I had often waited five times as long for a corporal—when a black Daimler rolled slowly round the far corner of the hangar and came to a stop 50 yards in front of us.

The King and Queen alighted, and after a brief chat with the Station Commander and one or two other senior officers began inspecting the crews going on the night's operations. The King wore the uniform of Marshal of the Royal Air Force, his sleeve leaving little doubt of who in the group was in the best position to pull rank. He and the Queen carried out the inspection with a touch of informality, exchanging a few words here and there as they made their rounds. The whole ceremony did not take ten minutes.

I had expected to see no more of them after the inspection, but again I was to be surprised. As their car disappeared once more behind the hangar, the Flight Commander announced that officers on ops that evening would not be following the customary practice of having their flying meal in the airmen's mess. Instead, at the King's request, they would join the King and Queen for tea in the officers' mess.

Accordingly, we found ourselves in the royal presence again a few minutes later, this time for a more extended period. One of the officers present had won the Distinguished Flying Cross a few weeks earlier, and the King had fittingly decreed that he would decorate him at a special investiture in the Tempsford mess. For some minutes the hum of conversation in the lounge was stilled. In a suddenly imposed moment of solemnity the recipient, a Wing Commander, stood before his sovereign as the citation was read aloud. The King then fastened the glittering cross on his chest, shook his hand, and exchanged a few words in a confidential tone of voice before concluding the ceremony.

For a further half hour we enjoyed the distinctly unusual pleasure of rubbing shoulders with the King and Queen at a cosy tea party. Then they had to leave—and we too had to leave. The parallel went no further. They drove back to Buckingham Palace in the Daimler; we took off on an estimated six hour and ten minute flight to visit the Maquis, waiting for us in a field about 35 miles south-southwest of Le Mans.

Much about Tempsford operations differed from Main Force ops. Firstly, no bombs; just canisters and packing cases laden with a great variety of stores: Sten guns, ammunition, explosives, detonators, timing devices, radios, printing presses, and crate after crate of carrier pigeons. Further; all operations were carried out low level, so as to avoid fighters and leave little or no record with the German radar crews of routes taken and numbers of aircraft involved. Ground observers would still see and hear us occasionally, of course; but the information thus obtained was often fleeting and generalized, and the variations which it was possible for us to make in our routes made it of limited value for their purposes.

Low level operations of this type at night meant restricting the flights to about one week as the moon was waxing to full and one more week as it waned. A fair amount of moonlight was essential, even if it came through light or scattered cloud; otherwise the low flying at night became hazardous in the extreme. As Dixon took us toward the French coast at about 300 feet—instead of the 12,000 or 13,000 I was used to—I had a distinct feeling that this business was risky enough.

We had flown out over Beachy Head and swung about 20 degrees west of south to run in west of Le Havre over the Normandy beaches, practically along the line of our first visit to France with the leaflets. Crossing just west of Courseulles, we swung back to south, skirting Caen, then coming to a course of about 170 degrees. We were navigating strictly by low level map-reading, a demanding enough science even by day. I wondered pessimistically how Dixon's navigator had any hope of tracing the one small field we had to find.

All of us kept a sharp lookout. At heights ranging from 50 to 300 feet it did not pay to wander over towns or other strong points; we presented too easy a target for light flak. Heavy guns obviously couldn't even begin to track us, and had no real chance of hitting us at this height, so we were not faced with the more common problem of trying to outguess predicted flak.

We began to pass over beautiful rolling country looking like some vast Currier and Ives panorama bathed in moonlight. Cottages and small fields, fences and stacks flitted by, seemingly almost even with our wingtips. The Stirling, flame and noise belching from its glowing exhausts, was an incongruous black intruder streaking across this peaceful, undulating terrain. Not a soul was to be seen anywhere, just rolling fields and the black smudges of thickets and copses.

All at once a small house appeared on a slight rise a few hundred yards ahead of us, looking very dark against the light texture of the surrounding stubble. The moment my eye lighted on it the door flew open, and in the bright yellowish light that streamed forth a man stood silhouetted, waving vigorously. I turned my head sharply as we passed and saw him again as he flashed into view behind the starboard wing, still waving.

"He thinks he's helping us by showing a light," Dixon explained.

I found the three-second scene touching. The Frenchman had exposed himself to serious punishment by his act, yet I was to see it repeated several times in different parts of France in the next three or four trips, and every Tempsford pilot had seen these mute and fleeting benedictions.

While the low flying carried with it, as always, the wonderful exhilaration of manifest speed, it exacted its own special brand of nervous strain as we peered ahead for power lines and other obstacles. After close to an hour of this, I learned a little trade secret of the Tempsford aerial provisioners. At night, flying low level, it was frequently difficult to see or to identify landmarks which could easily have been recognized in daylight or even from a greater altitude. Here the rivers of France were invaluable, particularly the broad silvery expanse which now slipped into view as we reached the Loire. Dixon and his navigator had intentionally overshot the area we were ultimately going to be making our drop in, and flown to the Loire to get a good solid fix only 15 or 20 miles from where the reception committee would be lying waiting. Turning upstream, the navigator soon got his fix at the junction of the Indre, and we steered a northwesterly course at 180 mph, calculated to bring us to the drop field in six minutes.

Now we climbed to 500 feet to expand our field of view, and stared intently all around, trying to spot the triangle of three flashlights that would identify our objective. When our six minutes were up, we circled briefly, trying to get our bearings on the terrain below, unable as yet to detect any sign of our Maquis friends. To me the whole experience still seemed so totally unreal that their absence came as no surprise.

After a minute's consultation with his instinct Dixon spoke: "Let's swing over past that little bush and try the field on the far side."

Over we swooped, and in sudden excitement I called "There they are!" as I saw the glow of lights just ahead of us. Dixon flashed a fast signal on our recognition light, and we all stared down at the red-paper covered lights below us to see who would respond. One light, incredibly, blinked "S . . . R," the agreed upon signal. I hardly breathed.

Now three black figures could be seen running into position on the field. In a few seconds they were in a line, shining their flashlights up at us. A man at one end flashed a double light, one in each hand, the signal that we should start our drop from the opposite direction and run down the line towards the double light. Dixon made a slow turn, carefully keeping them in view, and we crawled up to about 600 feet as we opened the bomb doors and started toward them. At that height, the chutes just had time to flare open and break the fall for a few seconds before the canisters landed.

As we ran in, the reception committee disappeared from my view, hidden by the nose of the aircraft. The bombaimer's voice came over the intercom as he dropped the canisters from the bomb bay in sequence, ordering the wireless operator to push the other cargo out the huge door at the rear end. Dixon held straight on for a second until the wireless operator confirmed that he had dumped the interior cargo; then we swung in a slow turn and came back for a good look at the field.

When we had first come on the scene the field had been empty. Then the lights had been exposed. On our first pass there had been three figures, and only three, visible. Now, as we came back, there were at least 20, some of them just emerging from ditches and thickets, running hard for the ghostly line of billowing canopies. In a matter of seconds men were detaching the tell-tale chutes and rolling them up, as others seized the heavy canisters and manhandled them rapidly towards a copse alongside a narrow road. We rocked our wings in salute, then nosed down to skim low over the fields again as we made for home.

***

MacRobert's Reply. After we had landed back at Downham Market this New Year's Day, Mackie told me a story I never forgot. It was a poignant tale, at once sad and uplifting, concerning a Scottish woman I had not heard of before, Lady MacRobert.

Lady MacRobert's husband died in 1922, leaving her with three sons to raise. When they grew up all three lads were drawn to flying.

One son, Sir Alasdair MacRobert, was killed in a flying accident in 1938. When the war broke out Lady MacRobert had two sons anxious to fly on operations.

On the 22nd of May, 1941, she suffered a second blow, receiving notification that Flight Lieutenant Sir Roderic A. MacRobert had been shot down and killed while flying his Hurricane on operations in Iraq.

As Mackie told the story it was easy to imagine the strain Lady MacRobert must have been under, with her only remaining son still flying on operations. I pictured her attempting to carry on at home—a home, incidentally, which she had thrown open to servicemen—praying fervently that he be spared to her, starting apprehensively at every ring of the telephone, at every glimpse of a telegraph boy, at the knock of any casual caller.

Her mother's prayers went unanswered. Sir Iain MacRobert was killed flying on operations less than six weeks after his brother Roderic, on June 30th, 1941.

Lady MacRobert's response to this culminating tragedy, after she had weathered its cruelest hours, came like a flashing ray of light from a magnificent spirit. She donated twenty-five thousand pounds toward the purchase of a Stirling, which, upon delivery, she presented formally to No. 15 Squadron, RAF, to carry on the battle. Proudly emblazoned on either side of the Stirling's cockpit, just below tile lofty canopy, was a message to fire a warrior's heart:

"MacRobert's Reply"

It was a reply indeed, a reply that echoed its own fanfare of heraldic trumpets.

Her response was epitomized in that one majestic phrase and gesture; but it went even further. With another twenty thousand pound donation Lady MacRobert helped pay for the purchase of four Hurricanes. Each of these aircraft bore the family crest, and three of them the inscription, "The MacRoberts Fighter" followed by the name of one of her three sons. The fourth bore the device "The Lady."

Lady MacRobert's sons, it is clear, came by their courage honestly. I often thought of that wonderful, indomitable woman.

Gelsenkirchen. At 4:30 that afternoon we sat in the briefing room and watched in the usual strained silence as the curtains swished noisily open to reveal route tapes running to Gelsenkirchen, in the heart of the Ruhr. Someone in the crew muttered: "Christ, Happy Valley." I responded with supreme confidence, "Piece of cake." Our target was the Nordstern oil plant in Gelsenkirchen.

I really did not feel the confidence I had expressed as I looked at the big target map in front of us. Heavy flak areas on that map were marked with red circles. The Ruhr was one solid turnip-shaped blotch of red, many inches wide, and a foot long on our map; and it had a deep belt of searchlights all round it, denoted by a continuous broad blue border framing the whole blob. Ruhr trips had one good quality: they were short. That was their only redeeming feature. Happy Valley was probably the most heavily defended industrial area in Europe. Apart from the hundreds of flak batteries and the dense concentrations of searchlights, it was well protected by swarms of night fighters, and it was extremely difficult on such a short trip to mislead them by routing as to the intended target area. When I said "piece of cake" it was just so much whistling past the graveyard; but I was to be reminded of it later.

We had skirted the fringes of the Ruhr's defences on more than one occasion, had seen that seemingly impenetrable palisade of searchlights, and knew only too well that to run through the heaviest belt of those defences—Gelsenkirchen was like another suburb of Essen—was going to be no picnic. Main Force was actually going to split as it approached our target area and attack the oil plants at nearby Wesseling and Scholven-Buer as well. All these attacks, and those delivered by the RAF in the days immediately preceding, were part of the co-ordinated allied bombing campaign against German oil plants initiated some weeks earlier, with gratifying success, by the Americans. These strikes were hurting the Germans, and their fighters were reacting accordingly.

Takeoff was late these summer nights. It was just after 11:00 PM when the Aldis lamp's green flash sent F Fox roaring down the flarepath. We crossed the coast outbound near Cromer, and climbed steadily to 22,000 feet in the clear night air.

Once we hit the enemy coast, the ever-present strain mounted rapidly to the higher level that was the concomitant of being in the enemy's ball park, blindfolded by night. I always waited tensely for the first burst of flak to stab at us, hoping it would not be too close. Once that first burst came up, and I recovered from the violent start that the sudden flash in the darkness always caused, I breathed a little easier and began the game that every pilot had to play, changing altitude, course, and speed, to throw off the next burst, counting the seconds carefully and watching to see where that next burst came; then varying the course again, being careful not to "balance" the pattern with a nice symmetrical correction to the other side. The German predictors were quick to average symmetrical evasions and fire a burst at the appropriate moment along the mean track.

The human system is incredibly adaptive, and what constantly surprised me, when I thought about it in safety on the ground, was how matter of factly we could play this deadly game, and even derive a certain nervous satisfaction from it, watching shells burst two or three hundred yards away, at the very spot you would have been had you not changed course as the gunners were launching their speeding projectiles on their way.

We thrust inland, threading our way through the welcoming flak, and Stan soon began reporting contacts on Monica, the radar set which he monitored in his cabin. It became apparent that Sam had positioned us well towards the middle of the bomber stream, and that the concentration of Lancasters was dense. In a way I hated these frequent radar contacts, for we always had to assume that they might be night fighters, and everyone strained unconsciously until one of the gunners came on intercom with something like: "Ah, I've got him, Skipper, it's a Lanc. He's three or four hundred yards dead astern and down just a little bit." On black nights they could not be seen at anything like that range. This night they could be spotted while they were well away from us. We had a second concern, however, even after the gunners identified the contact as a Lanc. The question uppermost in our minds then was: has he seen and identified us? The Fortress, of course, had a prominent single fin. Most of the aircraft with a single fin and rudder flying the night skies were German, and we wanted no "friendly" machine gun bullets put into us by mistake. If the friendly aircraft was slightly above you, the waiting period until you parted company was extremely tense, since it was easier for you to spot him than vice versa.

At a point about 20 minutes from the target we began to approach an outlying belt of searchlights which stood before us on either side of our intended track in two great cones. I feared and hated those baleful blinding lights more than anything else the Germans used against us. While in themselves they seldom caused death—although there were reported cases of pilots, particularly at low level, apparently becoming completely disoriented by their glaring beams and diving into the earth—they were all too often the harbinger of death. A pilot trapped in a large cone had little chance of escape. For long seconds on end the dazzling glare would render him helpless, spotlighting him as the target and making it almost impossible for him to see his instruments and maintain any sense of equilibrium. Meanwhile the searchlights' accomplices, the heavy guns, would hurl up shells in streams, and all too frequently the aircraft would explode or begin a crazy, smoking dive to the ground.

As I watched these two cones warily, I noticed that they were remaining stationary for 30 seconds or so at a time, leaving a corridor between them, then abruptly moving together and establishing one giant cone right in the middle of what had been the safe passage. Twice I saw them do this, and twice when they came together in the centre they trapped a Lancaster attempting to slip by. Each time the Lancaster was destroyed. It was an unnerving spectacle to watch, particularly when your turn to run the gauntlet was fast approaching. It was Hobson's choice with a vengeance. You could not fly straight into either cone while they were standing separate; that was committing suicide; and detouring all the way around the outside would have involved a major departure from the prescribed track and thrown out the aircraft's time over target by several minutes. You had no practicable alternative but to take the black void between the two cones, knowing that the lights would swing inward and illuminate some part of the safe passage every few seconds. You headed for the open spot and prayed that you would get through. I chose a spot slightly right of centre and sweated. We were lucky.

Hardly had we cleared this hurdle than Stan came on the intercom again to report another contact, a close one. This time we were not left long in doubt. In less than a minute our rear gunner, Johnny Walker, spotted an aircraft directly astern at a range of about 300 yards. This was approximately where Stan had predicted the contact would be found, but it was another 30 seconds or more before Johnny Walker and Bert Lester confirmed that it was a Lancaster. Then, for a minute or two, we seemed to be holding the same relative positions. I was reluctant to weave away if I could avoid it, since Sam's navigation thus far had kept us dead on track, and I preferred not to mar his handiwork. However, after another minute, Johnny Walker reported that the Lanc had closed further and was now just about 200 yards astern.

"If he comes any closer, any closer at all," I said, "let me know, and I'll weave off to the side a bit."

It was at that precise moment that Fate dealt us a card off the bottom of the deck.

The Lancaster abruptly stood on its wingtip and dived away. Directly behind it, and now directly behind us and in perfect firing position, was a Messerschmitt 410 which had been stalking the Lancaster.

As Johnny Walker shouted a warning and began firing himself, the air around us was instantly filled with white flaming shells that flashed past our windows with horrifying speed, and F Fox shuddered heavily to the pounding of a hail of close range cannon fire. Through the back of my seat I felt a rapid series of staccato blows that jarred us like the strokes of a wild triphammer.

I had instinctively thrust the control column forward and twisted the ailerons to dive into a violent corkscrew; but in the second it took to initiate the manœuvre, F Fox absorbed heavy punishment from the torrent of shells the Messerschmitt's cannons poured into us. Before I had 15 degrees of bank on, the starboard inner engine burst into great leaping flames and the intercom went dead.

As we rolled into the dive to starboard, the heavy vibration of a long burst fired from our mid-upper turret shook the instrument panel in front of me into a great blur; it was as though the instruments were mounted on the sounding strings of some giant lyre. With remarkable presence of mind, Bill ignored the tracers flying around his head, and moved to feather number three at the same time as he activated its fire extinguisher. I was dimly aware of his actions, and of the frightening flames that gushed out of the engine and were snatched back across the cowling as I rolled to begin my climb to port.

The firing ceased as suddenly as it had started—on both sides. With some difficulty I levelled up, after a fashion, and tried to take stock of the situation. F Fox was sickeningly sluggish and unresponsive; but for the next two minutes that problem paled into insignificance as I struggled to stop her swift descent, and watched Bill fight to get number three feathered so that we could get the fire under control. We had been told frequently that a fuel-fed fire, blown against the interior of the wing by the slipstream, could eat right through the main spar in as little as two minutes. If the main spar went, our chances of getting out of the aircraft as it cartwheeled earthward would be remote. Bill was unable to coax the recalcitrant propeller to feather properly, although the blades did rotate to the point where the propeller was turning over at a low speed.

Meantime J. B. had clambered back to find out what had happened in the rear of the aircraft. For all we knew, the four crew members behind the mid-upper might have abandoned the plane—or been killed.

F Fox continued to lose height, and without warning number three began to wind up. In moments it was up past its safe maximum and was overspeeding with a terrifying banshee wail. As it screamed itself into hysteria, the fire, which had been dying down, flared up in all its fury again.

Scared half out of my wits by the flames, and the knowledge that they were only inches away from enough gasoline to blow us into eternity, I tried vainly to remember what one did with an overspeeding propeller. In a moment Bill suggested throttling back the other three, and I strained to pull F Fox's nose up at the same time so that the overspeeding propeller would be carrying a substantial load.

It worked. Like a screaming circular saw suddenly deprived of power the propeller began to slow down, its terrifying note gradually subsiding like some manic thing being quieted. As it sank back below normal speed, we shifted the load onto the other three engines, staring appraisingly at number three and trying to gauge whether that fire would kill us with an explosion. Although it was not extinguished, it had subsided again with the propeller, so I turned my attention momentarily to the task of coaxing F Fox to hold height.

As though cursed with a devilish spirit of its own, number three began to overspeed again. I knew this nerve-wracking phenomenon, with its continually rising crescendo of shrieking sound was a condition which could not long endure. The propeller shaft would let go in a short time, and when that happened, in a Fortress, the propeller from number three would fly into, or perhaps through, the nose or cockpit. Despite the fact that the manoeuvre resulted in a partial stall which then lost us more precious altitude, I had no alternative but to throttle back again, haul the nose up, and try to force some load onto number three. As I did so, the flames were flaring above the cowling once more. The technique worked again, soothing the maddened outcry of the propeller and coaxing its speed back within a range the engine could tolerate. Again F Fox mushed down in a weary stall, the inevitable product of the unnaturally nose-high position coupled with the loss of power. Bill and I bent once more to the task of restoring the power very gradually, so as not to precipitate another runaway, and nursing the weary aircraft into a normal attitude.

As we levelled up, the air around us was suddenly filled with a hail of tracers again, and once again I threw F Fox into a corkscrew. But this time we could only manage a travesty of the prescribed manœuvre, and we would have died then and there but for the good shooting of Johnny Walker. A Ju 88, drawn by the irresistible sight of fire aboard a wounded prey, had stalked us and closed to finish us off. But the German pilot had reckoned without Johnny Walker. Hollering into the dead intercom in a fruitless attempt to warn me, Johnny drew a careful bead on the German and, in the face of the fighter's overpowering weight of fire, traded lead so accurately that the German was shortly forced to break off.

F Fox had absorbed more punishment in this second combat, although nothing like what she had taken the first time. She had lost even more of her characteristic responsiveness, and her struggle to fend off the clutch of gravity was palpably less successful. Another result of the second attack, however, was that it forced us to dive again, and this in turn had immediately started number three winding up. Once more the fire flared wickedly, ugly tongues of flame visible from a great distance at night, and again we went through our scary exercise, stalling the sluggish aeroplane to get the screaming propeller back under control. The second attack, therefore, inflicted additional structural damage upon us, re-kindled the fire in number three, and cost us altitude we could not afford to give away. It did one other thing: it convinced me that it would be foolhardy to try to make our way through the main flak and searchlight defences over the target in the condition we were in. Night fighters too were clearly in the stream in force. The Ju 88 had picked us up within minutes of the first attack, and I felt it would be simply asking for it to count on escaping from a third attack in our present condition. Although we were now no more than ten minutes away from the target, I coaxed F Fox into a gentle turn and reversed our course.

Bill went forward to get me a proper course from Sam, and again I surveyed the situation with what few crumbs of equanimity I could muster. Our most worrisome problem, apart from the smouldering fire which kept threatening to flare and spread, was the generally precarious performance of the aircraft. Flying on three engines with the fourth propeller properly feathered is one thing. It is quite another doing it with an engine which is windmilling and refuses to feather, and in an aeroplane which has been torn open and battered to the point where its aerodynamic efficiency has been seriously compromised. Pulling an aeroplane through the sky with an engine windmilling is much the same as pushing a stalled car while leaving it in gear. The drag is tremendous, and the net effect is to subtract and waste a substantial amount of your remaining power. When I turned F Fox about, we were down to 15,000 feet, having lost close to 7,000 feet in the two combats and the ensuing struggle with the burning engine. We were still losing height at about 500–700 feet per minute, were still without intercom, and were seriously limited as to manœuvrability.

As Bill and I were setting the remaining three engines to the most power we felt we could call upon them to deliver for a protracted period, and trying to trim the aircraft into the best attitude for its sorry condition, I felt a tap on my shoulder and looked round to see Hembrow, the German-speaking special wireless operator, standing just behind my seat. He looked dishevelled and more than slightly shaken. (In fact he had been slightly wounded, with a cannon splinter in the back of the shoulder.) His terse message registered indelibly on my brain as he raised his voice and called above the noise: "The wireless operator's been hit . . . And I've been hit . . . And we all want to go home."

This trusting message, implying that I could somehow wash out the balance of the exercise, and ordain safe delivery to Blickling Hall despite fire, battle damage, and anything else that might follow, made me feel rather fatherly. I reached back and clapped him lightly on the shoulder and told him everything was okay, that we were heading for home.

Then the first piece of good luck to come our way since takeoff manifested itself—the intercom came back on, although it remained intermittent and undependable. Actually it was not luck as it turned out, but good work by Stan, assisted by J. B. In a few minutes I had some knowledge of what had happened. Stan had been badly wounded, including at least two splinter wounds in the head which caused him to lose a lot of blood and subjected him to a great deal of pain. J. B. had promptly decided that Stan should be given an injection of morphine, and prepared to administer it; but Stan had insisted on struggling to repair the intercom before submitting to the injection. I hoped within the next few minutes to be able to make up my mind as to whether we would be likely to make it back across the North Sea or whether we should bail out and take our chances while we were over land.

It was not to be an easy decision. Time seemed almost to stand still, measured only by the intervals that elapsed between the repeated overspeedings of number three engine, which I came to loathe and fear. Time after time it went through its hellish performance, causing the flames to spring up fiercely again, and forcing us to lose precious height in each stall. I aged ten years, worrying about how long the starboard wing would stay on, and at one point ordered everyone to prepare to abandon the aircraft, so that they would at least have their chest packs on if F Fox came apart in the air. (It was at this juncture that Bill discovered that my chute had disappeared in the jinking.) However, as we neared the coast, I could not defer the decision any longer. I had to make up my mind whether we would try to make it across the North Sea or whether it would be better to have the crew abandon the aircraft, bailing out while we were over land. We had fallen from 22,000 to 6,000 feet by this time, but in the denser air F Fox was now finding her strength again, and had almost ceased losing altitude. I decided the whole crew should try to make it to England, and got Sam to work out a course for Woodbridge, on the coast in Suffolk, one of our three big crash dromes.

Over the water I told Bert to get the proper colours of the period ready for the Very pistol, thinking of our troublesome intercom and radio. Bill and I now felt justified in making a very slight reduction in power to ease the strain on the three good engines, which had laboured nobly but were showing the effort in their cylinder head temperatures. After a further tense wait the English coast appeared ahead, and in a short time we were approaching Woodbridge. Sam had brought us to it as straight as a homing pigeon, and my biggest remaining worry, or so I thought, was that at any moment the main spar on the starboard side might let go.

I called the tower repeatedly as we approached, and although our reception of their response was extremely disjointed, I gathered that we were cleared to land. To make doubly sure, I told Bert to fire the colours of the period several times and follow with a signal indicating that we had wounded aboard. I flashed the appropriate letters on our recognition light, then began to concentrate on the all-important task of getting F Fox safely on the ground.

I kept remembering that the main spar behind number three had been subjected to the effects of what amounted to a giant blow torch playing on it intermittently for an hour and three-quarters, and as I pictured its possible condition in my mind's eye, I was at pains to avoid increasing the wing loading with any steep turns in the circuit, much as I wanted to get on the ground and far away from the 2,000 gallons of gasoline and that seemingly unquenchable fire smouldering a foot or two in front of it. I offered up a silent prayer that the undercarriage would come down when I pressed the selector. F Fox had absorbed a lot of cannon shells—I had felt them striking home—and there was a distinct possibility that the electric motors or cables which activated the undercarriage mechanism had been damaged. I had not dared try it earlier, seeking to avoid both the additional drag and the vibration it produced swinging into place.

Now was the time to find out. Bert fired another signal from the Very pistol, and after ordering the rest of the crew, with the exception of Bill, to take Stan and get into their crash positions, I turned gently toward the flarepath and flipped the undercarriage selector switch. Immediately I could hear the whine and then feel the reassuring drag effect indicating that the wheels were dropping out of their nacelles; the undercarriage motors seemed to be okay. In a few moments the green light on the instrument panel glowed: undercarriage down and locked. I stole a glance away from the flare path and peered into the gloom below the inboard engine nacelle on my side. The port wheel looked all right. Bill was having a more difficult time on his side. The smoke and intermittent showers of sparks made it difficult to see anything in the darkness. But in a few moments he straightened up in his seat and gave me a thumbs-up. I prepared to make the best landing I could.

We touched down very lightly, and for a few brief seconds I began to relax. But our troubles were not over. One of the German fighters had shot our right tire into useless pulp. F Fox vibrated roughly and began sinking lower and lower on her wounded side. I had a terrible vision of the starboard wingtip catching and the aircraft cartwheeling into one final detonation. In a second or two we were down to the hub on the right wheel, and beginning to veer to that side as the hub dragged more and more heavily. I tried to correct the swing with a touch of brake, only to discover that we had no brakes—our hydraulics had been shot out. Immediately I applied a burst of throttle from the starboard outer to see if I could straighten our course that way, but F Fox was beyond responding; she hurtled on, continuing to veer to the right. I sat clutching the control column with both hands and practically bending the rudder bar with my foot as I tried vainly to check the swing with maximum left rudder.

Out of the darkness 50 yards in front of us, the silhouette of a Lancaster suddenly loomed up directly in our path. As I threw my left arm over my face we collided with the other aircraft at 75 miles an hour, severing it completely a few feet to the rear of its mid-upper turret with our right wing. F Fox spun around violently for two or three seconds and shuddered to a halt a short distance further on. Bill and I both snatched at the master switch to cut everything off, then snapped our belts free and turned speedily to open the side windows to escape.

My window jammed. I gripped it fiercely and tugged twice more. It stuck fast. Bill had wrenched his window open and was disappearing through it, so I flung myself to the right side of the cockpit to follow him out. His foot slipped as he thrashed clear, and his heavy flying boot came back into my face like the kick of a Clydesdale. I never even felt it, but twisted through the window like a limbo dancer and sprang rearward from the battered starboard wing like an Olympic athlete.

Fast as Bill and I were, the others had had a few seconds head start and had been covering ground. They had boosted Stan out the rear door and were many yards ahead of us, running for all they were worth. When Bill and I had sprinted 60 or 70 yards I turned for a moment to look at F Fox, and remember thinking that the person who had warned us about the vulnerability of main spars had clearly had no idea of how rugged the Fortress's was. True, the outer 25 feet of F Fox's wing had been splayed open in the violent collision with the Lancaster; but the centre section was still in place and still intact.

I turned to join the other members of the crew, who were now 30 or 40 yards further on. As I panted up to them, I called out to J.B.: "Where's Stan?"

He motioned behind him to a dark bundle lying on the ground. I hurried over and took a look. Stan seemed to me to be unconscious although his eyes were half open. Even in the semi-darkness I could see that his face was as white as parchment and his hair ominously matted.

"Oh the poor bastard . . . he's had it," I said.

This was not an example of my best bedside manner, of course; had I not been labouring under a considerable strain myself I should not have been so tactless. My sympathy and concern were genuine. (Although rather heavily drugged, Stan was still aware of what was going on, and heard my pessimistic prognosis. It made him mad, he told me later; but not as mad as he got a short time afterwards in the station hospital, when a chap wandered in beside him by mistake, saw Stan, and immediately began to throw up.)

Off to the side another Lancaster, apparently in dire straits, was emulating our performance, firing Very lights as it swung toward the funnel. After our own experience, we kept a wary eye on the Lanc—which also proceeded to swing out of control on landing and head in the general direction of F Fox and the Lancaster we had clobbered.

As the ambulance came hunting for us, the last card of the hand was turned over: the Tannoy [loudspeaker] gave vent to a strident announcement warning all ground crew to keep clear of the Lancaster we had just cut in half, advising in stentorian tones that it had a 12,000 pound high explosive bomb aboard.

I peered across to where the truncated Lancaster squatted, now pointing skyward at an unnaturally sharp angle, and guessed thankfully that we must have missed the bomb by about two feet as we slashed through the aircraft. The third aircraft had meanwhile piled in a short distance from ours. Shaken, I climbed into the second van and we were speedily borne to sick quarters to see the MO.

If you were involved in a crash, even if you walked—or ran—away from it, the rule was that you had to be given a medical inspection by the MO. In fact, the inspection varied considerably in scope and thoroughness, depending on what had happened and how busy the doctor was. We had to wait some time while they began looking after Stan. When it was my turn, the doctor called me in, looked at me, and said: "Were you hurt?"

"No, not a scratch," I said.

"You may not have a scratch, but you look as though you could use this," he rejoined, pouring what looked like about four ounces of service rum into a graduated beaker. "Toss that off," he said.

I took the medication as directed, and was unable to get any breath for approximately two minutes. But he was a better doctor than this rough-and-ready sounding treatment suggested. In half an hour my incipient case of the shakes—which he had doubtless spotted—was gone.

After everyone had been thus inspected, we went over to the mess hall for our customary reward of bacon and eggs. As I walked toward the steam table, a pilot standing with a small group ahead of us detached himself and came rather uncertainly toward me.

"You the pilot of that Fortress?" he asked.

"Yes I am," I said, "who are you?"

"I'm the pilot of the Lancaster you chopped in half," he said with a little laugh, sticking out his hand. "We were standing underneath the kite when you swung and came heading for us. We had a 12,000 pounder sitting in the bomb bay over our heads. I'll bet we raced out of there faster than you flew in."

While we waited to pick up our food, he told me that they had been attacked by a fighter just before they reached the target. In the course of the combat the fighter had shot out the Lanc's hydraulics, effectively preventing him from opening his bomb doors and getting rid of his load. His crew had been on the ground only a few minutes when they saw our Very lights and watched F Fox come in to land. Like us, they had thought everything was all right when we touched down safely; but in a moment they had realized the peril they were in. I could imagine the thoughts that went through their minds as they saw the lights of F Fox curving through the night towards their huge bomb. I suppose that for ten seconds they were more intensely frightened than I was—difficult as that is to visualize.

After we had eaten, we were directed to an empty Nissen hut not too far away. For an hour I lay on a cot vainly trying to relax and get some sleep; but my mind was too full of the night's events. I kept re-living the fire, the fighter attacks, and the crash. Eventually I decided to get up and go for a walk. I rose quietly, taking care not to disturb the others, and tiptoed out the door. Outside, I could see that we were only a few hundred yards from the field, and all at once I felt the urge to go back and see F Fox. I had walked no more than 50 yards when I heard a slight sound and turned to see the rest of the crew strung out behind me in Indian file.

We found F Fox without any trouble. Now she sat peacefully in the grey dawn light, the tumult of her final hours—for one glance told us she would never fly again—all too easy to recapture from her dreadful appearance. Under her wing I sank onto my knees and thanked God for bringing us home alive. No one offered any comment on the Skipper's unusual reverence.

10

Nothing to Do but Keep Going

from GABBY: A FIGHTER PILOT'S LIFE
by Francis Gabreski as told to Carl Molesworth

If ever there was a fighter pilot's fighter pilot, it was Francis "Gabby" Gabreski. He grew up in a small town in Pennsylvania, the son of hard-working Polish immigrants, and his love of flying was sparked in 1932, when he was thirteen years old and his father took him to the National Air Races in Cleveland. That year the young Gabreski witnessed the swashbuckling Jimmy Doolittle coax the bumblebee-shaped GeeBee to a dramatic win in the Thompson Trophy Race, then the world's ultimate closed-course pylon competition.

Six years later, and still smitten with the aviation bug, Gabreski scraped together enough money for a few flying lessons at an airport near the Notre Dame University campus, where he had enrolled as a freshman. Gabreski's first tentative stabs into the sky did not show any particular promise, but the thrill of flight, of controlling a winged vehicle through the air and looking down on nature's bounty, planted an undying seed.

Dire economics and the press of studies conspired to interrupt Gabreski's flight instruction. But, in his sophomore year, with war clouds on the horizon, Army recruiters came to campus, and Gabreski was sold on joining the Air Corps. With Uncle Sam footing the bill, Gabreski's personal finances would not be a problem, and he could always go back to finish up college. Little did he know that the dashing Jimmy Doolittle, his boyhood hero, would become, first, his theater commander and, second, his personal friend.

Although it is hard to imagine that one of the world's highest-scoring aces would have nearly washed out of primary flight training, this was precisely the reality faced by a young and uncertain Gabreski yearning to join the ranks of vaunted fighter pilots. Struggling to master the demanding Stearman PT-17 Kaydet, Gabreski was given a last chance to prove himself with an army check pilot. The night before his scheduled "elimination" flight, Gabreski sought strength in church, where he prayed more fervently than ever before. The prayerful evening was a turning point in Gabreski's flying life. From that point on, he would not be timid but self-confident—letting go of any inhibitions and giving it his all.

Despite the adversities on the way there, Gabreski had found his place—a member of the 61st Fighter Squadron of the famed 56th Fighter Group, based at Halesworth, England. Commanded by the superb leader Hubert "Hub" Zemke, the 56th achieved recognition as one of the outstanding fighter units in the 8th Air Force for its high number of air-to-air victories. In fact, the 56th became known as "Zemke's Wolfpack."

In November 1943, shortly before the events described in this excerpt, Gabreski became an ace by shooting down his fourth and fifth enemy aircraft, twin-engine Me-110s. During his seventeen-month combat tour, he was credited with a total of twenty-eight air-to-air victories, making him among the leading American aces of World War II. Later, while flying jets in Korea, he scored another six and a half victories.

As this excerpt demonstrates, the fighter plane Gabreski flew most in the European theater, the Republic P-47 Thunderbolt, was "one tough piece of machinery." Nicknamed "the Jug" for its barrellike appearance, the aircraft was amazingly resilient. The rugged Thunderbolt could take incredible punishment and still return its pilot to base. Also, the aircraft could dive without a mandatory speed limitation such that it permitted disengagement from enemy fighters in hot pursuit. The P-47 was uncommonly adaptable to and adept at its various missions—air-to-air combat, close air support, and ground attack. Gabreski's skills flourished in this classic tactical fighter.

In the final analysis it is, of course, the heart of the pilot that makes the difference. Gabby Gabreski, the small-town kid imbued with traditional values and touched by the dream of flight, believed in what he was doing and threw everything he had into his combat flying. As described in this excerpt, Gabreski was angling with just his wingman when confronted by a swarm of approximately forty enemy fighters. His reaction was characteristic: he plunged ahead because "there was nothing to do but keep going."

P.H.

On November 29 we went out again, this time escorting B-17s in toward their target at Bremen. I was leading White Flight of the 61st on the left side of the Fortresses at 30,000 feet above a solid overcast when Blue and Red flights radioed that they were being bounced.

I called for White Flight to break into the attackers and turned sharply to find myself nose-to-nose with about *forty* 109s. I looked around and saw that only my wingman, Joe Powers, had followed. Forty to two, not my kind of odds, but there was nothing to do but keep going. We went through and then turned to attack eight of them about 2,000 feet below us. Just as I was getting into position for a shot, Joe called in that there were more 109s behind us and coming fast. I pulled up out of the dive and used my airspeed to zoom away from the 109s. As soon as we were clear I picked out eight more 109s below and turned to try another bounce.

This time we had clear sailing. I picked out a straggler and opened up on him at 600 yards. He still was carrying his belly tank, and it burst into flames when my shots hit it. I continued firing short bursts until I was about 200 yards away and could see that he was a goner. Smoke and flames belched from the 109 as it spun down into the clouds, obviously out of control.

I swung away to the right and picked up four more enemy fighters. I was dead astern when I opened fire on another one carrying its belly tank, and again it burst into flames. Smoke and glycol poured from the 109 as it dove at a slight angle for about ten seconds; then at about 24,000 feet it rolled over and dove straight down into overcast trailing smoke and fire. Another sure kill.

About this time I saw a flash out of the corner of my eye. I looked back to see that Powers had caught a 109 trying to jump me and blasted him off my tail. That was typical for Joe. He was as good a wingman as ever flew with me, and I flew with some great ones. Sadly, Joe was killed in action while flying a P-51 in Korea early in 1951.

November had been a great month for me, but the first day of December nearly brought my combat career to an end. On this day I was leading the full group on a ramrod to Solingen. Lt. Norm Brooks was my wingman. We made landfall over the Dutch island at 27,000 and rendezvoused with the B-17s at 1142. About half an hour later the action started.

We could see lots of contrails around us, and I began to hear calls from a bomber box that was under attack in the rear of the formation. I turned our fighters back to help them, and before long I spotted seven 109s below us lining up for an attack. I led White Flight down after them, but they spotted us quickly and dove away. We gave up the chase at 22,000 and climbed back up to the bombers. As we approached them I spotted an Me-110 and attacked it from above. I saw no hits from my gunfire, but the 110 rolled over and dove away vertically.

I chose not to follow him down when I spotted a lone B-24 under attack by a mixed group of 109s and Junkers 88s. The Ju-88 was a twin-engine light bomber; very fast. The Luftwaffe was beginning to use 88s as interceptors, often armed with rockets. Like the Me-110, the Ju-88 carried a rear gunner. Again I made a diving attack. I opened up on an 88 at about 600 yards and fired a burst at him with no visible effect as I closed in to point-blank range. Suddenly he whipped over in a snap turn that carried him under me to the right. I was so close that his turbulence rocked my plane, and I broke off the attack. In seconds I could feel my engine lose power and see oil spattering on my windshield. The 88's rear gunner had hit me!

I throttled her back and dropped down to 12,000 feet. Brooks stayed with me, weaving above as we headed back toward the coast. My heart was in my throat as I watched the oil pressure gauge and listened for signs that the engine was failing. Instead, the engine held together and I was able to climb slowly back up to 24,000. In about forty-five minutes we reached the coast. Then I got another shock.

Brooks called to say that *he* was having trouble. It seems his propeller had become stuck in high pitch, which meant that he wouldn't last for the flight home across the North Sea. He was going to lose a little altitude and then bail out while he was still over land. Jeez, what next? I felt bad for Brooks, but was also worried about myself. What would happen if my engine failed while I was over the water? Normally, my wingman would be there to help the air-sea rescue guys find me, but now I didn't have a wingman. There was nothing to do but go it alone.

It was a long flight across the water at 180 mph, but my trusty P-47 carried me home. I sadly reported on Brooks's fate but was pleased to be informed that he, too, had made it back. He had been able to regain his prop control after he left me, and had come home alone.

Later, when my ground crew was going over HV-A, they dug a 20-mm slug out from between two of the engine cylinders. It was an explosive bullet, but for some reason it hadn't gone off. Someone grabbed a camera to snap a picture of Doc Hornig and me looking at that slug and marveling at my good luck. I was glad to accept a shot of Doc's post-mission "medicine" that day, too!

By this time the winter weather was upon us, making operations very difficult. The 56th flew only five missions in the first two weeks of December. Either the weather would be too bad over our bases to get in and out, or it would be too bad over enemy territory to allow an effective mission—sometimes both. But one of those five missions, an escort to Emden on the eleventh, would prove memorable to our squadron and especially so for me.

I was flying as Keyworth Blue One in one of the P-47s, 42-7871. The group was attacked over the Frisian Islands at 30,000 feet before we had even reached rendezvous with the B-17s. The 62nd took the brunt of the attack, and our other two squadrons pressed on toward the bombers. By the time we spotted them the Big Friends were already under attack.

Our squadron approached from the rear of the formation and saw about forty Me 110s between us and the bombers, lining up to make rocket attacks. It was the kind of setup a fighter pilot dreams about: We were above and behind the enemy, flying a superior aircraft, and we had a full load of ammunition. All I had to do was turn our fighters to the right and lead them down.

Nothing is ever as simple as it looks, I guess. Just as I was turning in behind the 110s I saw a bright flash above me to the left. We've been jumped, I thought. Two P-47s were falling in smoke and flames, and I wasn't about to be next, so I broke off the attack and zoomed up and away. When I looked back at 30,000 feet, I realized I was alone. Later I found out there had been no bounce. The two P-47s, flown by Lts. Edward Kruer and Lawrence Strand, had collided in the turn. Because of my position out front, I was the only pilot in the squadron who didn't see what happened. The rest of them continued their bounce on the 110s, and they shot down a bunch of them.

I knew it was dangerous to fly alone in a battle area, so I started looking around for some P-47s to tag along with. Instead, I spotted three more 110s flying in string formation about 5,000 feet below me. I couldn't resist the bounce, even though I knew better, so I pushed over and dove after the last one. I opened fire and kept shooting until I was close enough to see the crew bailing out. I was about 50 yards behind when they jumped from their burning plane, and it fell away trailing thick smoke.

I recovered at 23,000 and spotted a formation of P-47s; at least they looked like P-47s to me. But when I drew closer to them I could see they were 190s. Their radial-engine profile had fooled me. Lucky for me, they must have been looking the other way, because I was able to turn tail and get away without them chasing me.

By this time my fuel supply was getting seriously low, so I decided it was time to head home. I turned westward and flew for a few minutes before I spotted an Me 109 passing below me in a direction about 75 degrees from me. I held my breath, hoping he wouldn't see me, because I didn't have enough gas to stick around and fight with him. I was almost ready to breathe easy when I saw him make a sharp upward turn and start coming toward me.

I was so low on gas that I felt I shouldn't try to run at 100 percent throttle, which was 52 inches of manifold pressure. So I said to myself that I would try to run this guy out of ammunition. Pretty brazen of me, but I felt the best I could do was present him a difficult shot. As he closed in behind me I nosed the P-47 down to pick up some speed with the throttle at 43–44 inches. When he got close behind me, I would pull up and then kick the airplane over about the time I thought he was ready to shoot. When I saw the muzzle flashes from his guns I would present him with a 90-degree deflection shot, about the most difficult there is.

It worked the first time. I made kind of a chandelle, came down again in sort of a lazy eight as I watched what he was doing. I didn't look into my cockpit at all then. I just kept watching him, making sure he didn't get too close. I made another turn with my nose down, picked up speed, and went back up again. He did the same thing. It worked again. He had fired twice and not hit me, so he was running himself out of ammunition.

The third time I came up, kicked it off from the side, and he started firing again. But the moment he started shooting I realized he had his bead right on, because I heard an explosion in the cockpit. He hit my rudder pedal and shot it away. Part of my flying boot was shot up, too. My engine lost power, so I figured it had been hit, too. I said to myself, well it's the end of the road, I'd better get out of this mother.

I was at about 20,000 feet. I didn't look at the gauges, but it appeared to me that my engine was dead. I nosed the plane down to keep up my airspeed and began to roll my canopy back so I could bail out. The canopy was open about a foot when I looked at my gauges and saw that I still had some manifold pressure, and that my rpms were still up about 1,500. As it turned out, he had hit the turbocharger unit and knocked it out, which had caused me to lose power at high altitude. Once I realized I still had some power I gave up the idea of bailing out and decided to try again at getting home. The guy in the 109 had other ideas, however.

About this time I realized my foot was numb and I began to worry about how much that exploding shell had injured it. I didn't want to look at it because I was afraid I might pass out if there was a lot of blood. My first job, though, was to get away from that 109. I pulled the canopy closed and pushed over in a dive toward a bank of clouds I could see below me. It didn't make any difference what those clouds had in them—hills, mountains, or whatever. I was going to get into them before the guy behind me could finish me off.

I reached the clouds just in time, as the 109 was closing in on me. I immediately went on instruments and turned west toward England. Periodically I would come up out of the clouds to see where the 109 was. He wasn't giving up, but he was way back there skirting around the clouds looking for me. Finally I ducked back into the clouds and stayed there for about twenty-five minutes. I didn't know if I'd have enough fuel to get back to England, so when I got out over the water I called Mayday and raised air-sea rescue. A controller told me they had a radar fix on me and advised me to maintain my present heading.

So I kept going for all I was worth. By that time I was pretty low, so I couldn't really tell where I was. I just kept looking for landfall and hoping the controller was giving me good directions. I leaned out my fuel mixture, decreased rpms to the minimum, pulled my manifold pressure all the way back to 26 inches, and prayed. Eventually I saw the

English shoreline ahead, and within minutes I landed at Manston, an RAF recovery field on the coast near Margate.

I got the P-47 down okay and taxied in just as the engine quit. Only then did I work up the nerve to take a look at my foot. I wore fur-lined boots like the bomber crews had, and the one that was hit had a big gash across the bottom of it. But my foot wasn't injured at all! The impact of the shell hitting my boot had numbed my foot, but no shrapnel had hit me.

11

Turn on the Lights

from **THE MAGNIFICENT MITSCHER**
by Theodore Taylor

Marc Andrew "Pete" Mitscher not only grew up with naval aviation, he helped to build it. Looking at his inauspicious early years,
one could hardly have imagined that the lanky Oklahoman would
end up among the U.S. Navy's most accomplished and revered
four-star carrier admirals. So deficient was he as a midshipman
that the Naval Academy booted him out. The obstreperous lad was
readmitted only through the intercession of his politically connected
father. Finally, in 1910, Mitscher graduated from Annapolis, albeit
as the 107th in a class of 130.

An interest in aeronautics soon changed Mitscher's life. He
sought and received a transfer to the fledgling flight school at the
Pensacola Naval Air Station. In the fall of 1915, the first formal class
was started at the flight school with all of thirteen prospective
naval aviators, Mitscher among them. Here he distinguished himself, thriving in the hands-on environment of flying. By June of the
following year he had completed the course and thereby became
the thirty-third naval aviator.

With the United States entering World War I in 1917, Mitscher
wanted to be in the thick of the action—a combat assignment in
France. But the orders never came, the brass claiming that
Mitscher's services were too valuable at home. Mitscher was able
to begin making his mark shortly after the war, when, because of

his acknowledged aeronautical expertise, the Navy chose him as one of the pilots for the daring attempt to fly across the Atlantic.

In May 1919, three gargantuan flying boats—designated "NC" for "Navy Curtiss"—took off from the Newfoundland coast for Europe. Although Mitscher's ungainly beast was damaged in rough waters en route, dashing his hopes of completing the journey, his colleague in the adventure, Lieutenant Commander A. C. "Putty" Read, flew on in one of the other aircraft and made it to Lisbon. (This was eight years before Charles Lindbergh made his solo non-stop crossing.) For his contributions to the collective effort, Mitscher was awarded the first of the three Navy Crosses he was destined to receive during his distinguished career.

Aviation's golden years, the fabled period between the two world wars, witnessed the aircraft carrier's emergence as an important component in the naval fighting mix. During this time, Mitscher served in senior positions aboard the *Langley* and the *Saratoga,* the first and third flattop, respectively, in the U.S. Navy's fleet. On the eve of America's entry into World War II, Mitscher received one of the service's coveted assignments—he was to be skipper of the *Hornet,* the newest of the U.S. carriers. Five months after the Japanese attack on Pearl Harbor, that ship, under Mitscher's brilliant command, became immortalized in naval history as the platform that launched Jimmy Doolittle's Tokyo Raiders, flying the army's B-25 medium bombers.

A few months later, Mitscher and the *Hornet* were at the Battle of Midway, the most pivotal of carrier battles. On the morning of June 4th, the antiquated Douglas TBD Devastator torpedo bombers of VT-8 strode off the carrier's flight deck, their flight crews intent on inflicting heavy damage to enemy ships. Skimming above the sea without benefit of fighter cover, the cumbersome TBDs lumbered unswervingly toward the massed Japanese fleet, falling victim as so much fodder to the shipboard batteries and the deadly Zeros. Despite the relentless barrage, the aircrews would not be deterred; each aircraft stayed on target, pressing the attack.

The entire squadron was decimated, all fifteen aircraft shot to pieces and all but one of the thirty pilots and gunners lost. The valiant flyers had failed to score even a single hit. However, this crushingly painful sacrifice was not in vain, for VT-8's low-level attack diverted the enemy's attention to the surface as Douglas SBD Dauntless dive-bombers from the *Enterprise* screamed in from high above with virtual impunity. The Japanese carriers were sunk; the U.S. Navy won a resounding victory. The heroic airmen of the *Hornet's* Torpedo Eight had achieved their goal after all. And Mitscher nominated them all for the Medal of Honor.

For Mitscher, many battles were yet to come—at places like the Solomon Islands, the Marshall Islands, Leyte Gulf, Iwo Jima, and Okinawa. But the events and decisions at the First Battle of the Philippine Sea in June 1944, described in the excerpt that follows, reveal best the depth of character of this military commander. As the leader of Task Force 58, Mitscher sent his pilots up to intercept enemy aircraft, which they did with overwhelming success—the lopsided air battle was dubbed the "Marianas Turkey Shoot." Participants included Commander David McCampbell, skipper of VF-15, destined to become the leading naval ace of all time.

Not satisfied to have simply mauled the enemy's air armada, Mitscher sought to get at the source of the aircraft—the carriers. He launched a contingent of attackers, an admixture of torpedo, dive-bombing, and fighter planes. After the launch, it was ascertained that the Japanese fleet had widened its distance from Mitscher's battle group. Although Mitscher cancelled orders to launch additional attackers, he held steadfast in not recalling those aircraft already embarked. They could engage the enemy and get back, he reasoned. There was an opportunity to strike at the heart of the Japanese fleet, and he would not let it pass.

His men succeeded in knocking out the carrier *Hitaka,* but by the time they neared the battle group on their return it was dark. Regulations forbade illuminating ships at night in hostile waters where enemy submarines might be lurking. At the same time, without illumination the returning American pilots would have to ditch in the unforgiving sea, for most of them a fate tantamount to death. The sailors aboard the task force's many ships, strewn out across the sea, wondered what their admiral, commanding from the *Lexington,* would decide to do.

Protocol called for the task force commander to convey orders to his chief of staff, who would then see that they were implemented. Mitscher's chief of staff at that time was a nonaviator, a surface officer by the name of Arleigh Burke. Earlier in the war, Burke had successfully led destroyers in night actions and had acquired the nickname "31-Knot Burke." Yet, Mitscher was loath to have someone without flying experience as his chief of staff. When Burke reported for duty to Mitscher in March 1944, the taciturn admiral, never known as a man of many words, gave Burke the cold shoulder. It took time for the two men's relationship to warm as they developed enormous respect for each other.

On that fateful evening of June 21st, the admiral turned to his captain and gave the order: "Turn on the lights." It was Mitscher's way of saying the subs be damned; our pilots come first.

Not long after the war ended, Secretary of the Navy James Forrestal offered Mitscher the position of chief of naval operations. But the hardened combat veteran declined. He would not accept a desk job; he wanted to remain at sea with his fellow naval aviators. Eventually he became commander of the Atlantic Fleet, a job in which he served until he succumbed to a heart attack two years later.

P.H.

A TINY THUNDERHEAD OF BATTLE had appeared from the direction of Guam at 0530. Two or three bogeys had been spotted on the radar screens, and fighters from the *Monterey* had darted after them. The squawk box connecting Flag Plot to the Combat Information Center reported the results: "Tally-hoed two Judys; splash one."

Not enough to cause even momentary interruption, the sprinkle of action was duly transcribed by a yeoman who sat at a desk in Flag Plot. There was nothing to indicate this was really the beginning of such a robust day as June 19, 1944—the day of the "Marianas Turkey Shoot."

Mitscher had breakfasted in his sea cabin about 0630, after strolling out on the wing of the bridge to look at the disposition of the force. His staff insists his conversation that morning, if recorded, would not have filled a medium-sized memorandum blank. In spite of certain knowledge that enemy planes would soon arrive, he acted as though Task Force 58 were on routine practice maneuvers off the Virginia capes.

At 0714 *Belleau Wood* fighters patrolling over Guam radioed that many bogeys were taking off, and asked for help. Mitscher nodded, and Hellcats were launched from a half dozen carriers. In the brief battle that ensued, the pattern of the day was set: Thirty Navy fighter planes knocked down thirty-five enemy aircraft. Mitscher's loss was one Hellcat.

Then, at 0950 radar screens from one end of the sprawling task force to the other picked up large bogey targets. The battle was on. Mitscher said to Burke: "Get those fighters back from Guam." Burke relayed the orders and the Guam battlers rolled over and headed for the task force. At 1004, the *Lexington*'s bugler hurried through his general-quarters call, competing with the bong-bong-bong of the warning bell. Sailors throughout the big ship raced through passageways as watertight doors banged shut behind them—some to the flight deck, some to damage-control stations, others flopping into gun tubs topside. The air officer's voice was strident and urgent. To this clamor was added the coughing, sputtering, then roaring, of engines. Color flashed as busy figures scurried among the aircraft on deck—plane handlers in blue shirts and blue helmets; plane directors in yellow shirts and helmets; hookmen in green; chockmen in purple; firefighters in red, accompanied by two Frankensteinian apparitions in asbestos suits. In the ready rooms, pilots sat up to watch the ticker tape as it fed information to the screens in front of them. Some pilots had already gone up on deck to man their planes. On every carrier in the task force, the same carefully controlled frenzy was being repeated.

Mitscher sat in his swivel chair viewing the action on the flight deck below. J. R. Eyerman, the *Life* photographer, stopped on his way to his battle station to take a quick picture of the man in the chair.

Scarcely raising his voice, Mitscher asked, "Are you excited?"

Eyerman's pulse was pounding. He ventured a meek, "I guess so."

Mitscher turned, his eyes dancing, and in a firm, measured voice said, "Well, *I'm* excited." But when Eyerman developed his negatives, he found he hadn't captured Mitscher's suppressed excitement at all.

The planes were away as fast as they could be launched. Mitscher gave orders to the task force to send all bombers and torpedo planes to the east to orbit, thus making room for the fighters to land, refuel, rearm, and take off again. Meanwhile, fighters were being vectored out from all the carriers by their CIC fighter directors.

An alert sailor on the *Yorktown* transcribed the patter of his ship's fighter-director officer:

1015: Large bogey at 265–105 miles on course 090 at estimated angels 24 [24,000 feet].

1017: Scramble all ready rooms. Disengaged side to the east.

1025: Coal 1, 2, 3, and 4 have been launched and instructed to go to angels 25. [Coal 1, 2, 3, and 4 were divisions of *Yorktown* fighters already in the air.]

1026: Bogey now at 260–95 miles.

1037: Friendly planes have tally-hoed bogey at angels 15 to 25.

[*Essex* Hellcats, led by Commander David McCampbell of Air Group Fifteen, had made the first interception of the oncoming Japanese planes.]

The fight raged from 90 miles out on in close to the fleet, with Japanese planes "falling like leaves," as Commander McCampbell reported it. A few Japanese bombers, though, came relentlessly on and scored a minor hit on the *South Dakota,* and one made a suicide attack on the *Indiana.* The sky action held the attention of Mitscher and the task-group commanders, but could not entirely divert them from the knowledge that the bogeys were from enemy aircraft carriers that were enjoying complete immunity.

At 1103, Reeves said he wanted a search and attack group from his task group, already airborne, to go out 250 miles in an effort to find the Imperial carriers. Mitscher signaled back enthusiastically: APPROVED X APPROVED X WISH WE COULD GO WITH YOU.

But Reeves, because of jamming caused by the huge number of aircraft airborne and using radio, could not get his message through to the bombers and torpedo planes that awaited instruction while orbiting to the east. And shortly thereafter Mitscher recalled them. "Tell 'em to drop their bombs on Guam and Rota on the way back," he said to Burke. This would pit the air strips and make it more difficult for the bogeys to shuttle between the islands and their carriers.

At 1109, a new crop of bogeys—estimated at sixty-five planes—skimmed into the radar screens. CIC located them at high altitude; range, 130 miles. The fighter director, doing one of the finest jobs of the war, vectored out enough strength to decimate them. The pilots landing on the *Lexington* and other carriers to regas and rearm were in high spirits.

Down in Fighting Sixteen's ready room, one sweaty pilot yelled, "Hell, this is like an old time turkey shoot." His chief, Lieutenant Commander Paul Buie, overheard the remark, and the phrase "Marianas Turkey Shoot" was born.

From 1130 to 1430, sporadic raids were met. Claims of kills were approaching the fantastic even when allowance was made for exaggeration. Throughout, Mitscher stayed on the wing of the bridge, while Burke, Hedding, or Widhelm periodically emerged from Flag Plot to pass information to him, get a decision, or obtain his initials on a non-routine dispatch. Lieutenant Commander Joseph Eggert, USNR, the staff fighter-director officer, co-ordinated the immensely complicated air defense perfectly.

Four Judys attacked *Lexington, Enterprise,* and *Princeton,* and were loudly contested by every trainable gun in the task group. Two torpedoes splashed into the water, bubbling toward the *Lexington,* but missed the flagship by a wide margin.

By 1430, the heaviest enemy strikes were over and Mitscher began requesting the task-group commanders to report the results. As the replies flowed in over the TBS and by blinker, the slaughter didn't seem possible. Ozawa had fed planes in recklessly from both carriers and island bases. The early-afternoon score indicated more than three hundred Japanese planes destroyed, an air victory beyond all expectations.*

But Mitscher received the reports with little comment. He was more concerned, and had been all morning, with the groups of enemy carriers somewhere to the west. No amount of destruction of planes could entirely make up for the fact that the enemy fleet had escaped damage. Not one task-force plane had come within sight of the Japanese formation.

At 1500, Spruance, realizing that the enemy force had lost its weapon of attack, signaled what amounted to a release. At that moment, Mitscher could look southeast and see smoking Guam, barely fifteen or twenty miles off the *Lexington*'s beam. The miles between his carriers and Ozawa's carriers had been opening all day. The situation had not changed appreciably since dawn. Mitscher was between the enemy land bases and the Japanese carriers down-wind from him.

He detached Harrill's group, which was low on fuel, and prepared to steam for the enemy with the remaining groups. Permission to put the task force on a westerly heading did not arouse much elation on the *Lexington*'s flag bridge, however. Most of the staff thought the best opportunity for sinking the Japanese fleet had been missed in two days of east-and-west shuttling.

Sporadic raids were still occurring and destruction of Japanese planes continued. Individual totals were staggering. Commander McCampbell's VF-15, from *Essex,* accounted for seventy enemy planes, for example. On *Lexington* Lieutenant (j .g.) Alexander Vraciu, USNR, took the LSO's cut,

---

*An estimated 346 were lost on June 19 according to Samuel E. Morison's *History of U.S. Naval Operations in World War II,* Volume VIII (Boston, Atlantic-Little, Brown & Company, 1953).

bounced to the deck, and beamed as he crawled out of the Hellcat's cockpit. He held up six fingers and Mitscher waved from the bridge. Vraciu was an ace of the carrier war. Six "turkeys" had fallen under his guns in less than eighteen minutes. His total score was now eighteen Japanese planes.

Mitscher left the flag bridge and made his way down to the flight deck to congratulate young Vraciu personally. He shook his hand, then moved out of the way as photographers focused their cameras from every angle. Then he said, with evident embarrassment, "I'd like to pose with him. Not for publication. To keep for myself."

At 1630, Admiral Spruance signaled: DESIRE TO ATTACK ENEMY TOMORROW IF WE KNOW HIS POSITION WITH SUFFICIENT ACCURACY X.

But as the sun set over the Marianas, Mitscher and his staff were not optimistic about finding the enemy. Until 1900, occasional bogeys roamed into the formation, but they were either chased away or splashed. The Admiral came off the wing and sat down on the transom to look at the night orders Burke had prepared. Then he briefly discussed what might be done the next day. He decided not to launch searches that night because of the distance involved.

Finally Mitscher stood up and stretched. "You know," he said, "tomorrow I'm going to get a haircut. Personally, I hate barbers. I hate them like hell. But all the same, tomorrow I'm going to get a haircut." Then he parted the blackout curtains and disappeared toward his sea cabin.

Just after breakfast the next morning, Commander Ernest Snowden went up to the flag bridge and offered to lead a group of Hellcats in a search for the enemy.

"They're a long way off," Mitscher said.

"I'll use volunteers," Snowden replied. Then he briefly outlined a plan to load the Hellcats with five-hundred-pound bombs, with delayed-action fuses.

Mitscher seemed receptive. He said, "You'd better take a bomber with you." Some of the bombers had radar sets in them. Mitscher was concerned about navigation on the long flight.

Finally, he said, "I've got a search out that should be back about eleven hundred. If I don't get anything, I'll send you out."

Snowden, who was General "Hap" Arnold's son-in-law, went down to the fighter ready room and chalked twelve numbers on the bulletin board, with his own name beside the first. Then he turned to the pilots: "Gentlemen, this is strictly volunteer. Chances are less than fifty-fifty you'll get back. I need eleven people. My name is on the top of the list." Snowden left the ready room, and when he came back about a half hour later, all the numbers had names beside them.

The early-morning search group was recovered shortly after 1100, having found nothing. Snowden ran up to the bridge, and the Admiral nodded his okay. Then, as Snowden walked toward the ladder, Mitscher called after him: "I want you to go back and tell those boys that if you make contact and anybody gets shot down, I'll come and pick them up even if I have to steam the whole damn fleet up after them."

Snowden's long-range search group was launched at 1200. They went out 475 nautical miles—on the longest search of the war up to that time—and then Snowden turned them back toward the task force. There was not a sign of the Japanese fleet. At 1512, during the three-hour return leg, Snowden heard an *Enterprise* plane radio a contact to the task force.

Back on the *Lexington*, Mitscher slid down from his chair and followed Burke into Flag Plot. Seconds later, Burke was on the TBS: "Indications are our birds have sighted something big."

Mitscher waited for verification, along with information about distance, course, and speed. It came finally. The enemy was about 275 miles away. At the same time—1548—Burke was back on the TBS:

Have received following. Enemy fleet sighted 15–02 N, 135–25 E, speed 20 knots. Course, 270. Reception was poor. Anybody heard different transmission check position, course and speed. Anybody heard different transmission contact Commander, Task Force 58.

Gus Widhelm was exuberant. He had wagered two air-group commanders a thousand dollars the Japanese fleet would be sighted.

If Mitscher launched a strike now, it would be late afternoon before the planes could reach the enemy and completely dark by the time they could get home. He could count on heavy losses. Operating at such extreme range, many planes would run out of gas as they searched in the dark for their carriers, and would be forced into the sea. Each second of indecision, however, brought nightfall closer and reduced the chances of success.

Mitscher conferred with Burke and the other senior staff members, but Burke felt the Admiral had already made up his mind. Then Mitscher gave the order to launch planes. The ticker tapes in the ready rooms recorded the range and bearing—all the information the pilots needed— and the squawk box ordered: "Pilots, man your planes." At 1553, Mitscher informed Spruance he intended to launch everything he had. His Action Report said later:

> The decision to launch strikes was based on so damaging and slowing enemy carriers and her ships that our battle line could close during the night and at daylight sink all the ships that our battle line could reach. It was believed that this was the last time that the Japanese could be brought to grips and their enemy fleet destroyed once and for all. Taking advantage of this opportunity was going to cost us a great deal in planes and pilots because we were launching at maximum range of our aircraft at such time as it would be necessary to recover them after dark. It was realized also that this single shot venture for planes which were sent out in the afternoon would probably be not all operational for a morning strike. Consequently, Fifth Fleet was informed that the carriers were firing their bolt.

By 1630, the first deckloads were away—eighty-five fighters, seventy-seven dive bombers, and fifty-four torpedo planes. As they dropped out of sight, a second message came in from searchers, locating the enemy fleet sixty miles farther away. It was a stunning blow. At best, the original position gave the pilots an even chance in returning to the task force. The new position would strain the last ounce of fuel, and make night landings inevitable. If Mitscher didn't recall the planes, the casualty list was sure to be heavy.

After rechecking the charts, Mitscher decided not to recall them. However, he did tell Burke to cancel the second deckload and inform Admiral Spruance that the rest of the planes would be held until morning.

Mitscher's decision to launch planes that afternoon has received much attention, but his decision not to recall the first deckload of pilots was far more difficult. It hung over him until midnight.

A few minutes before sunset, Task Force 58 pilots found small Japanese units and then finally reached the wildly maneuvering enemy carriers. Ozawa had lost most of his fighters in the previous day's shooting, but launched what he had as the American dive bombers and torpedo planes attacked. Although the attacks were not co-ordinated, there was little interference. In the shadows, it was difficult to see how much damage was being done, although the inter-plane radios chattered enthusiastically. Actually, only one carrier, the *Hitaka*, was sunk. Two had been previously downed by submarines, and in addition, two oilers had been sunk.

Then the planes started home, but not in usual formation. They flew independently, or flocked together in any order for company. Mitscher had been out on the bridge wing since he launched them and ate his dinner from a tray. Every minute or so, he'd look at the sun's position, and check the big, luminous-dialed watch on his left wrist. At the turn of dusk, the loudspeaker in Flag Plot announced: "Attacks completed. Two CV sunk." Ralph Weymouth, a bit optimistic, had sent the message as the planes flew toward the force, now shadowy in the twilight.

Mitscher changed the axis of the fleet and spread the task groups to a distance of fifteen miles apart. By then, the pilots were within 70 miles. They had picked up homing signals and were visible on the task-force radar screens. But it was very late. Fuel tanks were almost dry. Mitscher informed Spruance of several course changes he planned to make after recovering the pilots who managed to reach the task-force disposition. He told Spruance he intended to steam the task force in a direction that would enable recovery of the pilots who had gone down in the ocean, and he also urgently requested Dumbo planes to join the search for pilots. Mitscher was facing the worst disaster in naval-aviation history.

He added speed until the carriers were surging along at 22 knots. By 2030, planes were sighted, scattered without pattern in the western sky. To the south were rays of lightning, and some pilots headed toward the false beacon. At 2045, a few aircraft began to orbit in confusion, their red and green lights flashing.

Mitscher knew their fuel supply was almost exhausted. They had to be brought in. Now the sky was filling up over the task groups. The pilots knew the task force was down there—they could even see the wakes of the ships—but there was no way to distinguish the carriers.

Ernest Snowden ran up to Gus Widhelm: "We gotta give these guys some light."

Admiral Mitscher slipped down from his swivel chair and walked into Flag Plot, sitting down at the very end of the transom. He lit a cigarette and looked up at Captain Burke.

"Turn on the lights," he said.

Task Force 58 suddenly leaped from the darkness, temptingly visible to any nearby submarines.

Searchlight beams climbed straight into the sky; others pointed toward the carrier decks. Glow lights outlined the decks; truck lights flashed on mastheads in the outer screen. Cruisers threw up a procession of star shells, flooding the ocean with light.

Said one carrier pilot, Lieutenant Commander Robert A. Winston, USNR: "The effect on the pilots left behind was magnetic. They stood open mouthed for the sheer audacity of asking the Japs to come and get us. Then a spontaneous cheer went up. To hell with the Japs around us. Our pilots were not to be expendable."

Then the planes started coming in. They were trying to locate their home ships. Mitscher said, "Tell 'em to land on any carrier."

Some made landing approaches on cruisers and battleships. More ran out of gas and made controlled water landings. Some glided right into the paths of destroyer searchlight beams. The destroyers were working overtime. Through the din could be heard the mournful beeping of the whistles on pilots' life-jackets. Men adrift!

Six planes settled safely on the *Lexington* but the seventh refused a wave-off. He was high, but cut his engines and landed, bouncing over the barrier and plowing into a row of parked planes on the bow, sparks and flame lighting up the deck. A rear-seat gunner in one of the planes that had just landed was killed by the propeller; another body was pulled from the wreckage.

Mitscher sent for the pilot, who was unhurt. A raw bundle of nerves and fear, he approached the man seated on the flag-bridge wing.

"Do I understand you refused a wave-off?" Mitscher asked.

"Yes, Admiral," the pilot answered, "my hydraulics were shot away. I didn't have enough gas to go around again."

Mitscher looked at him for a long time. Then he said, very gently, "Son, you always could have gone into the drink."

In ten minutes, an incredibly short time to clear up the strewn wreckage, Flight Deck Chief Prather had the *Lexington* ready to operate again, and the planes began landing. On *Cabot, Yorktown,* and *Bunker Hill,* and all the other carriers, the tumultuous drama was being repeated.

Several carriers had so many planes on the flight deck that airborne craft couldn't be landed. Their Captains ordered planes pushed over the side.

Although he had set a precedent for these rescue procedures in the Battle of Midway, Mitscher's decision to light up the fleet in the Marianas stands in naval-aviation history with the surface Navy's "Damn the torpedoes! Go ahead!" That night, Mitscher endeared himself to every man who wore gold wings, and won the admiration of all sailors. When the account of what had happened reached the press, Mitscher acquired new and greater stature. In stories about the Admiral words like "compassion" and "humanitarian" began to accompany appraisals of his fighting ability.

Two hundred and sixteen planes had been launched. By 2230, when the last of the surviving aircraft landed and Mitscher once again turned the task force after the enemy, only a hundred of the planes that had taken part in the strike were left. It was impossible rapidly to count the survivors and tally the missing. By early morning, it was estimated that eighty planes had gone down in the sea or been destroyed in landing accidents. Twenty were estimated to be combat losses. Rescues continued throughout the night and into the next day. By dusk of June 21, all but sixteen pilots and twenty-two crewmen had been rescued.

Meanwhile, at 0450, on June 21, Mitscher informed Spruance he did not think it would be possible to close the enemy at a speed greater than 15 knots. Fuel shortage would not permit them to move faster, and the recovery of the pilots had taken the force a good 60 miles farther away from Ozawa's battered remnants.

During the morning, Mitscher reorganized Task Force 58, sending a carrier group with the battle-line forces chasing the fleeing enemy. As the day wore on and other searches were futilely launched, it became increasingly evident that the Japanese would probably get away. Admiral Spruance canceled the search at 1920 that night.

But there was gloom on the flag bridge of the *Lexington*. Mitscher had gambled at the last moment. He had won, but his winnings were small compared to what they might have been. A considerable portion of the Japanese fleet had escaped. He summed up the battle in his Action Report: "The enemy had escaped. He had been badly hurt by one aggressive carrier strike at the one time he was within range. His fleet was not sunk."

So ended the Battle of the Philippine Sea in flag country of the U.S.S. *Lexington*, June 21, 1944.

THE KOREAN WAR

12

MiG Alley

from CHECK SIX: A FIGHTER PILOT LOOKS BACK
by Frederick C. Blesse

Frederick C. "Boots" Blesse's autobiography is a virtual definition of the fighter pilot. In it Blesse's love of flying and inveterate desire to engage in combat are absolutely explicit; he shows rather than tells exactly what it is that distinguishes the hunter and the hunted in aerial combat.

An earlier work, *No Guts—No Glory*, encapsulated Blesse's attitude toward air combat and became a tactical manual whose concepts are still valuable today. In *Check Six*, Blesse's almost ingenuous exuberance celebrates what he considered at the time to be the most important event of his life, scoring his fifth victory and becoming an ace. Blesse writes with the simple directness that characterized his combat mode; he keeps his pen as "balls to the wall" as he had kept his throttle.

In the life-and-death struggle that characterized the F-86 versus MiG-15 battles in Korea, surviving 100 missions was enough for most pilots. But Blesse found himself with four confirmed victories and 95 missions. He could have gone home, with honor, after only 5 more missions, but he was determined to become an ace, and extended for 25 more missions to make sure he had the chance.

That chance came on September 4, 1952, with Earl Brown, now a retired lieutenant general, flying as wingman on Blesse's 104th mission.

The pair, flying their silvery Sabres, had made two passes through MiG Alley without any contact. Blesse spotted two MiG-15s high, as they almost always were, with their superior altitude capability. The two enemy planes showed fight—not always the case—and turned into Blesse's flight of two. Blesse moved into range and "lit his fuselage and right wing with my .50 calibers." It was enough; the pilot ejected, and Blesse was an ace.

On the climb out, Brown on his wing, Blesse was aware that he had a long way to go over enemy territory and he said a little prayer: "Lord, if you have to take me while I'm over here, don't do it today. Let me get back and tell someone I finally got number five."

Blesse went on to get five more before returning to the United States—but not before getting forced down himself. On his 123rd mission, on October 3, 1952, he was at the end of his patrol and low on fuel when he spotted a flight of four MiGs. In a long, rolling, descending dogfight, Blesse managed to shoot down one of the MiGs, making him a double ace. But he had consumed too much fuel, and his only option was to head for a rescue rendezvous point, Peng Yeng Do Island.

It was typical of Blesse that, out of fuel, deep behind enemy lines, and faced with an ejection and then a hoped-for rescue at sea, his primary concern was that his gun camera film which would confirm his tenth victory, would be lost. Fortunately, Captain Robbie Risner, another hero of two wars, had seen the burning MiG-15 go down.

Blesse was rescued by an air-sea rescue amphibian and went on to a successful air force career, serving a combat tour in Vietnam and later retiring as a major general. After having known him over the years, it was a treat to be able to interview him for a television series. He came across on camera as he was behind the stick over the Yalu—direct, confident, and aggressive, well aware that if there's no guts there's no glory—but that you still have to "check six"!

W.J.B.

When we approached MiG Alley, basically northwestern North Korea, it was wall-to-wall MiG-15s. Everywhere you turned there was a flight to deal with. My squadron got in a big melee, coming out the other side with three kills, a probable, two damaged and not a single wingman lost. Though I got one of the kills (my third), this was over-shadowed by the electrifying effect the fight had on the outfit. There were no more doubting Thomases. All we had since the reorganization was a few guys getting sporadic kills, but on 6 August it was teamwork and tactics that carried the day. It was obvious even to those of little faith that what we had done for the 334th made the squadron a successful fighting unit.

There had been only two flights scheduled that day, one to the north sector of MiG Alley and one to the south. The other flight leader was Lieutenant Chick Cleveland whom I had promoted to command beyond his rank. Chick and I flipped a coin to see who got which one. He went north and I took the south. When we got back, it was easy to tell who had fired and who hadn't by looking at the black powder smudges around the gun ports. When I saw Chick's airplane coming in with no smudges, I got on the radio and said, "How about going over to D channel?" He switched so we could talk without bothering anybody. I told him there were MiGs everywhere, "How'd you do?" After a long silence, I heard loud and clear in a disgusted tone, "If they sawed a woman in two, I'd get the half that eats." Chick was our youngest flight commander, an outstanding pilot who distinguished himself in every possible way. He got four kills along with several probables and a couple damaged. He was made an honorary member of the American Fighter Aces Association ("The Ivory Ace," 99 44/100ths percent pure) and retired a three-star general.

While the other squadrons got about one or two apiece and had a few flights separated, we came home together and had more victories. After that, everybody in the outfit practiced without being told. At last they could see that it worked. During that month our squadron got 11 kills with another 17 in September. Our tactics changes had paid off hand-somely. For a while at least, we ruled the roost!

After my fourth kill on 20 August, plus a probable and three dam-aged. I was coming up on 95 missions and rotation. I wanted that fifth kill so bad I could taste it. The group commander, Colonel Royal Baker, came around every evening, telling me I ought to go home. I had done my duty. I owed it to my family to come home. Other aces had warned me about Baker; he was really too immature to be a good group com-mander. He felt as though we were in competition with him, not working for him. He was a one-man board of inquiry every time someone came back with a kill. I finally told him it took me my whole life time to get where I was and that I not only didn't want to go home, I wanted to extend for 25 more missions. He finally left me alone and directed his campaign against one of the other aces.

Korea made you feel lousy; tired of the huts, roaches, uncomfortable bunks, poor food and no women. But it was the only place you could get this kind of experience. I put in for another 25 missions and it was approved.

I had been caught up in the Ace syndrome long before I got to Korea, so wanting that fifth kill was not new to me, though it was to quite a few other guys. Many would get close and wrestle with the problem of whether to go home or extend for 25 more missions, hoping to get that last MiG.

One pilot got to 94 missions with four kills. He had been writing his wife for weeks telling her when he was going to be back and suddenly he got in the middle of several fights, coming back every day with a MiG. Then, at 95 missions, he had to extend. He decided to send her a telegram which read, "Dear Joyce, I'm at 95 missions. I have four MiGs, must get fifth MiG to become ace. Have decided to extend 25 missions. Be home in about two months, (signed) Joe." He thought that ought to do it—surely she'd understand how important this thing was to him.

About four days later a telegram arrived for Joe. Opening it up, he read. "Dear aspiring ace: I, too, have made an important decision. I am going to have a baby in nine months and seven days, and if you want to be in on it, you better get home!" Joe never made ace!

Flying my 104th mission on 4 September 1952, I got my fifth victory. Earl Brown ("Brownie," I called him) was my wingman and had been with me during at least one other successful flight. I liked Brownie. He was a fine pilot, cool under pressure, knew his job to the nth degree and had a good sense of humor. We all used to kid about having sweaty palms which we thought was an indication the MiGs would be flying that day. I'd often rub Brownie's short haircut, telling him what good luck he brought me. I rubbed it on 4 September 1952.

We had made a couple of passes through MiG Alley with no contact. Suddenly I spotted two '15s about 11 o'clock high. "Padlock," I called to Brownie. That meant I had my eyes on enemy aircraft and that from here on he was responsible to check six for us both. "Roger," Brownie countered.

We dropped our external tanks and began increasing speed as we cut to the inside of a very lazy turn the MiGs were making. "You're clear," Brownie barked. Suddenly the leader began a sharp turn into us and the hair prickled a little on the back of my neck. One of us wasn't going home. As he turned toward us, I pulled up steeply and rolled over, following him around the turn and through the dive that followed. "You're clear," Brownie assured me once again. The MiG leader's wingman was thrown off in a reversal and headed for the Yalu River and safety.

In the next turn, I was in range for a shot and lit up his fuselage and right wing with my .50 calibers. Suddenly it was over—he ejected! It all happened so fast it took me a moment or two to realize I had just gotten Number Five. Before I could even think "Ace," the words "You're clear" jolted me back to reality. Old Brownie was out there doing his job and saving my ass from being picked off while I thought of the wrong things. As usual, fuel was low and it was more than time to get out of there. I thought of a hundred good things about Brownie right then but all I said was, "OK, Brownie, I got it. Let's go home!" It was no accident he got three stars before he retired.

As we climbed out, I thought of all the enemy territory we had to fly over to get home. In the back of my mind a little prayer began popping out, "Lord, if you have to take me while I'm over here, don't do it today. Let me get back and tell someone I finally got number five." It was the realization of a dream that I had since I was a kid, and over the years came to mean more to me even than becoming a general officer in the Air Force.

Up to this point I had earned a few Air Medals and Distinguished Flying Crosses for my two Korean tours. In the past, in Korea, when one became an ace it was customary to get a Silver Star so the Fifth Air Force commander, Lieutenant General Glenn O. Barcus, came down personally to present it to me. George Davis was killed in action after 14 kills so Gabby Gabreski, the USAF's top living ace, was leading the active Korean aces with 6.5 kills. In the Fourth Group, Harry Thyng and Cliff Jolley both had five.

During my 107th mission on 8 September, I jumped a flight of 12 with just my wingman, and I recall radioing to him, "If these guys have read Chapter Two, we're not going to be here very long." We pressed on into the rear flight, which turned off. I watched to see if they were going to turn back but they just kept going.

We flew up fairly close to the second flight and they broke off, again watching to see if they'd come back but they kept going as well. Now we were down to two on four, which isn't too bad. Suddenly the second element broke off and I was sure these guys would turn into us. Nope, they went off like the others so we attacked the two-ship flight. The wingman broke away. I shot the leader down after a half loop and a couple of turns then went after the wingman and got him also. It was getting easier.

News of the two kills brought Harry Thyng and Cliff Jolley out to greet me in the parking area. Throwing his arms around me, Colonel Thyng said, "Damn, Boots, it's about time somebody in this wing was the leading ace." He was referring to Gabby Gabreski. It was just a competitive situation, since Thyng was commander of the 4th Wing at Kimpo and Gabreski had the 51st Wing at Suwon.

On 15 and 17 September, I got the eighth and ninth red stars painted under my canopy, but in getting number nine, I almost lost my wingman. We had closed in on a MiG-15 and were getting fairly close. My wingman, to keep from getting thrown too far out in the turns, was crossing back over from outside to inside each time I made a tight turn.

On one of those crossovers, he was coming underneath just as I was firing and tearing some pretty good size pieces off the MiG. A big hunk of his stabilizer came off, went underneath my airplane and got sucked into my wingman's airscoop. It just corncobbed his engine, taking off all the compressor blades, leaving him with nothing but a whirling dervish that gave no thrust. He had to shut it down and eject into the water. We got a chopper out there, picked him up and brought him home with no injuries. He was the only wingman I had who didn't come back in his own aircraft.

On 3 October 1952 for my 123rd mission, two away from going home, I took a wingman who had only a few missions. There were seven or eight of us who used to get into the MiGs quite a bit and we found if we could get a new guy in action during his first eight or ten missions, he turned out to be a pretty darned good combat pilot. On the other hand, if he went up and back, up and back for 25 or 30 trips and never saw anything, he was apt to wind up a little less aggressive than we wanted him to be.

We cruised around looking for MiGs, but we didn't see anything. I mean everything was dead. Number Four developed fuel problems so Three took him home. As we got down close to Bingo (just enough fuel to get home with a small margin of safety) we turned around and started south. We had quite a bit of enemy territory to cross before "going feet wet" over the water. As we leveled off at around 31,000 feet, about 200 miles from home, I saw a flight of four MiGs at our six o'clock, out about a mile or two. We were getting fairly close to the water so I nosed over a bit to pick up speed. We didn't have the fuel to fight so I wanted to get over the water and continue home.

I think the lead MiG pilot realized what was happening because he started firing his guns. The 23s were ineffective, but when he fired that 37 you could see it coming like a Roman candle. I had the living daylights scared out of me the first time I "trapped" a MiG at my six o'clock, firing away. Well, my wingman had never seen an enemy airplane, so all he saw when he looked back was big cannon balls coming at him, even though the tracers were falling far short. Without thinking, he broke away from me, which was just what the MiG leader wanted. The '15 cut to the inside of the Sabre's turn and rapidly began to close the range.

One glance at the situation and I thought, "Christ, we don't have enough fuel for this." Nevertheless, I came around and radioed. "Put it in a spiral and keep at least four Gs on it; I'm coming down." He got his '86 in a spiral, with the MiG leader and his wingman in a trailing spiral trying to get him, while I fell in behind them with the other element of two MiGs behind me. We had a big daisy chain winding down from 31,000. As we hit 18,000 I was getting even more concerned about fuel—there wasn't enough of it left to do anything but break for home.

The second MiG wasn't doing as well as the leader, who was gaining on my wingman. He slid out, giving me the chance to get a couple of bursts off. A couple of pieces flew off, then I got a good burst into him. He rolled out right away and must have told his leader, who probably didn't want to be there by himself, and broke off as well. Now there was just me and the two MiGs behind me. I radioed a little more advice to my wingman, "Keep that thing at .9, get it over the water and head for home. Don't worry about me." He got out and made it back OK.

Meanwhile the third MiG started firing at me. It was easier for him since I had eased off a little to fire at the number two man. Seeing a couple rounds go by. I tightened my turn, reversed into him and we crossed at a pretty high angle. I held my turn, then rolled over in a dive. As frequently happened during those damn fights. I looked around after I pulled out and found I was all by myself. I knew two MiGs were there somewhere, but I couldn't find a thing.

I stayed in a tight turn for about 10 seconds, worried somebody was going to take a shot at me. Then I looked at my fuel gauge—1,100 pounds. If the winds were right, I'd make it with fumes, but if they were wrong, I'd have to try to land on the beach on Peng Yeng Do, a small island off the coast. I started climbing to save fuel. Around 11,000, I caught a glimpse of something out of the corner of my left eye—a MiG, coming down on me from 10 o'clock. "This is it," I thought, "school's out. I don't have any fuel to fight with this guy." For some reason he never saw me, diving right in front of my '86. As he came by, I looked at my fuel gauge, looked at the MiG and said, "Hell, it's a tossup anyway. Why not?"

Pulling about a 4-G turn, I climbed to the right and rolled off the top underneath him. It took about 25 seconds—I closed to 600 feet, fired and watched the MiG explode and begin burning, then saw the pilot eject. I rolled right back out on course, figuring it cost me about 200 pounds of fuel to shoot him down. There went Number Ten but I was down to 900 pounds. I hoped the camera film worked; otherwise, no confirmation.

The alert flight at Kimpo, led by Captain Robbie Risner, had been scrambled after hearing we were in a fight and short on fuel. A five-kill ace at that point, with another three MiGs to come, Robbie was one of the USAF's finest fighter pilots. About 13 years later, he was shot down in Vietnam, spending seven years as a POW under horrible circumstances, as described in his fine book, *Passing of the Night*. It was a good thing Robbie and his flight saw the burning MiG-15 or I wouldn't have gotten credit for my last kill. I didn't think I would make it back and my film would be lost with the aircraft.

I was still over North Korea. I called "Dumbo," the rescue flying boat that was always on station during our missions, and told him to orbit Peng Yeng Do Island. "If I can't make it home, that's where I'm going to try to land." If I could get 100 miles out at 39,000 feet with 300 pounds of fuel, shutting down the engine would allow me to glide back to base at 180 knots, putting me in the traffic pattern at 6,000 feet where I could restart and land. But I only made it to about 32,000 feet when I hit 300 pounds. Without tailwinds there wasn't a chance. Calling the base, I asked what the winds were and they replied. "Out of the southwest." Nothing could have been worse. I shut the engine off and began a 180-knot glide toward Kimpo Air Base.

As I passed 17,000 feet, I decided I'd become a POW if I stayed on this course. I had no relish for that, especially after Pyongyang Sally had broadcast the night of my eighth kill. "Just wait, Major Blesse, we're going to get you and when we do, we're going to hang you from the Han River Bridge." I changed course and continued my glide toward the west coast and the island. I called Dumbo again. "I'm probably not going to make it, so orbit between the shore and the island." He acknowledged.

I continued to glide down at 180 knots but the wind was against me. For awhile I didn't think I'd even get to the coast. At about 7,000 feet everything looked like it was much too far away so I restarted the engine and used my remaining fuel to climb as high as I could. At 13,000 the thing flamed out so I re-established a 180 knot glide, hoping I'd make the water. I had to cross a main supply route, and I drew a tremendous amount of enemy fire. Several times the flak bursts were so close one wing or the other would raise up. I had no choice but to be a predictable target—jinking would cost me airspeed and altitude—so I held my heading and hoped I wouldn't get "the golden BB" (a direct hit).

I finally crossed the North Korean coast at about 3,000 feet, but a half mile or so out over the water, I knew I was getting too low. "Time to get out," I thought, so I called Dumbo. "I can't go any farther; I'm getting out. Don't let my aircraft hit you." Instantly he radioed back. "Rog, we've got you in sight."

Then occurred one of the finest things that ever happened to me in the Air Force, something I'll never forget. We had a radio in wing operations, and when the guys weren't flying, they all went up there to listen to what was being said in the combat area. It wasn't unusual to find 15 or 20 pilots sitting around listening to what was happening on the mission. Chick Cleveland recalls that day well.

"I was in the operations room monitoring the squadron combat frequency on 3 October 1952 when Boots ran out of luck and fuel (but not judgment) after downing his tenth enemy aircraft. He was very calm as he headed for Chodo, an island in our hands in the East China Sea, for a planned bailout. Things were pretty tense in ops as the conversation on the radio made it apparent that our leader might not make it back.

"The special bonding that takes place between fighter pilots in combat made us feel that a part of us was up there with him. Five or six of us grabbed the mike and gave him some quick words of encouragement. All I could think to say over the radio just before his ejection was something like, 'Congratulations on number ten. We'll have a seat for you at the bar—see you when you get back.' His reply was equally original, like 'Roger.' And out he went."

I heard it from the listening end of my radio. Right after I told Dumbo I wasn't going to make it and had to eject, I heard, "Take it easy, Boots." Then another guy on, "See you at supper." And another, "Don't forget you owe me five bucks so get your butt back here." One message after another from six or seven guys. I remember very clearly a chill going up and down my spine and saying, "God, what a great bunch of guys."

My hands went to the seat triggers. BOOM! Explosive charges blew me and the seat, with parachute attached, into the slipstream. Out I went at about 1,200 feet, a little too low. I didn't want to get tied up with the seat so I undid my seatbelt before ejecting. The chute opened, pulling me away from the seat instantly. Almost immediately I went into the water. My throat burned in the salt water from a parachute strap abrasion. One of my pockets was open and all my maps and survival gear floated out.

After inflating my one-man raft I swam over and picked up my helmet, which for some reason had not sunk. Very carefully I put everything back in the dinghy, then climbed aboard myself. Just about the time I was set for the winter, the Dumbo landed and taxied over to me.

A line was fired out an open window, which I grabbed, and I was pulled over to the airplane and inside. As soon as I was in, the pilot hit the throttles to get out of there. Scrambling to my feet, I ran up the aisle to the cockpit . . . and started banging on the pilot's helmet. "Wait, a minute! My dinghy is still out there with all my stuff in it!" With a quick, disgusted look at me, he said. "Fuck your dinghy. They're shooting at me and we're getting the hell out of here!" My dinghy became a target for Risner's alert flight, which sent it to the bottom of the East China Sea with my F-86.

By the time I got back to Kimpo, word of my bailout had already gone to the Pentagon and a wire had come back which read, "Subject: Major Frederick C. Blesse. Subject officer will be returned to the ZI immediately before we have another Davis incident." This referred to George Davis' death in action the previous February. He had extended his tour voluntarily, as I had, and since he was the leading ace, the Air Force got some bad publicity when he was shot down. They didn't want it to happen again so my tour ended abruptly though I was two missions short of the 125 I had volunteered for. In any event, I was now the leading ace in Korea, and though I suspected it wouldn't last too long, I intended to enjoy every minute of it. The next day I was in Japan for a series of press conferences.

13

A Typical Fighter-Interceptor Mission in Korea

from **OFFICERS IN FLIGHT SUITS**
by John Darrell Sherwood

In his book *Officers in Flight Suits,* military historian John Darrell Sherwood set out to examine the culture of fighter pilots. The title reflects the fact that U.S. Air Force fighter pilots are regularly attired in flight suits rather than in traditional uniforms like those worn by most officers in the Army and Navy. Sherwood suggests that during the Korean War these "officers in flight suits" had a distinct lifestyle.

Sherwood states that the flight-suited officers, by and large, were not college graduates, came from families lacking social prominence, and, to a greater degree than others in the military, attained their officer status through a demonstrated ability to master the intricacies of highly sophisticated equipment—that is, jet fighter planes. According to Sherwood, the flight suit (a simple kind of coverall almost totally devoid of decoration or embellishment) signified certain characteristics such as proven skills, self-confidence, and informality.

To support his thesis, Sherwood draws heavily upon the experiences and recollections of a handful of fighter pilot veterans of the Korean War. The reader is introduced to some of these combat veterans, like Frank Tomlinson and James Hagerstrom, in the excerpt that follows. They are described as having shared concerns such as the hazards of bailing out over hostile territory. In the locker room, the nervous tension preceding a mission was deflected by boisterous horseplay. The lightheartedness of the locker room, however, was replaced in the cockpit with the dead seriousness of manipulating the controls of a North American F-86 Sabre.

In reviewing a typical "fighter sweep" or MiGCAP (MiG combat air patrol), Sherwood discusses the ways in which the Sabre pilots tried to overcome inherent drawbacks. Faced with limited fuel reserves, declining agility at higher altitudes, and imprecise radar vectoring, the "flight suits," as Sherwood refers to the Air Force fighter pilots, sometimes succeeded in overcoming the problems through innovative and courageous methods.

Sherwood contends that the "flight suits" in Korea enjoyed substantial latitude in their permissible behavior owing, partly, to the newness of the Air Force as a separate military service and the fact that the Air Force grew rapidly during the war with its uniformed personnel more than doubling. Also, the Korean War, despite ominous politically inspired hindrances in prosecuting the action, was a real shooting war being waged, in part, from remote airfields. Under the circumstances, some slack was cut for the fighter pilots. This phenomenon—highlighted by an approved dearth of political correctness—created, in Sherwood's view, an environment in which the fighter pilots could thrive and accounted for much of the success they achieved.

In the end, the Air Force is seen as a meritocracy in which those who perform the most and the best are rewarded accordingly. This opinion, perhaps a bit simplistic (after all, how many aces ever got to be chief of staff?), needs to be considered, for the question of how to maintain the esprit of fighter pilots is of critical importance. Whatever the origins of the motivation and success behind those who fly combat, Air Force fighter pilots during the Korean War proved they were at the apex of their profession.

P.H.

A STANDARD MISSION would begin at first light. After quickly throwing on a uniform, the pilots would wolf down breakfast, typically powdered eggs and black coffee. As unappetizing as this food was—especially for those hung over from too much drinking the night before—most pilots would force themselves to eat. "You always ate breakfast," recalled

Tomlinson, "because you might not get another meal for a while, especially if you had to bail out."

After breakfast, the entire mission would be briefed in the Combat Operations Briefing Room. First, the ground situation was described by the ground liaison officer. Then, an intelligence officer briefed everyone on flak, escape and evasion, and rescue procedures. The basic rule of thumb if you were hit was to try to bail out over the Yellow Sea or near the friendly island of Chodo. These areas were patrolled by the U.S. Navy's Seventh Fleet and were therefore much safer for the slow-moving rescue helicopters to operate over than the mainland. For those who had to bail out over the mainland, travel instructions, survival tips, and contact lists were provided but the chances of avoiding capture in these cases were extremely slim. FEAF Intelligence instructed pilots to head toward the coast, and then paddle out to sea in their survival rafts so that air-sea rescue could pick them up. Not surprisingly, no pilots shot down over the land portions of MiG Alley escaped capture.

After the intelligence briefing, a weather officer would give the weather forecast over the base, the mission areas, and the island of Chodo. He also gave the pilots a list of alternative airfields to be used in the event of emergency landings. Finally, the mission leader would explain the order of the day, or the FRAG order as it was called: "FRAG" literally means a "fragment" of FEAF's daily air order of battle. He would also assign "start-engine times, areas and altitudes to be flown, and special duties to be accomplished." At the end of the meeting, pilots would get flight maps, pasted on cardboard mats for ease of use, and code words to be used in the event of a bailout. Pilots would then break up into smaller groups and conduct informal meetings to discuss their individual roles in the mission.

The briefing, overall, not only informed the pilot of the day's mission, but it also was very much a part of the ritual of aviation combat. Many of these men had seen air combat movies such as *Dawn Patrol* (1936) and implicitly understood the symbolism of the predawn briefing: the danger, the patriotism, and, most important, the fact that some of the men in the room might not return. The emphasis on escape, survival, and evasion reinforced this danger.

If shot down, they would be expected to leave the security of the cockpit and survive alone in a harsh and dangerous environment. According to Bud Mahurin, "There were no known friendly civilians above the bomb line." North Korea was "Indian country" for these men—a harsh and dangerous frontier inhabited by a "savage" foe. To survive in this environment, all men were issued a standard survival kit which contained such items as food, a first-aid kit, and a .45-pistol. However, most men customized their kits to reflect their own personality and fetishes. Mahurin, for example, added "two pairs of heavy white sox, a change of underwear, a .22 caliber Savage folding rifle, and a roll of toilet paper." For Hagerstrom, the survival kit and his personal flight suit became an obsession and a mechanism for managing fear. Before he left the U.S., Hagerstrom purchased a pair of felt-lined Russell moccasin boots and a white bird-cloth flying suit lined with raw silk for maximum insulation. He also carried dried milk, berries, nuts, oatmeal, ten pounds of rice, sterno, a pot, a fold-up camp stove, a monocular, maps, shaving equipment, a sleeping-bag vacuum packed in a picnic-ham can, a shelter-half, and enough sulfa to cure pneumonia three times. In addition, he packed a radio, three batteries, and a special SAC issue .22 caliber Hornet rifle with a muzzle velocity of 4,000 feet per second, a range of 100 yards, almost no bullet drop, and no smoke. "The Hornet was the first thing in my backpack," Jim explained, "a pistol won't do it because a patrol with rifles would just stand off at 50 yards and shoot at you." If shot down, Hagerstrom planned to fight off any patrols which came after him until dark, when he could slip away. He had enough food to last thirty days and he planned to hike ten miles a day until he reached the DMZ. Why did he plan so carefully for a bailout? Hagerstrom claims it helped him not to worry: "The difference between panic and fear is pretty tight, and you can spread that line a bit by having one last chance."

After another cup of coffee, many pilots took a trip to the latrines to relieve themselves before the flight. Flight suits had acquired the unenviable nickname of "poop suits," and it was certainly more desirable to dispose of waste before a flight rather than during it. It was also not unusual for anxious or hung-over pilots to throw up before battle. Before one mission, for example, Leonard "Bill" Lilly leaned over the side of his F-86 on the taxiway and threw up; he then went up and shot down two MiGs.

After the latrines, all pilots proceeded to their aircraft to examine the maintenance logs, talk to the ground crew chief, and perform a preflight inspection. From there, the pilot would join his comrades in the locker room to suit up. The atmosphere before a mission was similar to a high school varsity locker room before the big game. "It was almost joyful," claims Earl Brown, "and guys would start to sing while they were suiting up": "Oh we sing, we sing, we sing of Lydia Pinkham, Pinkham, Pinkham, and her love for the human race. Wonderful compound, a dollar a bottle, and every label bears her face, her fucking face." They would also tease one another with such lines as: "Today's the day I'm going to get some MiGs." "How are you going to do it?" another pilot would respond. "You'll never know!"

The joking, though, ended as soon as the pilots hit the flight line and performed their final stationary check, a 360-degree walk around their aircraft. By this time, over three hours had passed since reveille, but there was still more to focus on before takeoff: all gauges, instruments, brakes, and surface controls had to be checked while taxiing out. Takeoffs were then conducted in four-plane formations "approximately five to eight seconds apart."

Once airborne, the climb to altitude is made at "near maximum power settings and the element does not move into close formation except to penetrate an overcast." The object here was to achieve a high speed of Mach .88 or above and an altitude of 43,500 feet before hitting MiG Alley. Because the MiG could get above the Sabre at any altitude, speed was tactically more valuable to a flight than altitude, for it emphasized the Sabre's rate of closure when attacking and reduced the MiG's rate of closure when the tables were turned.

A basic MIGCAP or "fighter sweep" contained either nine or twelve elements spread across MiG Alley. At least two elements would fly directly opposite the large Chinese air base at Antung, nicknamed "Antung Air University"; other elements might be placed between Antung and the Sui Ho Reservoir; and still others, east of the reservoir or farther south as a backup. These sweeps were often vectored to MiG flights by two radar stations—one just above Kimpo Air Force Base known as Dentist, and another on Cho Do, known as Dentist Charlie.

There were several tactical problems the Sabres confronted while in MiG Alley. First, their patrol time was extremely limited due to the 200-mile distance between the F-86 bases near Seoul and MiG Alley. F-86s, consequently, only carried enough fuel to loiter over the Yalu River for twenty minutes; however, aggressive pilots like Hagerstrom would try to "whittle down" their "bingo" state. When a pilot transmitted the bingo code word to his flight, it meant that he had only enough fuel to get back to the base, and would have to break off from a combat patrol. A high bingo was 1,500 pounds of fuel and a low bingo was 1,100 pounds, but Hagerstrom quickly discovered that these guidelines were conservative. "It was ridiculous to come up and only spend twenty minutes over the Yalu," he explained, "so I made a few calculations of my own and determined that I could make it back to base with 600 pounds: just to be safe, though, I used an alarm clock to tell me when to head on home." Nevertheless, Hagerstrom often "pushed the envelope" well beyond his own self-imposed 600-pound limit: on a mission where he shot down a MiG, he pushed it to 300 pounds, and on another, he actually ran out of gas taxiing away from the main runway.

Another problem which the Sabres faced was limited maneuverability at high altitudes. In the thin air of the stratosphere, oxygen-breathing jet engines begin to lose power, and a quick turn or a burst of gunfire from the .50 guns could cause an F-86 to lose speed and altitude in a hurry. Consequently, MIGCAPs flew racetrack patterns and made broad, 90-degree turns.

The final and perhaps the most vexing problem for the Sabre pilots was target acquisition. In general, the MiGs were very reluctant to "mix it up" with Sabres. The Sabres, therefore, often had to sneak up on the MiGs from behind to get a shot in, but this was no simple task. Clear air and lots of sunshine made spotting a MiG extremely difficult. Without visual references, the human eye tends to focus on a point eighteen inches in front of the nose. Often, sunlight reflecting off an aluminum fuselage was the only visual cue that a MiG was nearby, and your eyes constantly played tricks on you: a speck of dirt on the Plexiglass canopy, for example, could easily be mistaken for a distant MiG. Some pilots carried binoculars to improve their chances of spotting MiGs. Hagerstrom, before he left the States, had a special pair of half-mirrored, distance glasses made which enabled him to see at twenty feet what an ordinary person would see at ten. The optometrist told him they might permanently ruin his eyes, and he replied: "I don't give a shit."

As soon as a MiG was spotted, it became a race against time to maneuver to within 2,000 yards of the MiG, position the gun sight, and get a kill in before the bingo point was reached. F-86s only had enough fuel to patrol MiG Alley for twenty minutes, and any dogfighting limited that time even further.

Upon return to base, a pilot would immediately be debriefed on the day's activities. If the nose of his plane was black from gun smoke (an indication that an aerial battle had been fought), he would often be met on the tarmac by the squadron leader or even the wing commander and be asked to go over the kill as he emerged from the airplane. Later, more formal debriefings would occur in the operations hut, and on occasion "mission whiskey" or other spirits would be offered to the pilot by the flight surgeon to settle his nerves. The flight surgeon gave the pilot several ounces of whiskey for every mission flown, and generally this whiskey would be awarded to the pilot in large volumes at the end of every month: but occasionally, the spirits were actually doled out after a mission. "Thank God the doctors were also aware of the limits of human endurance and gave us a ration of whiskey to be used at the completion of every mission," recalled Mahurin. "If it had not been for the whiskey ration and the rest leaves in Japan," he claimed, "we would have had frequent crack-ups."

F-86 pilots flew roughly three missions a week and one hundred missions per tour. When a pilot completed his hundred-mission tour, he was immediately sent home. After every thirty missions flown, a pilot was given an Air Medal, and after one hundred missions, a Distinguished Flying Cross. If a pilot managed to do something spectacular like shoot down five MiGs, a Silver Star was awarded. Status in the Air Force, in short, was directly related to performance in combat and missions flown.

14

War Fighting Is Not Much Fun

from WINGS AND WARRIORS: MY LIFE AS A NAVAL AVIATOR

by Donald D. Engen

Don Engen has had many careers, both within the Navy, where he served in combat and as a test pilot, and without, where he has held executive positions in industry and served as administrator of the Federal Aviation Administration. He now is director of the National Air and Space Museum, my old post, and is busy massing support for the establishment of a new NASM facility at Dulles Airport.

Don's flying career was magnificent, and he writes of it in such exquisite detail that you think he must have had a full-time secretary recording every day of his life. He attributes the marvelous attention to detail to the ordinary demands of Navy record keeping, but one can only be grateful that he was able to record and recall his exciting life with so many exact particulars.

In this excerpt, Engen deals with his second foray into combat, this time in Korea, where he entered the war on June 3, 1950, flying Grumman F9F-3 Panthers. His first mission was a strafing attack on an airfield near Pyongyang, where he was momentarily tempted by the appearance of a Yak-9P fighter. With his usual disciplined will, he let the Yak go, staying instead in position as section leader. Even today, you can sense a certain wistful angst as Don recounts the story—he would have much preferred to have shot it down.

Instead, he destroyed another Yak fighter and a DC-3-like transport on the ground on his first strafing pass. The attack was one of several that virtually eliminated the North Korean air force as an operational entity.

Despite recognizing early on that the air war in Korea would be much different from his fighting in a Curtiss SB2C-3 in World War II, Engen threw himself into the action—and there was plenty of it. The carriers had to regain the proficiency they had enjoyed fighting the Japanese, and Engen's accounts of the hectic activity of damaged Vought F4U Corsairs returning, and Douglas ADs crashlanding on the deck, make outstanding reading.

The Navy had to learn how to use its new jets in combat, and Engen participated in a series of raids and reconnaissance missions at low level over North Korea. A typical two-plane combat reconnaissance flight would destroy three or four trucks, a bus, and, if one could be found, a locomotive. Engen would fly as low as 50 feet off the ground, well in advance of his wingman, who would follow behind at 500 feet. When Engen saw a target—tanks hidden under trees, a truck tucked into a barn—he would call it out and his wingman would attack.

In the heat of combat, life went on as usual in the Navy, and Engen amusingly recounts the ordinary bureaucratic problems that plagued the pilots' lives. He himself was struggling through a correspondence course on international law from the U.S. Naval War College—a course that seemed to contradict everything he saw going on in the theater. And he tells the sad story of the accidental death of a seaman who was killed when a high-explosive incendiary round blew up. Less than six hours after the accident, a telegram was received announcing that the late seaman's wife had just given birth to a baby boy.

This juxtaposition of combat action and vivid descriptions of life on board the carrier highlights Engen's book, which clearly delineates not only the extraordinary experience and capability of the man but also his essential compassion and humanity.

W.J.B.

USS *VALLEY FORGE* and HMS *Triumph* rendezvoused and with escorts proceeded north into the Yellow Sea to a position slightly above the thirty-eighth parallel, where we would launch to make the first combat sorties into North Korea. *Triumph* and *Valley Forge* operated as separate task groups, and at 0300 on July 3, 1950, we Navy pilots arose, ate breakfast, and went to the ready rooms to brief for the start of our part of the Korean War. I was scheduled to fly as section leader for Commander Harvey Lanham, who would be the airborne coordinator of the initial strike. Commander Lanham planned to reassign targets of opportunity should the prebriefed airfields not appear sufficiently important. Lieutenant Commander Bill Lamb of VF-52 was in tactical command of the high cover, and a total of sixteen F9F-3s would be in the air. VF-53 and VF-54, each with eight F4U-4s, and VA-55, with twelve AD-1s under the leadership of Lieutenant Commander Doug Hodson, would be the main attack group. That group was appreciably slower, so it took off first. The jets planned to overtake the main group and provide flak suppression as the main attack group began its initial runs.

The jets launched eastward into the half-lit, early dawn sky and rendezvoused en route to coast in across the western, low, flat islands and marshlands of North Korea. No one shot at us. I could see large ships anchored in Chinampo harbor, and many plumes of steam clearly marked busy locomotives in the early morning. Each engine pulled long strings of loaded railroad cars to destinations inland, and the country appeared to be oblivious to the attack that would start in minutes.

The F4Us and ADs began a long, fast, descending run-in to attack the main airfield at P'yŏngyang as our F9F-3s purposefully overtook them. Our F9Fs split into four divisions of four to comb the area for airplanes and to strafe any opposing gun emplacements on the airfield before the F4Us and ADs attacked. Lieutenant Junior Grade Leonard Plog and Ensign Eldon W. Brown of Lieutenant Commander Bill Sisley's division each reported making firing passes at airborne Yak fighters, and I could tell by their excited comments on the radio that each had made a kill. Everyone else was too busy with their responsibilities to say much. My job was to stay with CAG, regardless, and to provide extra eyes and support for him. I saw one Yak-9P that I was tempted to chase, but CAG pulled John Nyhuis and me back and kept me in position as his section leader. After CAG saw that the attack was going as planned, he let it continue without retargeting, and his section and mine dropped down from 20,000 feet to join the fray.

John Nyhuis and I made a strafing run from north to south on the airfield. Each of us could pick individual targets, and I used the large concrete parking ramp in front of the control tower as my general target and strafed and burned one Yak-9 fighter and a DC-3 look-alike on the first pass. John Nyhuis also strafed and left two airplanes burning. There was a lot of excited chatter on the radio about various targets, and there was very little AA that I could see, as we wheeled in the air over the airfield craning our necks for more airborne airplanes. The aerial war in North Korea, at least the early phase, was over almost before it began. The North Korean air force never launched more than hecklers again.

The F4Us and ADs completed their attacks on the hangars, airfield facilities, and airplanes on the ground. Their 1,000-pound bombs were decimating those facilities, and although it was July 3, not July 4, I caught myself thinking that those were high-order fireworks and that we had front row seats for a most unusual show. For twenty minutes we wheeled in and out of the low hung clouds over P'yŏngyang in complete aerial domination, and when our ammunition had been fully expended, we rendezvoused and departed to arrive back at the ship in time for the scheduled recovery. We vaguely heard our British friends over Haeju on our common VHF frequencies, and they were much more reserved on the radio than our pilots seemed to be.

Our low flying caused us to use more fuel than planned but each pilot had enough to make the recovery in *Valley Forge* as the jets overtook the returning force and landed first. The first Navy jet combat sorties were completed without incident and without damage to any U.S. aircraft. The ready rooms were full of excited pilot chatter as we were debriefed, and those who had not yet flown prepared for the next combat strike into North Korea.

I was fortunate that CAG flew on both the first morning flight and an afternoon flight, too, because that meant that I would fly twice. That afternoon we attacked P'yŏngyang airfield again, as well as a nearby major rail yard. John Nyhuis and I strafed another Yak fighter on the airfield and a locomotive that gave off a satisfyingly large cloud of steam as my 20mm cannon projectiles penetrated the outer skin and tubes of the boiler. On that flight I realized that this war was to be different from World War II. North Korea was too small a country to provide much in the way of large targets for long. That fact was further emphasized when John Nyhuis and I flew over a yellow 1941 Chevrolet convertible that was roaring down a dirt road, creating a high dust plume behind that could be seen for miles. The convertible's top was down, and a uniformed figure was hunched over the wheel, driving like Barney Oldfield. John and I wheeled up in the sky, reversed course, and rolled in on the Chevrolet from 5,000 feet. Yes, this was going to be a different kind of a war.

I stood the landing control duty in Primary Fly so that Howie Boydstun could fly on the second strike that first morning and again in the early morning of July 4. In addition to the fireworks over North Korea, we had our own fireworks back in *Valley Forge*. July 4 was one of those days that aircraft carriers do not like to have. During the first recovery that morning, an AD with minor AA damage came in high and fast and after the cut floated over the wires and barriers to pass by Commander Blackie Wienel and me in Primary Fly at eye level. Blackie hit the emergency alert switch to announce heads up on the flight deck for all to hear and to enable them to take cover wherever they could find it. The AD landed with a thunderous smash on top of the air group airplanes parked farther forward on the flight deck. Parts, propeller blades, and dust flew in all directions, and when everything came to rest, not one person had been hurt. The AD ended up askew on top of another AD, and both pilots eventually climbed out of their airplanes uninjured.

That "act" was followed by an F4U with moderate battle damage that could not lower one main wheel. The pilot made his approach for landing after all aircraft were on board. His hook caught a cross-deck pendant as his right wing slammed to the deck. No sooner had that occurred than the HO3S-1 helicopter manning the plane guard station aft of *Valley Forge* reported an engine failure and hit the water in a great splash. The helo pilot was rescued by the plane guard destroyer, while the mess on the flight deck was sorted out. Finally, another AD floated over the wires after the cut but remained low enough to hit all three barriers and then to end up in a mess of wire spaghetti on the flight deck just below Primary Fly. Again, no one was injured, but it was not a good day.

No one had been shot down in combat on July 4, but we managed to lose three aircraft and damage seven others in the second day of combat! For my way of thinking, that was not the way to start a war. It was immediately apparent that, among other things, a vital need existed for additional intelligence and better coordination. It was evident, too, that we would need to repair the airplanes that had been damaged because we had no replacements. The pilots of the air group also needed to do some deep thinking about carrier procedures. What was happening was a manifestation of our lack of flying earlier on the cruise. That lack continued to haunt us until August, when we had built up greater currency in the air. After our first days of combat, *Valley Forge,* in company with *Triumph,* returned to Buckner Bay, Okinawa, to prepare better for much more combat.

The F9F-3 was designed from World War II fighter experience, when the Navy was still trying to figure out what a jet fighter should be. Its four 20mm cannon were quite effective against many targets, but Rear Admiral John Hoskins must have pondered that he might have been better off with more F4Us and ADs. The jets provided an entirely new warfare capability and an effective deterrent to strikes against the force, but they used too much aviation gasoline, and we still had no jet fuel on board the ship. The tender loving care required by the jets was appreciably greater than that needed by airplanes deployed in World War II. But Rear Admiral Hoskins also knew that this was the first deployment of any Navy jet airplanes in the Pacific and that the war was providing valuable opportunities to test new procedures and the efficacy of those jet airplanes. He probably spent many sleepless nights, certainly in the early stage of the Korean War, weighing the pros and cons of the mix of aircraft with which he could fight this war. Soon, his answer to the need for jet airplanes would be a resounding "yes, we need them." Ultimately, the war forced a faster rate of introduction of jet airplanes and improved ordnance-carrying capability and taught us many lessons to hasten jet airplane acceptance.

By mid-July the war was going badly on the ground for South Korean and United Nation forces. The North Koreans marched south past Osan, and the Air Force had its hands full trying to interdict their supply lines from the north. Our TG 77.4 sortied from Buckner Bay on July 16 and moved north into the Sea of Japan to cover a diversionary landing of the 1st Cavalry Division at P'ohang on the east coast of South Korea. That flanking maneuver was designed to put more pressure on the North Koreans as they continued their determined drive south toward Pusan. HMS *Triumph* with the escorts moved into the Yellow Sea. North Korea was no more than 150 miles from east to west and some 240 miles from north to south. Its small size made us wonder all the more how a country could mount such a determined advance. We placed a carrier off each coast of North Korea so we could squeeze the

North Koreans harder. The Air Force was fully engaged in supporting the South Koreans at the front, and naval aviation forces were to carry the war to North Korea.

With the landing of the 1st Cavalry Division on the east coast of South Korea, we then moved up the east coast to target our efforts on port complexes of Wŏnsan and Hamhŭng, north of the thirty-eighth parallel, and those were virtually destroyed. Our intelligence was still poor, and returning pilots constantly brought in new information. We virtually did our own real-time intelligence gathering. A returning VF-51 pilot reported a large oil refinery in Wŏnsan. A subsequent strike by the F4Us and ADs destroyed that target, probably one of the largest we had seen to date.

For the remainder of July, Air Group 5 attacked new and different target complexes along the east coast of North Korea. Also, we set about to deny the North Koreans use of their transportation system, so vital to the support of their war in the south. Our F9F-3s provided new combat tactics, and we honed our ability to conduct road and railroad recce flights by flying at treetop height to clear all transport from a specific stretch of road or railroad track and to deny the vehicles and trains early warning of impending attack. A typical two-airplane combat recce flight would yield three or four trucks, a bus, and perhaps a locomotive. There was no aerial opposition in August 1950. John Nyhuis and I adopted this technique: I flew very low at about 50 feet, and he would loiter behind me at 400 or 500 feet; the instant I saw something, I would call him, and he would be in position to attack before the truck or tank could get off the road and hide in nearby trees. That worked well, but I frequently returned to the *Valley Forge* with Korean mud from my 20mm projectiles splashed onto the underside of my fuselage.

As the war progressed, our flight deck procedures and flying became more polished. We overcame the tactical rustiness from our previous lack of flying. We fighters launched in tactical divisions of four and then split into two groups of two after we struck at our major target. Our greater speed allowed us to cover much more area in less time than the propeller-driven airplanes. Of course, we had less time in the air as well, and that drove the need for better coordination. It also created challenges back at the ship for jet launch and recovery in coordination with the much slower propeller-driven airplanes. New single- and double-launch-and-recovery cycles were devised as a means to dovetail the differing operating requirements.

By late July the North Koreans pushed the South Koreans and our U.S. ground forces back almost to Pusan, the southernmost port in South Korea. We shifted our road recce into South Korea to support the Air Force. Its pilots were having to fly their combat sorties from Japan because Korean airfields were no longer available. Anything moving on the roads 23 miles north of Pusan was North Korean. That was our rule of engagement.

John Nyhuis and I flew our road recce flights and marveled at the large number of bits and pieces of P-51s and P-80s strewn beside the roads of South Korea and across the nearby countryside. Shiny aluminum wings and fuselages of Air Force airplanes stood out in marked contrast to the lush green countryside. Those airplanes were shot down or were brought down by the nearly invisible wires purposely stretched across valleys or roads by the North Koreans. We were alert for the wires, but we still flew low. On one road recce flight, using our technique of low-high, I was flying at 50 feet, following each turn in the road, and John was higher, a mile behind me. I came around a small mountain to be face to face with a North Korean truck coming down the road from the other direction. I saw the look of surprise on the truck driver's face, and I am not sure who was more surprised, he or I. The truck driver jammed on his brakes and skidded to a stop as I whizzed past, too quickly to shoot. A company of soldiers had camouflaged the truck with an improbable entire tree in the truck bed and was hiding under it. I quickly called John Nyhuis, and he dispatched the truck and the platoon.

As we flew more and more in the south, the F9Fs were coming back with the odd rifle bullet hole in the wing or fuselage. One pilot came back with a big chip out of the armored glass in front of his face from a single rifle bullet. The propeller-driven F4U-4 was a World War II design, which initially had had an engine-oil-cooler bypass installed to prevent ground fire from downing an otherwise good airplane. (That is, the World War II pilot had been able to bypass the oil cooler if that vulnerable part of the engine was hit by ground fire.) That feature was removed from the F4Us in the late 1940s because it was thought to add needless cost and complexity. That decision was coming home to haunt the Corsair pilots. Their airplanes would be hit by nothing more serious than a single rifle bullet, and then their engines would seize when all the engine oil leaked from the oil cooler. They then would be forced to land behind enemy lines minutes after being hit. The amazingly versatile helicopter performed many miraculous pilot saves, but at that juncture in the war helicopters could not be positioned close enough to the action to always be effective. We were losing many F4U pilots and hoped they were being captured, not killed out of hand.

We had a small Marine photo airplane detachment in Air Group 5. In late July one of those pilots, Captain Dave Booker, was shot down about 30 miles north of Seoul. Dave crash landed his F4U-5 photo airplane late one afternoon setting off a monumental search and rescue effort, which failed because of impending darkness. The next day the first airplanes airborne could find no sign of Dave. Several weeks later we heard him speak on Radio P'yŏngyang during a propaganda program. We recognized immediately that he was just telling us that he was alive, and whatever inane statement the North Koreans attributed to him was meaningless. Dave was the first pilot from *Valley Forge* known to be captured.

As July ended, *Valley Forge* and *Triumph* went into Sasebo, Japan, for ammunition and resupply. On August 1 the first naval aviation support from the States arrived. USS *Philippine Sea,* with Air Group 11 embarked, entered Sasebo harbor to coordinate combat information and operating procedures with *Valley Forge* and the task group commander's staff. They were a welcome addition to our meager naval aviation forces. We saw a number of old friends and acquaintances when Rear Admiral Hoskins sent us to *Philippine Sea* to provide our combat lessons learned to date. Commander Solly Vogle was commander of Air Group 11, Lieutenant Commander Tom Amen was commanding officer of VF-111, Lieutenant Commander John Butts—an old friend from VB-19 days—was commanding officer of VF-112, and Lieutenant Commander Jerry Lake—from my days at Mojave—was executive officer of VA-115. There were many other friends as well—Lieutenant Junior Grade William Barnes from VBF-19, now in a VC-3 detachment and flying F4Us, and Lieutenant C. A. (Buck) Weaver, friend from VF-212 days. Later, Buck would be shot down and killed.

Both *Valley Forge* and *Philippine Sea* were under way on August 3. We returned to the Yellow Sea for eleven days, and the *Philippine Sea* started combat operations in the Sea of Japan. During that time Commander Solly Vogle was shot down and killed. We also saw the senseless brutality of the Korean War. As we steamed at our launch position off the west coast of Korea, near the thirty-eighth parallel, we found the sea littered with hundreds of bodies of men. Each had been tied back-to-back with another man and shot in the head. Those bodies must have come from a river, or perhaps they were captives that had been taken to sea and executed. We could not tell if they were North or South Koreans. Regardless, that sight was a grim reminder that being captured was certainly not in one's best interest.

On August 12 Commander Harvey Lanham's division was launched in the late morning to coast in over the southwestern part of North Korea. We were on a road and railroad recce flight and split into two sections. CAG and Ensign Lou Simmons went north. John Nyhuis and I conducted our road and rail recce farther south near Kumch'on, where we found two heavily armored trains moving south through the delta toward Seoul. We immediately stopped them by strafing the locomotives. We were working over the remaining cars when John advised me that 40mm AA from the heavily defended trains was coming very close to me. I acknowledged his transmission, and we pulled up to put some distance between ourselves and those shooting on the ground before returning to our attack from a different direction. I never heard from John Nyhuis again. He simply disappeared after he made that radio call and never answered my subsequent attempts to raise him on the radio. I looked for an airplane on the ground or evidence where one might have crashed: there was none. John had simply disappeared. I called CAG, and he and Lou Simmons came down to look. We found nothing. Finally, reaching a low-fuel state, we departed for the ship. I hoped that John might have had radio failure and returned to the ship, but he had not. John Nyhuis had been shot down.

The next strike to be launched that day contained a search and rescue group of ADs and F4Us that returned to the area of Kumch'on, but no sign of John's airplane could be found. The next day I flew to the same area to look again but found nothing. To this day I do not know exactly what happened. He was simply missing. On the evening of August 13 *Valley Forge* headed toward Sasebo for brief resupply and needed repairs to the catapults and arresting gear. After a few days I wrote John's parents in Walla Walla, Washington, to tell them what I knew.

Returning to sea, Air Group 5 worked the east coast of Korea for the rest of the month, first to the south and then back up north again. While we hoped that the troops would hold and eventually break out of the Pusan perimeter, it was easy to see that North Korea was effective in sending so many troops and supplies to the south under the cover of darkness. Our four-plane night-fighter detachment from VC-3 under Lieutenant Commander Bill Henry proved invaluable at interdicting large truck convoys at night. Frequently, they would hit the lead few trucks and then the rear few trucks, to trap the remainder on the narrow road until daylight, when the first day strikes would finish off the convoy.

One day Lieutenant Commander Harley Thompson, operations officer in VF-51, attacked a train that happened to have explosives in it. His 20mm shells laced into one rail car, and as he flew over it, it disintegrated, blowing wood and rail-car parts everywhere. Harley's F9F-3 flew through the blast and out the other side, and when he had collected his senses and evaluated his situation, he found he was in deep trouble. He had one piece of 4-by-4 lumber stuck in the leading edge of his wing; there were holes in the fuselage and the wings; he was losing hydraulic fluid, as well as fuel, from some gaping holes that he could not see. He had almost blown himself out of the sky, but his engine was still running.

Harley, some said understandably, let the world know that he had a problem. On the VHF radio he broadcast, "I'm hit! I'm hit! I'm going in. I can't make it." All this was given in one continuous stream of chatter as he headed toward the Sea of Japan. No one could offer help because he would not stop talking on the radio. However, he did remain airborne, and when he finally paused long enough for someone else to have a chance to talk. I heard the cool crisp voice of one of our HMS *Triumph* Royal Navy friends, a Sea Fury pilot somewhere over the horizon, come on the radio. He said, "I say, old chap, why don't you shut up and die like a man." Harley made it back to the ship with some masterful flying, but it seemed that subsequently he talked less on the radio.

The North Koreans continued heavy use of their roads for resupply of their forces in the south during August 1950, and we stepped up our assault efforts on the roads. A typical combat recce flight would garner each section of two airplanes, three or four trucks, a bus, and, if lucky, a locomotive. There was no aerial opposition. We had the skies to ourselves, and the Air Force stayed close to the battlefront. The automatic antiaircraft (AAA) fire was definitely becoming more accurate, and it seemed as though every person on the ground had a rifle. We could see individual soldiers shooting at our airplanes when we flew low.

There are always anomalies when a war first starts. Peacetime administrative requirements are still in effect, even though you are fighting a war! Reports, accident investigations, and all manner of administrative minutiae confound those in battle until some higher echelon provides relief. We had to conduct an aircraft accident investigation if a .50-caliber bullet hit an airplane; other peacetime reports seemed just as pointless, and there was the continuing need for written examinations for promotion and the completion of required correspondence courses. Dave Pollock completed his written examinations for promotion to commander in the wardroom of *Valley Forge* between combat flights and was promoted at the end of August. I was fulfilling my correspondence course requirements from the U.S. Naval War College for promotion to lieutenant commander, and the course on international law particularly troubled me. It just did not ring true with respect to what we were doing in Korea. I was about to quit the course in disgust when fortunately the Navy did away with such requirements for promotion.

August brought another challenge. USS *Valley Forge* was limited in its air operations by the capabilities of its H-4 catapults and its arresting gear. Our jet airplanes always taxed those capabilities to their limits, and as a pilot you could feel the punishment in your body on the catapult shot or arrested landing. The ship could make 30 knots, but we needed in excess of 35 knots of wind across the deck so that we would not exceed the airplane's or the ship's catapult and arresting gear capabilities. In August some days the F9Fs could not fly because there was not enough wind across the deck, so we would simply stand down. That happened infrequently, but we pilots in VF-51 and VF-52 took some heavy ribbing from our friends in the F4U and AD squadrons when it did.

Commander Harvey Lanham's division now consisted of himself: his wingman, Ensign Bob Zaijicheck of VF-52: me from VF-51; and my wingman, Ensign Lou Simmons from VF-52. We had so few pilots that the intermingling of VF-51 and -52 pilots in the division was a means of sharing the combat sortie load.

By the end of August more and more pilot rescues and recoveries were being made by helicopter pilots. One of those rescued was VA-115's Lieutenant Commander Jerry Lake. Jerry was shot down and crash landed on a sandbar in the middle of a river in North Korea. He held off a platoon of North Koreans with his .38-caliber pistol, even though wounded, while his compatriots overhead tried to keep the enemy out of the river by strafing them. An HO3S helicopter made it in and picked up Jerry in a hail of enemy fire to return him behind our front lines. Many heroic tales, such as that one, did much to sustain the morale of the pilots. Helicopter pilots were special people, and tales of their exploits cannot give them the praise they deserve.

General MacArthur planned the invasion of Inch'ŏn in a bold move to cut off the North Korean army south of Seoul. We moved to the Yellow Sea to support that invasion, which was scheduled for September 15. While our operations in the Yellow Sea were not challenged by the Chinese or the Soviets, everyone was edgy about operating in this land-locked area. Late on the afternoon of September 4 a radar target was detected moving south seemingly out of Darien in Manchuria. CIC reported to Rear Admiral Hoskins that the bogey was tracking south over the Yellow Sea, approaching the force on a direct course. *Valley Forge* went to general quarters in preparation for an air attack, and an air-borne division of four F4U-4s led by Lieutenant Junior Grade Richard Downs of VF-53 was directed to intercept the bogey.

Faced with this oncoming threat, Rear Admiral Hoskins gave the order to the flight leader to make an identification pass and if fired on to return the fire. The bogey was identified as a twin-engine Tupelov bomber, a Tu-2, with Soviet markings. Downs made the first pass, and as he flew by the Tu-2, its tail gunner opened fire. Downs then instructed his following wingman, Ensign Edward Laney to fire back. Laney's 20mm fire was very effective and took large pieces out of the Tu-2. On fire, the bomber dove toward the water and then crash landed not far from an American destroyer in our screen. The destroyer pulled the only surviving crew member out of the water, but he promptly died. The destroyer reported that from the papers in his flight suit and from his appearance he was a Soviet pilot. Air Group 5 had just shot down a Soviet bomber!

Messages then flew thick and fast to Pearl Harbor and on to Washington. President Truman had been scheduled to make a speech before the United Nations denouncing the aggression in South Korea, and the State Department had one glorious mess on its hands. The Seventh Fleet had shot down a Soviet airplane that we thought was attacking *Valley Forge* in the Yellow Sea. In fact, the airplane might have been going to attack, but we would never know for sure. The comman-der of the Seventh Fleet directed that the body of the Soviet pilot be transferred to the fleet flag ship, where it was temporarily interred in the refrigerated meat locker.

Diplomats being diplomats, things were not resolved quickly. Washington and Moscow exchanged views, and the president did speak at the United Nations. Notes were exchanged. The Soviet pilot's body was transferred to *Valley Forge*'s meat locker. The Soviets would not admit that one of their airplanes had been flying over the Yellow Sea with the intent of attack, let alone that it had been near the U.S. task force. More diplomatic meetings were held, and more notes were exchanged. After weeks of this, the supply officer in *Valley Forge* palmed off the Soviet pilot's body on an unsuspecting supply officer in Sasebo, where there was a much larger refrigeration facility. We never learned if that vexing diplomatic problem was ever resolved, and I would not be surprised if that Soviet pilot's body was still in limbo.

Not all of our losses were in the air. On September 12 one of our ordnance men, Petty Officer Third Class Dominguez, and an ordnance striker were loading 20mm cannon ammo into one of our F9Fs on the forward hangar deck when one of the high explosive incendiary rounds blew up and killed Dominguez. There was no further damage. His death was particularly sad because just six hours after the accident the squadron received a Red Cross message that his wife had just given birth to an eight-pound baby boy, their third child. Petty Officer Dominguez had only $1,000 of life insurance so all of us in VF-51 chipped in and raised another $2,000 for his family. Life on board an aircraft carrier is tremendously complex and is not just about flying airplanes. Those sailors who maintained the airplanes and the many officers and enlisted men who manned the absolutely vital nonflying positions in our aircraft carriers deserved special credit.

General MacArthur's invasion of Inch'ŏn went down in history as a classic operation on September 15. The U.S. and South Korean Marines stormed Wolmi-do Island off Inch'ŏn in the morning and took it in a matter of hours. In the afternoon the Marine Corps and the Army stormed ashore with strong close air support. The F4Us and ADs from the carriers *Valley Forge*, *Boxer*, and *Philippine Sea*, along with Marine F4Us from the CVEs *Badoeng Strait* and *Sicily*, provided the close air support. *Boxer*, with Air Group 2 embarked, had just arrived from the States the night before and had no jet airplanes. The F9F-3s of *Valley Forge* and F9F-2s of *Philippine Sea* flew interdictory reconnaissance north and south of the landing. Over 200 ships were brought together under the command of Vice Admiral A. D. Struble as commander of

Joint Task Force 7. After the landing the ground troops moved across Korea, cutting the lines of supply for the North Korean army and enabling the U.S. and South Korean forces to break out of the Pusan perimeter and join them by September 27. More than one-half of the North Koreans were killed or captured.

On October 6, 1950, *Valley Forge* entered Sasebo harbor for our first port visit in a month. Everyone was grumpy from the daily flying routine, and the wardroom crackers had weevils. We would break the crackers in half to knock out the weevils before we ate them. After you have been at sea for a month, land can have a definite and different identifiable smell. Once ashore, trees and flowers have individual smells, and you detect the slightest whiff of perfume almost immediately. The Sasebo port visit was good but seemed too short as *Valley Forge* left on October 11 for our return to combat.

The rate at which we were flying was such that the ship had to refuel every third day to maintain the required supply of aviation gasoline. The jets still were using most of the aviation gasoline. We would rearm every other refueling day, now that there were sufficient ammunition ships deployed. Air Group 5 continued to pound the targets in North Korea, and Lou Simmons and I spent a lot of time on road reconnaissance. The weather turned much colder, and, in a way, that was a blessing at sea because we had more thrust in our engines and good wind for our jet launches and recoveries.

The days droned on. War fighting is not much fun. The thrill of coasting in over a hostile coastline and attacking a large target complex, or looking for an enemy fighter airplane with which to test your skills, can break the monotony, but the thrill soon disappears as the daily dirty drudgery of strafing trucks and looking for soldiers on the ground to kill, as they try to kill you, begins to dull your mind. One day melds into another, and administrative duties on board ship become chores to take your mind off tomorrow. At night you dream of improbable war fighting situations and wake to begin another day of the same slugging dirty war.

THE VIETNAM WAR

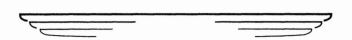

15

Ia Drang Valley and Holidays

from **CHICKENHAWK**
by Robert Mason

The title of this moving, action-filled book derives from the
author's trenchant observation of his own personality—chicken
before a battle and a hawk in it. No one could fail to be "chicken"
given the mortally dangerous conditions under which Robert
Mason and his colleagues flew. It is a tribute to his courage that he
became a "hawk" when Vietcong bullets ripped through his helicopter as he loaded wounded aboard.

The helicopter war in Vietnam was fought up close and personal, with danger awaiting every sortie. This was not death-at-a-
distance; it was combat at close quarters, with casualties occurring
at a frightful rate. Mason and his fellow helicopter pilots flew over
hostile territory day after day. They raced in at low altitudes that
kept them always in range of all the antiaircraft fire, from flak guns
smuggled down the Ho Chi Minh Trail to the mass discharge of
rifles. The basic nature of Army and Marine Corps missions invariably took the choppers into harm's way—to drop off troops, ferry
supplies, or pick up casualties in the very forefront of a firefight.

Mason's matter-of-fact approach to writing minimizes the hazards he encountered; he passes them off as a Humphrey Bogart
character might have done, with a stolid tough guy's casual acceptance of raw peril. Yet the missions were terribly risky, with every
flight going deep into enemy-held ground. All too often the pilots

were desperately tired from flying as much as twenty hours a day, yet when the call came, they went.

Despite the understated writing, as spare as the Spartan life they lived in the field, Mason's remarkable sensitivity is revealed time and again, never more poignantly than in the way he reacts to the dead and wounded he encounters. The author never became indifferent to the suffering he sees on most of his missions. Instead he generates an internal fire, a fierce resolve that lets him fly sortie after sortie, regardless of the danger or the fatigue.

On one mission, vividly depicted in the first of these two selections, Mason flies to where a Jeep had been blown up by a crude Vietcong mine, a howitzer round buried in the road and fired remotely. Mason has to land in front of the mangled Jeep, praying that his landing site is not mined, knowing that the same VC who blew up the Jeep are probably watching him through open gun sights. He then supervises the loading of two terribly wounded men and the battered remains of four others. He writes: "A grunt was crying. One of the wounded, his friend, had just died. The other was just barely alive. I wanted to fly at a thousand miles an hour."

Mason's writing carries us through the swirl of combat at a thousand miles an hour. It also makes us stop and think about the bravery of the men who had an impossible job to do, and did it, regardless of danger, equity or reward. There was very little "chicken" in Mason and his colleagues, but a great deal of "hawk."

W.J.B.

LA DRANG VALLEY. At six the next morning, we were back in the air for our zealous commander, whose entire air force consisted of our Huey and us.

It was a very beautiful morning for flying. I had a canteen cup of coffee with me while Riker took his turn at the controls. The coffee and the cool air cleared my mind. I felt much better after my night on the stretcher.

The day was bright. Deep-blue skies blazed over the shrub-covered hills and valleys of elephant grass. Below, on the side of one shallow hill, eroded ravines had exposed the red earth in a pattern that resembled a drawing of a tall-peaked hut, an aerial signpost set there to show us the way to the Montagnard village nestled in the jungle just a couple of miles beyond.

I sipped some coffee as we passed over the village. The familiar ground plan featured one hut in the middle of the village that was at least four times taller than its neighbors. I think this was the chief's hut. Parallel to this row of huts was another row of small cubical buildings that sat off the ground on four posts. There was one of these directly across from each dwelling. I saw these villages peeking out of the jungles and tangled hillsides all through the highlands. They seemed peacefully removed from the business at hand.

We landed at the hill and were briefed. Same routine as yesterday. The captain on the hill told us, "You gotta move the guys from this list of coordinates to this list of new coordinates." He handed me a piece of paper. "Keep your eyes open. The net is beginning to tighten up on those gooks, and they might get fidgety."

When he said "gook," I saw that dumb interpreter smiling broadly. On the way out of the tent I said, "How are you this morning?"

"Yes." He nodded.

Riker and I were pissed off about having to go out there and fly single-ship again. Where's the rest of our company? Why haven't we been relieved yet? The little sleep we got last night was not enough. We were both "off," and we were bouncing the Huey again. We finished moving the squads around by noon and returned to the hilltop for lunch and to pick up our new mission. On approach, I noticed that the kid had given up and moved his tent somewhere else. I shut down and the rotors were still turning when an aide from the tent ran out with a message.

"You got to get back up. A Jeep was just mined five klicks from here."

Reacher, who had just opened the cowling of the turbine to check something, slammed it shut as the four of us jumped back into the Huey while I lighted the fire. A medic jumped in as we got light on the skids.

The medic briefed us by talking through Reacher's microphone as we cruised over the trees at 120 knots.

"The Jeep was carrying six men from the artillery brigade. The two that were in the front seats are alive. The other four are either hurt or dead. They've got a prick-ten radio (PRC-10), so they can talk to us."

I saw the smoke ahead at the spot that matched the coordinates scribbled in ballpoint on the medic's palm. "There they are," I said.

We landed in front of the Jeep, or what was left of it. It was twisted like a child's discarded toy. The edges of the crumpled and torn metal were smoking. It had been destroyed by a howitzer round buried in the road and triggered remotely. Landing in front of the Jeep was dumb; there could be more mines. It was one of those cases where we trusted the ground guys to pick the spot. A Sergeant ran up to my door. He told me through my extended microphone that two of the guys in the back were still alive. "Should we put the dead on board?" His eyes were wide.

We nodded. They started loading up. The two wounded were unconscious, torn, bloody and gray.

One of the dead had had his right leg blown off with his pants. I didn't see the other body yet.

Some journalistic instinct struck me and I took a couple of quick pictures as the wounded were carried toward us. I got one shot of a grunt carrying a severed foot when I realized what I was doing. I stopped. It seemed like the ultimate violation of privacy. I never took another picture of wounded or dead.

I was twisted around in my seat, watching them load, directing Reacher through the intercom. The man that had lost his leg had also lost his balls. He lay naked on his back with the ragged stump of his leg pointing out the side door. A clump of dirt had stuck on the end of the splintered bone. My eyes shifted away from his groin, then back. Only the torn skin from his scrotum remained. Riker looked sick. I don't know what I looked like. I told Reacher to move him back from the door. He could fall out. The scurrying grunts tossed a foot-filled boot onto the cargo deck. Blood seeped through the torn wool sock at the top of the boot. The medic pushed it under the sling seat.

I turned around and saw a confused-looking private walking through the swirling smoke with the head of someone he knew held by the hair.

"A head? Do we have to carry a head?" I asked Riker.

The kid looked at us, and Riker nodded. He tossed it inside with the other parts. The medic looked away as he pushed the bloody head under the seat. His heel kicked the nose.

"We can't find his body. I don't think we should stay to look for it. Is his head enough?" a grunt yelled.

"Absolutely. Plenty. Let's go," Riker answered.

I flew toward Pleiku as fast as the Huey could go. Reacher called from the pocket that "One-Leg" was sliding toward the edge of the deck. I had him tell the medic, who put his foot on One-Leg's bloody groin. That kept him from sliding out, but the torn skin of the stump flapped in the wind, spraying blood along the outside of the ship and all over Reacher as he sat behind his machine gun.

A grunt was crying. One of the wounded, his friend, had just died. The other was just barely alive. I wanted to fly at a thousand miles an hour.

Riker called ahead so we could land at Camp Holloway without delay. We went by the tower like a flash and landed on the red cross near the newly set-up hospital tent. The stretcher bearers ran out to unload the cargo.

I could see that they had been busy lately. There was a pile of American bodies outside the hospital tent.

The other wounded man died.

We had lost the race.

The stretcher bearers' technique was to cross the cadaver's arms and then, with a twist, flip it off the deck onto the waiting stretcher. I watched as two specialists unloaded One-Leg. They dropped him in a grotesque heap on the canvas. The sun glinted off a gold band on his left hand. The specialists were laughing. About what, I don't know. Maybe they were so accustomed to their job that they thought this was hilarious. Maybe it was nervous laughter. Regardless, their nonchalance was too much for me. I jumped out and made them stop before they got to the tent. I braced them on the spot and yelled and yelled and yelled.

"Okay, a company from the First of the Seventh [1st Battalion, 7th Regiment, a First Cav unit] is trapped here," Shaker pointed to a spot between the Ia Drang River and the Chu Pong massif on the big map in our briefing tent. "Charlie has them completely pinned down. The grunts say that Charlie can't overrun them, but they have some bad wounded to get out." Shaker paused a moment while he checked his notes. "I'm going to take five ships out tonight. There's no moon, so the darkness will be our cover." He stopped to suck on another cigarette. He smoked even more than me. Chain smoking made him look nervous, but I don't think he was. I think he was so intense because he was the only black platoon leader in our battalion. He took another puff and began reading the names of the crews and their ship numbers. I didn't listen too carefully because I knew that Riker and I were going to sit this one out tonight and get some rest. Then I heard, ". . . and Riker and Mason in eight-seven-nine."

"What?" Riker exclaimed. Shaker seemed not to notice.

Shaker looked at his watch. "It's 1730 now. Eat some chow and be on the flight line ready to crank at 2000 hours." He turned to leave, but stopped. "Those of you not on the mission tonight will stay in the company area on standby." As he left, the crowd broke up, and I heard rumblings of disappointment about having to hang around. Apparently there were some good bars in Pleiku.

Riker looked as unhappy as I felt. It seemed that our earlier debriefing had fallen on deaf ears. We had got back from our marathon mission with Grunt Six just two hours before. Shaker knew we had already put in eight hours of flight time today and twenty hours the day before. What was he trying to do, kill us?

"No, I'm not trying to kill you." I had caught up with Shaker on a sidewalk in the adviser compound. "Mason, you're new to our unit and fresh out of flight school, and I'm responsible for your training. You need all the night flying you can get."

"But—"

"You got some sleep last night, right?"

"Yes."

"So be ready to go at 2000 hours." He left before I could even get started. I wanted to tell him how miserable I felt, how tired I was. But I got angry instead.

Fresh out of flight school, my ass! I said to myself as I walked back to the mess tent. Need night time, hey? Want to see if I can hack it? Well, let's just see if I can hack it! I now had a goal that superseded survival.

The NVA allowed us to land without opposition. They even waited for the crew chiefs and gunners to get out to load the wounded. When they were sure we were on ground and busy, they opened up. The thing that saved us was the moonless night. As I sat in the cockpit, I remember not being able to see the two Hueys in front of me at all. All our position lights were off. The only light was the faint-red glow of our own instrument panel—until Charlie started shooting. Bright-red tracers streamed in from the dark tree line at the front. They couldn't see us, so they sprayed the whole LZ indiscriminately. The grunts scattered and started firing back.

Shaker yelled, "Yellow flight, take off!" Then he went. He didn't realize that his crew chief was still outside trying to get to another wounded grunt. Stranded, the crew chief was going to be a grunt for a few hours.

We had got four on board before Shaker yelled. The two ships behind us were empty.

We took off single file into the tracers. The NVA were firing at our noise, and they were hitting. From where I sat, it looked pretty bad. I was on the controls and veered quickly left and right as I took off, thinking I could actually dodge the bullets. As I dodged, the world became distant. There was no sound. The burning red globes streamed past me. I banked hard to the left as soon as I saw the dim horizon, and the red death left me and licked up, looking for the others.

The sound came back and I heard the chatter on the radio. Four of the five ships had been hit. We were the exception. Amazingly, no one had been hurt.

There were still eight wounded to get out back at the LZ, along with Shaker's crew chief.

We flew back to Pleiku and dropped off the wounded. En route, Shaker instructed two ships to join him on the return flight. Riker and I were chosen to try our luck again.

Back over the LZ an hour later, Shaker was told by the grunts that the LZ was too hot, so he elected to land about two miles away and wait.

I remember being so keyed up with adrenaline that I wanted to go back in, regardless. I even thought Shaker was chicken.

We stayed strapped in our seats with the Hueys shut down. The clearing was pitch black. This LZ had been taken earlier in the day and was supposed to be secure, but no one believed it. We stayed put.

The adrenaline high I had produced during the action was now wearing off. I sat in my seat watching little white spots drift in front of me. I felt drained of my strength. The undefined world of my dark surroundings mingled with my black thoughts. Somehow this has to stop, I thought. I can't think straight. If the VC don't get me I will. What's Shaker thinking of sitting here in the middle of nowhere? Riker and I did not talk.

I heard a small observation helicopter (H-13) over the spot where the trapped men waited, a scout from our 1/9 Cav squadron. I imagined the pilot bristling with Western .45s and cowboy boots, having a waxed mustache and a firmly set jaw, glaring down into the darkness, looking for signs of the NVA. Theoretically, he would fly low and slow, so the VC would shoot at him. Then, if he survived, he could locate them for the artillery or gunships. Fourteen of the original twenty pilots of that scout unit would be killed in less than six months.

He circled, invisibly. There was no reaction from the NVA. He grew tired of this passive search, and either he, or his crew chief started shooting down into the jungle with a hand-held machine gun. His tracers formed a tongue of flame arcing down from nowhere. That worked. After a few of these bursts, the NVA opened on him. Tracers leapt out of the jungle to a spot where they guessed he might be. When they fired, he stopped. They had just given away their position. Minutes later mortars *whumped* in from somewhere near where we sat. They kept it up for almost five minutes. The whirlybird went back to check it out. He fired into the jungle again and flew even lower than last time, but he could not draw fire. Either the machine gun had been wiped out or the enemy had gotten smart. We would have to find out which.

Shaker sent his gunner back through the blackness along the parked ships to tell us it was going to be one ship at a time: Crank up and wait, and monitor the radios until he got out.

We waited while both Shaker and the next ship got in and out successfully. We were last.

The approach was eerie because I did it without lights. The large landing light and even the small position lights would make excellent targets. The machine gun was apparently out of action, but the grunts were now saying there was some sniper fire from the tree line. I was on the controls, and I decided to keep going. I talked on the radio to a grunt who promised to switch on a flashlight when I got closer. I lined up on the general area and made a gentle descent into the darkness. The grunt on the radio talked me down.

"Okay, now left. You're doing great. No sweat. Keep it coming like you are. Let down a little. I think you should go more right. Okay, you should see the flashlight. Can you see the light?"

"Roger." The dull glow of an army flashlight with a special filter on it popped into existence below me, making the man holding it a target.

A single point of light in pitch blackness doesn't tell you much. You could be upside down for all you know. Without other references to compare it with, the light seemed to drift around in the blackness. I kept my eyes moving, not staring at the light. Disorientation was a common occurrence at moments like this. It was never clear to me just how I did manage, but the ship touched down in front of the flashlight; the skids hit the ground gently before I realized that I was that close. Apparently we got no sniper fire on the way in. Of course, I would know about it only if we got hit or if the grunts told us.

We picked up all the remaining wounded, which amounted to two stretcher cases and one walking. The guy with the flashlight jumped on board, too, just before we took off.

I was very cautious on takeoff and avoided the old machine-gun position by making a sharp turn as we cleared the trees. The Huey was low on fuel and therefore light. I stayed low for a while to accelerate and then pulled the cyclic back hard to swoop up into the night sky. I switched on our position lights so that any other aircraft could see us, and 3,000 feet and thirty seconds later we saw fifty-caliber tracers sailing up, glowing as big as baseballs. I switched off the lights, and when we became invisible again, they stopped firing.

Holidays. Nate and Resler and I went to town one morning. There was nothing up that day, so we hung around in the bars and watched the girls. Nate claimed he was immune to Viet clap, so he had most of the fun.

Something did come up, but since we weren't there, the company left without us. We got back early in the afternoon to a ghost camp. Everyone except the Bobbsey Creeps were gone.

"Big battle going on just north of Lima," said Owens. "Where were you guys? The major is pissed. Did you have a pass? It's hot out there. Really, the major is really pissed."

Nate thought the time was right to open the canned ham he had been saving for Christmas. We had a quiet party. The ham was good.

Just after dawn, Leese busted in through the door flap. "The New Guy was killed."

"What?" said Gary.

"The New Guy. You know, the replacement. He got shot through the head. Hey, you guys, get ready to get out there."

I wondered if I would amount to that much of an utterance someday. "Mason got shot through the head. Hey, you guys, get ready to go out there."

"What's going on?" I said.

"It's hot," said Leese. "Lotta automatic fire. All in same area where we've been farting around for the last two weeks. Yesterday Charlie decided to fight. It's already hot again this morning. You guys are supposed to crew the next two ships coming back. Mine is fucked. Nate, you and I take the next ship, and Bob and Gary the one after that. Okay?"

There was an hour between Leese and Nate's departure and the arrival of our ship. Resler and I were alone in our corner of the tent. I smoked. Resler cracked his knuckles.

"There's some islands out about twenty miles from Qui Nhon," said Gary.

"I know."

"Twenty miles away. Completely uninhabited, too." "How do you know that?" I said.

"I've heard."

"Terrific."

"Do you ever think about quitting?" Gary asked.

"Sometimes."

"Me, too. Sometimes. Guess that makes us chickens."

"Maybe. But we do go fly, don't we? That's got to make up for feeling chicken."

"Yeah, I guess it does." He paused. "And when I'm flying the assaults, I start feeling brave, almost comfortable, in the middle of it all. Like a hawk, maybe."

"I do, too. When I'm in the middle of it. But times like now, I'd quit at the slightest excuse. So what am I? A chicken or a hawk?"

"You're a chickenhawk." Gary smiled.

"Yeah." There was silence. Yes, I thought. We're both scared out of our minds. It felt like we were near the end of our wait on death row.

"Hey, guys, it's your turn." Wendall ducked into the tent. The palm-tree isle, the bronze nubiles, popped out of existence. "The crew chief is patching some holes, the ship will be flyable in just a minute." Wendall looked kind of pale. "The old man wants you to join the gaggle at Lima. They've got some more missions to fly today. I hope it's better for you guys."

The crew chief, along with the maintenance officer had inspected the ship. The holes in the tail boom were a concern because the bullets could have gone through the tail-rotor drive tube or the control cables. They had not. The crew chief covered the holes with green tape that almost matched the olive-drab skin. It was now our ship.

The sky, as if on cue, was overcast. At the An Khe pass Gary had to drop to within fifty feet of the road to maintain visibility. We landed at Lima.

"What's that all about on the road?" I asked Connors. As we circled Lima on our approach, we had noticed a crowd of men around a big pile of something covered with canvas next to an overturned mule.

"A grunt mule driver lost control and flipped over."

"Was he hurt?"

"No. Killed."

"You and Resler are Red Four," said Leese. He hurried back toward the front of the gaggle. Lima was crawling with activity. Troopers moved around in small groups, looking for their assigned ships. A few Hueys were out over sling loads, hitching up. A Chinook made an approach slinging in a fat black fuel bladder from the Golf Course.

"Shall I put my men on board, sir?" a Cav sergeant asked me.

"Yeah, Sergeant. Let them get on." I looked forward at the other squads moving toward their ships. "We're leaving pretty soon."

He turned. "Move it!" They were in place in about fifteen seconds, I think.

It was a monster gaggle—forty or more ships—the kind I hated the most. And we were flying the four position again. We would have to fly hard to keep up with an outside turn, and flare like hell when the gaggle turned our way. Plus, the ship was a dog. When we took off, she hung down in the turbulence of the choppers in front of us, straining her poor guts out. We caught up to the gaggle at mission altitude and watched the prep going on. Smoke trailed in long streamers drifting off to the west. Air-force jockeys streaked away back to their base, their job done. Our gunships worked the area with their rockets and flex guns. Gary flew, so I just watched the show and smoked a cigarette. Kinda like being at a movie. The grunts behind me were screaming at each other over the cacophony of the ship, smiling, laughing, smoking cigarettes, scared out of their brains. The ships in the gaggle rose and fell on the sea of air. Formations always looked sloppy when you were in them because no two ships were ever at the same altitude. From the ground you got a flat view of the V, and it looked better. One of the noises on the radio was the Colonel.

"Yellow Four. Pull in closer. You call that a formation?" The Colonel was flying above us, being a colonel. There's a reason why they do that, we said. It's from the word itself: colon(el), or asshole. They do exactly what you would expect them to.

"Guns ready?" Gary asked. We were now dropping fast, having crossed the initial point, a meager hut near a tall hedgerow that marked the beginning of the final leg of the assault. The LZ was two miles away.

"Ready."

"Ready."

"Fire at my order only, unless you see something obvious. Don't shoot into the huts."

"Yes, sir."

"Yes, sir."

Can't fire into the huts. If you fired into the huts, you might kill a VC.

As we swooped toward the ground for the low-level run, I put my hand gently on the cyclic; my feet rode the pedals; my left hand touched the collective.

"Flare."

Fifty feet off the ground, Gary was doing well. He flipped the tail past a few trees just when I thought he'd hit them. The gaggle mushed and bounded into the LZ. The troopers leapt out firing.

"Yellow One, it's too hot ahead of you. Recommend you pedal-turn and go back out the way you came." That was one of the Dukes, the gunships making runs at something at the far end of the LZ. The guys up front were yelling that there was a lot of shooting going on, but I couldn't see any back our way.

"Roger. Flight, we're going out the way we came. Wait your turn." The flight leader lifted to a high hover and turned to fly back over us. Each ship in its turn leapt up and flew back over us. By the time it was our turn, the first ships were already calling in hit reports. As we joined up, the ship ahead of us was hit, showering bits of Plexiglas back on us.

Next I heard *tick-tick-tick,* and new bullet holes appeared in the Plexiglas over our heads. Gary pulled full power trying to get higher, but the ship was a dog even when empty, so we lagged behind the others. *Tick.* Somewhere in the air frame.

At 1,000 feet or so I lit a cigarette and contemplated the new holes. Bad place for 'em. It'll leak if it rains.

We didn't make it back to Lima. We were pulled out with the other three ships in the Red flight for a couple of emergency extractions. Gary and I followed Farris and Kaiser in Red Three to get some wounded out of a hot LZ. The other two ships went somewhere else.

Farris orbited a couple of times to make sure there was no firing going on. We were supposed to wait until the grunts secured the LZ.

"All clear, Red Three." I heard gunshots in the background as the trooper talked on the radio to Farris. Farris did, too.

"You're sure?"

"Affirmative, Red Three. You're clear to land." Of course, he was lying. I would've lied, too, in the same position.

As we made our approach, Farris took the spot I was headed for, so I had to fly a hundred feet past him. I landed in a grassy spot in front of a hedgerow. I saw troopers low-crawling all over the place.

"Secure, my ass," said Gary.

Two bent-over men ran toward us carrying a stretcher. Sand sprayed out of the grass near them, and they went down. The body in the litter shifted like a doll.

"Fire from the front," I radioed to Farris.

The stretcher bearers got back up and made it to the side door, where the crew chief quickly jumped out and grabbed one end of the litter and shoved it across the deck. Another few rounds hit the dirt in front of us. I looked at the radio antenna of the grunt leader swinging around behind the hedgerow. "Fucking liar."

Another litter had been hauled to our other door, and the gunner was out helping. We were locked to the ground. Farris called that he was leaving. "Come on! Come on!" I yelled back between the seats. Two walking wounded rolled on board. The grunt leader stood up for a second and then hit the dirt. All I heard was the whine of our turbine. No shots. Just little puffs of sand in the short grass. At the hedgerow, a man held a thumbs-up. He pointed to a man at his knees and shook his head. For the first time, I noticed the body. Of course it was a body.

Strands of intestines had followed the bullets out of his guts and were lying across his abdomen. He could wait a little longer.

I was up. Pedal-turn. Nose down. *Tick*. Go. *Tick*. Climb.

The four wounded lived.

We spent a rainy night back at good old Lima. The new bullet holes leaked.

16

Wabash Cannonballs

from 100 MISSIONS NORTH
by Kenneth H. Bell

This thrilling story of a Republic F-105 sweep over North Vietnam is an accurate representation of the terrible contrasts in that war. On the one hand there were the combat crew members, professionals, aggressive and determined to do their duty regardless of the personal sacrifice involved. On the other hand, there was the mindless interference from the White House, from the Pentagon, and from higher headquarters, interference that made the combat pilots' job almost impossible and sometimes resulted in punishing aircrews for positive results.

In this excerpt, Ken Bell puts us in the cockpit of his Republic F-105 Thunderchief during a combat mission that almost ended in disaster; he was saved by the heroic actions of a Boeing KC-135 tanker crew who put their lives—and their careers—in jeopardy to save him.

In one of the great ironies of warfare, the strategic campaign against North Vietnam was undertaken by tactical fighter bombers, while the tactical campaign in South Vietnam employed hundreds of daily sorties by Boeing B-52s, strategic bombers converted to iron bomb droppers. For much of the war the great preponderance of missions against the North were flown in F-105s, the famous Thuds. The aircraft was originally intended as a supersonic long-range nuclear bomber to be employed by the Tactical Air

Command. In Vietnam, it proved to be the fastest, toughest strike fighter of the conflict, and it suffered the greatest rate of loss because it was sent in mindless raids against heavily defended targets.

In Bell's excerpt, a spell of miserable weather had frustrated all attempts to locate a downed colleague, code-named Tomahawk Four. Bell and his colleague, Ted Tolman, working with the redoubtable Colonel Jacksel Broughton, created a plan that would give them another chance to search for the downed pilot, Joe Abbott, and at the same time perhaps force the recently quiescent MiGs to fight. A flight of F-105s would be launched against a perennial target, a transformer site near Hanoi, while another flight would be used to provide MiG cover. If the weather broke, they might be able to find their downed friend. If they did not locate him, they would at least have a chance to attack the target and perhaps lure MiGs into combat.

The search was conducted at low altitudes, where the F-105s burned fuel at a furious rate; eventually their fuel state reached the point that if the MiGs showed up, they would not have enough fuel to engage.

Bell's account of his rendezvous with his tanker, White Anchor 66, is gripping. By the time the tanker arrived, deep in hostile territory, he was down to two hundred pounds of fuel, within seconds of a flameout. Just as he moved into position to take on fuel—he flamed out. Now Bell, the tanker pilot, and the boomer had to attempt the seemingly impossible: refueling a 105 that had been transformed into a heavyweight glider.

They pulled it off, to the credit of all concerned, and when Bell got back he wanted to put the crew in for a commendation, with a special recommendation of an Air Medal for the boom operator, whose skill had saved the day at literally the last second. Bell's request was refused, for the tanker crew had "overextended themselves beyond the limits set in their operating procedures."

Once again, it was Headquarters versus the combat troops.

W.J.B.

In the early morning hours of 3 May 1967, we were tired and frustrated. We had made repeated attempts to destroy the transformer site near Hanoi, with only limited success. We had taken some cutting losses in the process and had seen the attempts to rescue four of our best crews fail when they should have succeeded. Our combination MiG sweep and rescue mission, as exciting and refreshing as it was, had been foiled by the weather, and hope of rescuing Tomahawk Four was growing dimmer by the hour.

Our frustration continued. After hours of planning, the morning MiG sweep mission was delayed only to be ordered to go at the last minute. As expected, the weather was terrible, and the MiGs sat it out safely on the ground, so the strike force returned to try again in the afternoon. Ted Tolman and I were in charge of all of the special flight planning, and we were worn out but willing to try anything that might work to get us off of top-dead-center.

When Colonel Broughton landed we put our heads together and came up with an interesting plan. We would use one flight of F-105s to provide our own MiG cover on a mission that would have the appearance of another strike against the transformer site. If the weather broke and we got through, so much the better. If not, we could divert the strike flights to alternate targets and use the cover flight to locate the position of Tomahawk Four and troll for MiGs simultaneously. In either event, we would have one flight of clean F-105s poised and ready for a MiG fight if the North Vietnamese adhered to their operational pattern.

Ted and I went to work planning the details while Colonel Broughton talked to the boss and Seventh Air Force. After a few last minute changes and a flurry of phone calls, headquarters reluctantly agreed to let us fly the mission.

Colonel Broughton led the cover flight as the force commander. I was flying his wing, and Ted Tolman was Three with Paul Sheehy on his wing as number Four. We were Wabash flight leading five other flights, tired but eager for a fight. The mission code word for MiGs was Hurdy Gurdy, and the Wabash cannonballs were armed and ready to face the music, red eyed and grinning.

Halfway down the ridge, we had to abort the strike mission because of bad weather. On command, the force turned in place to go to their alternate targets. Wabash flight headed for the foothills, eager to look for MiGs and make a last, desperate attempt to locate Tomahawk Four. Joe Abbott had been down for almost three days, and his trail was surely getting cold and lonely.

When we reached the foothills, Wabash flight split into two elements and started to fly a racetrack search pattern. After several turns, we received a very weak beeper signal that responded to our initial command but faded quickly. We continued the search for almost thirty minutes without success—no beeper and no MiG interceptors. We had worked our way down to low altitude and I was burning fuel like crazy. I was tempted to suggest that we concentrate on finding MiGs but I kept my mouth shut. Finding Joe Abbott was important but I sensed that we were flailing away at low altitude for nothing.

Wabash Lead sent Three and Four back to the tanker for fuel. It was necessary to split our coverage in order to continue the search effort. Without the support of the element we were more vulnerable to attack and far less effective as MiG hunters. Lead was determined to find Joe Abbott or MiGs, and I was obliged to hang on and do my job as a wingman. I kept glancing at the fuel gauge and wondering what we were going to do if we did get tapped by MiGs. Low on fuel, we would be asking for a fight we couldn't finish.

"Wabash Two, fuel state?" Lead asked.

"Roger, Wabash Two is bingo-minus-five [2,500 pounds of fuel remaining, about twenty-five minutes of flying time]. Suggest we punch tanks and save some drag, over." Without our drop tanks we would not be very useful for subsequent rescue cover, but I sensed that we needed to save fuel in case we ran into trouble looking for a tanker.

"Roger, drop tanks, ready now," and away they went to the foothills below. Both the airplane and I breathed a sigh of relief.

Lead was cutting it close and I was getting nervous. When I reached 2,000 pounds of fuel remaining I called it, and we started back to the tanker. With luck, I could make an emergency recovery at Udorn if we missed the tanker, but I didn't have enough fuel to screw around in the process. When Wabash Lead asked for a vector to the closest tanker there was total silence. Suddenly, not a soul could hear us and we were left to fend for ourselves. Even Wabash Three and Four had apparently disappeared and were silent.

We started an immediate climb and headed for the Red Anchor refueling rendezvous point that had been assigned to us during the mission briefing. I had 1,500 pounds of fuel remaining, and the fuel flow meter indicated that I was burning 6,000 pounds per hour, 100 pounds per minute. At that rate, we had about ten minutes to wake up the airborne control net and find a tanker able to help us.

Wabash Lead switched to Guard Channel, and we turned our transponder beacons to the emergency squawk position. Suddenly, we had more help than we could use, including some from our own Number Three man.

"Wabash Lead, this is Three. We're outbound from the tankers heading zero-four-five for the search area. Have you at twelve o'clock on a DF steer, over."* We were heading southwest so Ted's report was encouraging. But we couldn't see the tankers, and our range to them was uncertain.

I checked our position, and we were over the Plaine des Jarres in Laos, the headquarters of the enemy Pathet Lao Army. My fuel was dropping steadily. At just below 1,000 pounds, I reported my fuel state to the leader. He wasn't exactly fat either; he only had 200 pounds more than I did.

We started receiving urgent radio calls from Red Crown and Ethan Charlie, two airborne command posts; from Brigham Control; and from points as far away as Udorn Tower in Thailand. Several tankers also tuned in trying to help us, but the net effect was zero. Lead finally lost his cool and gave a stinging all-points lecture about radio discipline, and the radio got quiet quickly. I was trying to save fuel, but my gauge was knocking on 500 pounds.

"Wabash Lead, Two is at five hundred pounds and hurting," I called with all the cool I could muster. My call prompted another open-mike lecture from Lead on the stupidity of two perfectly good F-105s going down over Laos because someone at a radar console couldn't get their thumb out of their butt long enough to find us a tanker.

White Anchor 66. "Wabash flight, White Anchor Six-Six has your beacon at ten o'clock, forty miles. We're heading north at twenty-four

---

*Radio Direction Finder. It uses a needle in the cockpit to point to the transmitting radio and show a bearing to the station.

thousand, turn left to zero-niner-zero degrees and you should have us at your one to two o'clock position and closing, over."

We turned and started a gradual descent as Wabash Lead froze the airways again, "EVERYONE EXCEPT WHITE ANCHOR SIX-SIX SHUT UP!"

I only had 200 pounds of fuel, and I was looking so hard for the tanker that my eyes were burning. "Wabash flight, White Anchor Six-Six has a visual. You're slightly high at twelve o'clock, less than five miles and closing fast, over."

We crossed over the tanker and Lead started a steep turn to the north to join-up, but the tanker was slower and we overran him. When I finally spotted the tanker, he was at our seven o'clock position and 1,000 feet below us. I had to do a high yo-yo maneuver to keep him in sight. My fuel gauge was bumping zero, and I could feel the engine beginning to surge. I was within seconds of a flameout.

I pulled the nose up and over in a tight left turn to try to drop in behind the tanker. I moved the throttle but there was no response, the engine was spooling down at 65 percent and I was out of fuel. I punched my mike button, "White Anchor, toboggan. Go down, *Go Down*. I'm flamed out!" I felt helpless. I was still overrunning the tanker slightly and too far ahead of him to drop down into the trail position. It was difficult to stay above him and keep him in sight. I was desperate, "Come on fellows, give me a chance and toboggan, get the nose *down!*"

Finally, the tanker pitched over and started to accelerate. I eased down into the refueling position behind him. For a split second, I was in perfect position and steady behind the boom. I held my breath and said a prayer.

The boomer began to align the refueling boom nozzle with my receptacle just as the tanker began to inch away slowly. I thought, "Come on, boomer. Stab me now." The tanker slowed down slightly and the gap between us stabilized. Split seconds seemed like hours, and I felt myself tense up all over.

"Looking good, Wabash Two. Hold her steady, boom coming out now. Boomer has a contact and *connect*, over!" The nozzle moved into the receptacle, and the locking latches closed with a sharp clunk. I almost went limp.

The boom was locked into the receptacle, and my aircraft was being towed as the tanker began to pass fuel. "Hallelujah, praise the Lord and that beautiful boomer," I shouted out loud to myself. "We did it!"

When fuel started showing on the fuel gauge, I went through the air start procedure, and the engine came back to life quickly. At 500 pounds, I hit the boom disconnect switch and moved out to the side to let Wabash Lead have a turn. Within seconds, he was in position and taking fuel. After Lead got enough fuel to make it home, I moved in again for a top-off and we dropped down and headed for Takhli.

The feeling that came over me as we left White Anchor 66 was a combination of embarrassment, joy, pride, relief, thanks, and humility. I was so proud of the tanker that I could have kissed the whole crew on both cheeks, especially the boomer. They had stuck their necks way out for us and done a superb job under enormous pressure. The fuel they gave us reduced their own reserve and put them on the ragged edge of making it back safely.

"White Anchor Six-Six, this is Wabash. Good show, old buddy. Leaving your frequency. Thanks a bunch, see you at Channel Forty-Three. Wabash go button three and check in, over!"

"Wabash Two, roger."

The force of what we had done hit me hallway home as we were descending for a landing. In a way, I felt foolish because we had really done it to ourselves, but I was relieved that I wouldn't have to explain the unnecessary loss of an airplane.* The thought of spending time as a prisoner of war because I had failed to speak up when I knew we were putting ourselves in crack was enough to make my skin crawl. "Shake it off and count your blessings," I thought. "Skill and cunning had won again, but only by the skin on my rosy red ass."

We tried to submit a commendation for the crew of White Anchor 66, with a special recommendation for an Air Medal for the boomer, but their detachment commander discouraged us. I was shocked when he explained that the recommendation might result in a reprimand rather than a commendation because it would reveal the fact that the crew had overextended themselves beyond the limits set in their operating procedures.

The detachment commander apologetically suggested that we limit our thanks to a pat on the back and perhaps a personal letter of appreciation in the interest of keeping the episode out of official Strategic Air

---

*The aircraft, F-105D S N 62-4329, was subsequently lost by the 354th TFS during a crash landing at Takhli on 5 October 1967.

Command (SAC) review channels. It was hard to believe but we decided to think it over.

A few days later, I discussed the matter with Colonel Broughton, and we decided to submit the commendation anyway. We were convinced that the crew deserved official recognition, and we were willing to test the wrath of SAC headquarters to see that they got it. I figured they would appreciate our effort even if they did get their knuckles rapped, and the process might serve to air out a system that sounded a bit too autocratic and stuffy in the first place.

We submitted the commendations but they disappeared in the system. Suffice it to say, the courage and resourcefulness of White Anchor 66 over the Plaine des Jarres that afternoon will live on in the annals of war as a memorable accomplishment.

17

The Bombing Campaign and Dick Wyman

from OVER THE BEACH: THE AIR WAR IN VIETNAM

by Zalin Grant

The Vietnam air war was the evidentiary ideal for critics of aerial bombardment in search of proof for their theory that bombing does not succeed and, if anything, strengthens the enemy's resolve. In the first of two excerpts from Zalin Grant's book, in which he deftly uses the naval aviators aboard the USS *Oriskany* as a window on the whole of the Vietnam air war, this theory is given credence. As is discussed, the United States, an acknowledged technological leader and military superpower, made little progress in stanching a far less sophisticated adversary despite years of attacks from the air.

The mathematical models, embraced by Defense Secretary Robert S. McNamara, that forecast the collapse of the enemy upon the delivery of an allocated tonnage of bombs, failed to come close to catching the essence of the real situation. Something in the calculations was missing altogether. In his obsession with statistics and probabilities, McNamara arrogantly overlooked the human factor, arguably the single most important element in any warfare analysis.

Indeed, Grant points out that the North Vietnamese were exceedingly motivated, willing to sacrifice anything in the struggle to repulse a foreign power, to die rather than live under a regime imposed by outsiders. Although Grant does not draw the parallel, this same sense of purpose was arguably not unlike the impassioned efforts mounted by the American people when threatened on various occasions with foreign domination. Putting aside the venality and ruthlessness of North Vietnam's leaders, perhaps it is a refreshing thought that the people of a poor and backward country can outlast a mighty power. This idea might offer sustenance to a just David among the community of nations confronting an evil Goliath.

As told elsewhere in Grant's book, the Vietnam air war was prosecuted in the most idiotic of ways. Rules of engagement, imposed by politicians far removed from the heat of battle, were next to suicidal for the American airmen charged with implementing the tasking orders. Late in the war, with White House frustrations peaking, the game plan was radically changed for a short time in Linebacker II, a high-intensity bombing operation unlike any other during the war. Many American airmen thought that Linebacker II, which profoundly impacted the North Vietnamese, ought to have been the type of air campaign the United States waged from the beginning.

With the success of Linebacker II, the debate over the efficacy of the Vietnam air war took on a new twist. Some observers to this day suggest that victory would have been attainable, and much sooner, if airpower had been applied consistently in such a manner. Others adhere to the contention that the will of a determined people transcends the power of bombs. Both sides in the debate have apt historical examples to use in support of their respective arguments. And the debate rages on.

In the second excerpt from his book, Grant offers a first-person account by a carrier-borne fighter pilot, and the reader gets as close as the written form allows to the soul of this rare breed. We fly along on a spine-tingling dogfight against a wildly gyrating MiG that smashes into the ground after being savaged by a Sidewinder air-to-air missile. Soon afterward, the victorious lieutenant, a hero for the time being, finds himself reluctantly having to escort a couple of congressmen who have junketed to the *Oriskany.* The real-life protagonist would much rather have been flying than catering to the clownish characters from Washington. During the congressmen's tour, the naval aviator hears his admiral give a gloomy assessment of the war, confirming suspicions he has had for some time.

Through it all, what comes across is a sense that the airman's calling is the camaraderie shared with his fellow pilots. There was the exhilaration of flying all out, on the very edge of the envelope, along with the depressing prospect of losing the war. Yet, nothing altered the constant of the squadron, its men, his brother fighter pilots. It is telling that when the matter of a medal for the MiG victory was broached, the airman responded that he did not care one way or the other if the Navy awarded him a decoration. He was aboard ship with his squadron mates.

P.H.

THE BOMBING CAMPAIGN. With the buildup of the American nuclear arsenal after World War II, theories on how to wage a war took on an increasingly abstract coloration. Nuclear strategy was based almost entirely on psychological considerations. No one wanted an atomic war—that was madness. But America's enemies had to know that it possessed the means of annihilation, a credible retaliatory threat, to protect the country's security. It was not surprising, then, that McNamara's theory on how to wage a conventional war against North Vietnam was a modification of the nuclear strategy. America would give the North Vietnamese an example of what it could do to them and they would be cowed by the possibilities of such overwhelming power.

But the difference between an iron bomb and a nuclear weapon was the difference between extensive destruction and total annihilation, and a threat was only credible if the threatened believed they could not survive the consequences with acceptable losses. The North Vietnamese based their strategy not on abstract theory but on past experience. They had not the slightest doubt that America was the most powerful country in the world. But the French, too, had been powerful, and the Vietnamese had won by pursuing a military strategy based on nothing more complicated than endurance. They had outlasted the French.

Two days before the air war began on March 2, 1965, the North Vietnamese leadership began methodically to prepare the country for the bombing. They had three factors to consider. First, the safety of the population must be given priority and, to the degree possible, the security of the industrial base; second, the transportation network had to be kept open so that the war could be supported in the South; and third, an antiaircraft system should be developed not only for protection but also to make it costly for the Americans to wage the air war. A decision was made to evacuate nonessential personnel from Hanoi and Haiphong. Foreign observers who were persuaded America was fighting a war narrow in scope thought the evacuation order was an overreaction on the part of the North Vietnamese, or perhaps was being used as a psychological step to prepare the population for war, but the Central Committee of the Communist Party acted as though the destruction of the cities was a foregone conclusion and told the people to get ready for a long war. *The bomb shelter is your second home* became a national slogan. A goal was set to provide three shelter spaces per person. The North Vietnamese claimed later to have dug twenty-one million bomb shelters. Whether the figure was correct or not, Hanoi and Haiphong quickly took on the look of a concrete beehive. Hundreds of thousands of circular one-man shelters were spaced at six- to thirty-two-feet intervals along almost every road. Two and a half feet in diameter, about five feet deep, the shelters were made of prestressed concrete, with two-inch-thick lids that were left ajar for quick occupancy. Half-buried communal shelters, made of cement and brick with roofs of tin and earth, were scattered throughout the country. Shelter upkeep was added to other Sunday housekeeping chores. The manholes filled with rain during the monsoon season and had to be drained. Larger shelters had to be swept and cleaned, and repaired after near misses.

The population's reaction to the air-raid sirens varied with time and the changing bombing patterns. At first, loudspeakers placed on street corners gave a running commentary about the attack, and air-raid wardens were there to make sure each person was in his proper shelter. But as months passed and the bombing became routine, few bothered to run to the shelters until the antiaircraft guns started booming and bombs were whistling down. The wardens urged people not to mill around or sit on the ground to watch the fireworks, but without much success until the heavy bombing of the cities began in 1967, and then the alerts were taken seriously.

If North Vietnam's long-war strategy were to succeed, it was imperative to keep the traffic flowing to the South. Needed was a massive repair system. Youth brigades were established for the day-to-day repair of roads and the building of alternate routes to be used as detours. Teenagers, boys and girls, worked at night, filling in bomb craters with dirt carried in bamboo-woven baskets, painting white posts along the sides of roads to guide truck drivers who moved without lights, being careful to defuse the delayed-action bombs that had been dropped to interrupt their work.

The kids could handle filling in craters, but bombed-out bridges presented a more serious matter. North Korea had faced the same problem fifteen years earlier in its war with the Americans; and North Korean advisers soon arrived to teach the Vietnamese six ways to move a truck across a river after a bombing attack. The simplest bridge was constructed of bundles of bamboo and stalks tied together to float on water, with wooden planks laid across and lashed to the stalks, something that cost practically nothing and could be replaced with little effort. A more sophisticated version was built by bringing together flat-bottomed canal boats, about three feet wide and sixteen feet long, and laying a roadway of bamboo and boards across them. These pontoon-type bridges were hidden along riverbanks by day to prevent their being bombed and brought out at night. Rivers that were wide and fast-flowing were often crossed by ferry boats operating from a system of piers and heavy cables. Materials to repair bridges and ferries were stockpiled nearby. Seldom did traffic stop longer than a day or two after an attack.

This did not mean the bombing was not exacting a heavy toll. By 1966, it took about five hours to drive the crater-filled obstacle course that the sixty-five miles of road between Hanoi and Haiphong had become, as opposed to two hours before the bombing began. A Western reporter estimated that four days were needed, driving only at night, traveling at a speed of ten miles an hour, to traverse the four hundred and fifty miles from one end of North Vietnam to the other. With delays caused by fresh craters and recently destroyed bridges, the trip could take much longer.

Repairing a railroad was harder than fixing a highway. The North Vietnamese decided to concentrate on keeping the railway that ran from Hanoi to China in good working order. With the help of Chinese laborers, they built a third rail into China, so that rail cars adapted to the Chinese standard gauge could move directly onto the narrow North Vietnamese tracks. To compensate for the damage inflicted on the railroad, they expanded their already elaborate inland waterway system. Farmers were told to clear rivers to a depth of five feet, so that shallow barges could use them, and later the call went out for a fourteen-foot dredging of certain rivers. Barges became a frequent target for bombing. From 1965 to 1968, U.S. pilots reported they destroyed or damaged 23,978 "water vehicles"; and in early 1967 they began seeding the country's rivers with mines.

With so many planes daily flying overhead on armed reconnaissance missions, as the Americans called them, camouflage became an art form. Drivers attached branches, palm fronds, and banana leaves to the roofs of their buses and trucks. Jeeps were covered with a fishnet in which leaves were inserted. Saplings were pulled over and tied to conceal pontoon bridges. Few jobs were as dangerous as that of truck driver. Trucks traveled alone or in small groups to avoid being spotted from the air. Besides having mechanical breakdowns, they frequently got lost because of detours and the lack of signs on bombed roads. But the material continued to reach the South. If it couldn't be moved by truck, barge, or by train, then a bicycle with a bamboo frame attached to carry six hundred pounds could be pushed a distance of one hundred and seventy-five miles in eighteen days.

North Vietnam's limited industrial base was made up of about a thousand enterprises. Of these, nearly two hundred were large, relatively modern plants controlled by the central government. A machinery factory, for example, built in 1958 with fifteen million dollars in Soviet aid, was one of the most important of Hanoi's plants. Spare parts, lathes, tools, electric motors, and so forth were made there. After the bombing began, much of the plant's equipment was scattered around Hanoi, broken up into fifty separate workshops. To a Cuban writer, the gutted machinery factory had an air of emptiness and desolation, yet some workers continued to operate around-the-clock on the bulky machinery left in place.

A similar evacuation of other factories was carried out. While most of them continued to operate, production steadily declined. Exports of coal dropped by half; the country, once an exporter of cement, became an importer. Prewar gains in the textile industry were halted; both the quality and quantity of cloth fell, with the army demanding vast supplies of new uniforms, leaving the civilian population with small amounts of the worst possible material for their personal use.

Although an iron bomb could do little damage to an unmechanized farm, food production declined because the communist party transferred farmers to other war-related activities. The pig was the country's most important meat supply, and the pork ration remained the same as before the bombing—ten ounces per person each month—but even this low amount was rarely available. A sugar ration of about one pound a month was issued only to mothers of newborn babies. Fish, *nuoc mam* (the national condiment), and flour were seldom seen. Two boxes of matches and a bar of soap were distributed every three months. To try to offset the deficiencies, the government ordered pharmaceutical factories to increase their production of vitamin pills.

The personal hardships caused by the bombing were many. Still, it did not denigrate the tenacity of the North Vietnamese, which even their opponents grudgingly respected, to point out that theirs was already a culture of deprivation and hardship. To describe the difference in attitudes toward daily life separating Hanoi from New York, for example, where a power failure lasting a few hours in 1965 rated a *Time* cover story, was difficult indeed. The North Vietnamese were tightening their belt, as the saying went, but it was a belt that originally came with few notches, and this could not be minimized in searching for an explanation of their resilience.

They tried, as much as possible, to protect their industries by putting defensive weapons nearby. The surface-to-air missiles, however, had not proved very effective in the usual sense. By early 1967, a total of fifteen hundred SAMS had been fired, bringing down only thirty-one planes. The reason could be partly laid to successful American jamming techniques and evasive aerial maneuvers. But also at blame was the incompetence of Vietnamese technicians, many of whom were barely out of their teens and were assigned to the sites with little training. A Russian adviser complained that they fired the missiles like machines guns.

Nevertheless the missiles inadvertently proved their worth in another way. They drove American pilots down into the range of antiaircraft weapons that the North Vietnamese could fire to good effect like the machine guns to which they were accustomed. The explosions of the thirty-seven- and fifty-seven-mm flak looked to pilots like smudged popcorn outside their Plexiglas cockpits, with the heavier eighty-five- and one hundred-mm fire taking on a darker, more ominous color. The North Vietnamese discovered that positioning their guns in formations of triangles, diamonds, and pentagons concentrated their fire and gave them a better chance of catching a dive-bombing airplane in a deadly cone of exploding shrapnel.

Early on the North Vietnamese also recognized the value of another weapon. The spectacle of the richest country in the world bombing one of the poorest, whatever the political ramifications of the conflict, left many people, including friends and supporters of America, uneasy. After the war, North Vietnam's leaders boasted that they had manipulated the antiwar movement to their own ends. Propaganda was a legitimate weapon of war and since the North Vietnamese were, as they saw it, fighting to win over a much stronger power, one could hardly blame them for taking whatever steps they could to influence world opinion. If a movie star or a college professor, spurred by conscience or ideology, or any combination of the two, wanted to help publicize what she or he considered the essential injustice, if not the criminality of American policy, then Hanoi was often ready to issue a visa. Western journalists who proclaimed an allegiance to objective reporting were another matter. In North Vietnam's opinion, one objective view existed: America was wrong. Hanoi did not consider it helpful for a reporter to suggest otherwise, even if he included the on-the-other-hand qualifications in his story, which generally served as basis for his claim to objectivity. The Agence France-Presse was allowed a reporter in Hanoi but his dispatches, whether from self-imposed or official censorship, carried none of the probing bite of his AFP colleagues in Saigon. British journalist James Cameron was permitted to tour the country in 1965, and he wrote a series of articles sympathetic to North Vietnam. No American reporter, however, had been invited until Christmas, 1966.

Dick Wyman. I wasn't supposed to go. I was the spare. Out of five airplanes from our squadron, three went down on the flight deck with malfunctions. Cal Swanson and I wound up being launched. We got over the beach and Swanson's radar failed. The flight leader operated off the radar and the wingman was visual. It was standard practice to turn the lead over to the other airplane when someone's radar went down. So I had the lead. Or was supposed to have it. Swanson didn't resign himself to flying as my wingman—he wanted it both ways. He started giving me instructions about where to find the MiGs.

"Let's go to Wichita," he said. That was the code name for an area of North Vietnam. "Let's go."

We got there and saw nothing. He had another suggestion. I ignored him. I spotted an A-4. I radioed the pilot to ask if he had seen anything. "Yes," he said, "I've got a MiG here." About that time I saw him. He was in front of me. We passed head on. He rolled and I rolled and started down after him.

"I'll get him," Swanson said.

He tried to get on the MiG's tail. The pilot went into a sharp turn and pulled his nose around. He started firing at Swanson.

"Get him off my tail!" Swanson yelled. "He's shooting at me!"

I pointed my nose up and pulled the trigger.

"Is he still behind me?" Swanson asked.

"No," I said, "we're going the other way."

I was running him hard. Each time I came down and tried to put a Sidewinder missile on him he reefed into me. When he did that, I had too much of an angle and couldn't get off a shot. I made four passes. He was running out of gas. His buddies had left him. I think he was just trying to get home. As I came off a pass, Bob Rasmussen zoomed down and fired a Sidewinder. The missile almost homed in on me. The MiG broke. The Sidewinder exploded harmlessly. The MiG was hard to see because of the camouflage. "I'm not taking my eyes off you," I said. Good eyesight was crucial to a fighter pilot. One of the problems, I think, was that Swanson and Rasmussen lost sight of the fight.

We had started at sixteen thousand feet. Now we were at treetop level. The MiG had done everything right. He was outmaneuvering me. Then I came down on him and was almost at the point of overshooting him when he started a reverse. He must have realized it was too soon. He went back into his turn and tried to reverse again. That let me get on his tail. I fired a Sidewinder. The missile took off two-thirds of his left wing. We were fifty feet off the ground. He hit the rice paddy and exploded in a fireball that shot higher than my canopy.

I was about to run out of gas. I radioed for a tanker. He was pretty far offshore and he refused to fly closer. "I've got orders not to go over the beach," he said.

"I don't want you to go over the beach," I said. "I just want you to come closer, so I don't run out of gas before I plug in." An admiral was listening to our transmissions. He ordered the tanker to get in there and give me some gas.

The *Oriskany* asked if I wanted to do a victory roll over the ship, to celebrate the shootdown. "I don't know," I said. "Stand by one."

Swanson was flying beside me. He nodded his head, "Yes, do it."

"Roger, I'll do it," I radioed the ship.

"You are cleared for a port side victory roll," the *Oriskany* said.

After a mission one normally came around the starboard side at six to eight hundred feet and broke around to make a landing pass. This time I was going to come by the port side just above the flight deck, pop the nose up, roll the airplane all the way around, then break out of that and land. I started my maneuver. Swanson had not said anything on the radio, but he later told me he tried to signal me with his hands that he was going to roll around me as I did mine. If so, I didn't see it. I went into my roll and suddenly I saw an airplane inches away, ready to land in my face. I thought my wing was going to break off on his belly, it was that close. I nearly died of fright. When I landed, everybody on the flight deck said, "Jeez-sus, you really came close to getting killed on that one." Dick Schaffert, who missed the MiG at the beginning of the dogfight, joked that his only consolation was that Cal and I almost ran into each other on the victory roll.

"I don't think I can get you a Silver Star for that," Swanson said after we landed.

"Skipper, I could care less," I said. "I got a MiG. That's enough for me."

Reporters came out to the ship for interviews. Swanson did all the talking. It sounded as though he had fought the fight and pushed the MiG in front of me where I finally shot him down. He said we fell into the alternating passes as we'd been trained. But there was no alternating, except once when he got in front. As he knew, he made a gross error by giving the MiG a shot at his tail. I didn't care, though. I knew how it had happened.

On my first MiG encounter with Bellinger, I thought the pilots were Vietnamese. This second time, I'd bet my shirt and overcoat they were North Koreans. It was such a drastic change in the way they flew, the tactics they used. Bob Rasmussen and I talked about it and agreed that we would have liked to see the pilot get out safely. He fought well. But he had too many guys against him. We were like a pack of dogs on a deer. So I wasn't wild about seeing him get killed. But it was a big high to shoot down the plane.

I received a Silver Star. After the ceremony, Bryan Compton said, "Goddamn, Dick, I'd like to have you in my squadron." That meant more to me than the medal. He was the best. If you had a tough mission, you prayed he was leading it. Funny thing was, Compton later made admiral and during peacetime everybody hated him. What a mean, ornery bastard of an admiral he turned out to be! But on Yankee Station he was loved, because nobody was a better strike leader.

After I got the MiG, two congressmen, one from Georgia, the other from Maine, came aboard the *Oriskany* for a briefing on the air war. Since I'd become a little famous and was from his home state, I was assigned as the escort officer for the Maine congressman. I had no idea about the importance of public relations in those days, and I was irritated to be taken off the flight schedule. You got points for flying missions. I hawked the ready room and took anybody's flight who was sick or couldn't make it for some reason. This way I got ahead of the others. When it was noticed that I was ahead, I would be assigned to take an airplane for maintenance to the Philippines, which was like extra leave, and I could spend the time partying.

The admiral was set to see the two congressmen at eleven o'clock that night. I expected a big gala briefing to be laid on to impress them. We walked into the war room and there was the admiral, his chief of staff, his aide, and that was all.

The admiral said to me and the other escort officer, "You can stay or leave. Whatever you choose."

"Thank you, sir," I said. "I'll sit in."

"Gentlemen," the admiral began, "this is not going to be a briefing with colorslides and flip charts. We don't have the time."

That impressed me. He wasn't going to cozy up to the politicians. He was direct and matter of fact. He began describing the air war and what we were trying to do.

The Maine congressman stopped him. "Admiral, how much longer is it going to take to win this war?"

The admiral looked at him for a moment. "We know if the guy starts out from North Vietnam with ten pounds of rice," he said, "we're going to stop all but one pound from reaching the South. If he starts with ten bullets, he'll only get one down there. Beyond that, there's nothing we can do. Air power cannot stop that last pound of rice or that last bullet from reaching South Vietnam. So we'll have to stay here long enough to make him decide it's not worth starting with ten pounds to get one pound to the South. Or we'll have to decide whether it's worth our time to stay here that long."

The two congressmen looked like they'd been hit with a blackjack. They sat there stunned, not wanting to believe but knowing he had no reason to lie. Neither of them asked another question. The ballgame was over. Probably nothing had a greater impact on my thinking either. Until now I had believed somebody would come up with the magic answer and we would win. But here was an admiral saying it wasn't going to happen.

After the briefing I took the congressman back to his room. He was due to leave the next morning.

"Good night, sir," I said. "I'll see you bright and early."

"Hey, Dick," he said, "have you, uh, have you got anything to drink around here? I'd really like something to nip on."

"Sir, you know that alcohol is illegal aboard ship."

"Yes, I know. But have you got any? I'm not too fussy.'

I had never met a congressman before and didn't realize that a lot of them drank like fish. I thought he was trying to set me up. I could see him going back to Washington and calling a news conference to expose illegal drinking on Yankee Station. "Lieutenant Richard Wyman, a Silver Star winner, was caught redhanded by Congressman . . ." I played dumb.

"No, sir. I don't have anything. Maybe the admiral does. I could ask his aide."

"Come on Dick. Where is it?" He was getting desperate.

"No, sir. Not me."

How the poor guy got to sleep on that noisy aircraft carrier I don't know. He left the next morning probably thinking I was the straightest arrow he had ever met, a fighter pilot who didn't drink.

18

The Inferno

from **A LONELY KIND OF WAR**
by Marshall Harrison

No one has improved upon the profoundly simple and often repeated cliché that war is hell. But Marshall Harrison's gripping account of a gruesome skirmish in the Vietnam War confirms the accuracy of the truism. Flying an OV-10 Bronco in Vietnam as a forward air controller, known as an FAC, Harrison's job was to designate targets for air force tactical fighters. Given the veil of jungle growth, it was a difficult mission. From his perch just above the battlefield, he had a unique perspective on the daily scrimmaging, which on one eventful day turned into a veritable inferno.

Harrison describes the situation as a U.S. Army company is ambushed by North Vietnamese regulars. Senior army officers are circling overhead in command and control helicopters, called "slicks." There is no shortage of orders being transmitted to the pinned down troops below. Meanwhile, the Americans are incurring an alarmingly high casualty rate as the enemy engulfs their position. Valiant rescues are attempted by medevac helicopter crews, but they are shot down, the burning hulks of their overturned aircraft serving as an expression of the battle's hopelessness.

Even the helicopter gunships, an aircraft type first deployed in the Vietnam War to provide enhanced protection for ground forces, are of little use in this scenario as the dense jungle canopy obscures the clever enemy. The gunships fire blindly into the brush, their relatively small caliber rounds coming to rest harmlessly in the jungle floor. These aircraft are themselves fodder for enemy gunners shooting into the sky with impunity.

The enemy, devoid of any air assets in this engagement, has merely turned nature to its advantage—using the landscape's thick foliage as an effective shield. The only chance of salvation is the heavy firepower of Air Force fighters. Because the ground fighting is at close quarters, extra caution must be exercised to ensure that no friendlies are accidentally clipped by the cannon, bombs, and napalm. The situation is further complicated since thunderstorms are rolling in, and the FAC is unable to make any visual contact with the ground forces owing to the jungle canopy. Fortunately, the American soldiers can ignite flares emitting colored smoke to delineate their position.

The outcome of battle not infrequently hinges on the deeds of a few people or even a lone individual. With terrified and contradictory transmissions occupying the radio channels, reports of growing casualties, a battlefield littered with fallen aircraft, no way to see what is happening on the ground, and tracer bullets screaming past, normal emotions can easily degrade a person's usefulness. The difference between victory and defeat, or between rescue and catastrophe, is often the ability of a central player to somehow suppress the natural human tendencies and press on with discipline against seemingly insurmountable odds, operating with coolness under fire.

P.H.

I DIDN'T HAVE TO USE THE MAP to find the scene of action, for the sky was filled with helicopters, mostly slicks carrying brigade and battalion staff. No one had requested USAF support, so I climbed until I felt reasonably confident that I wouldn't be involved in a midair collision. Once there, I pulled the throttles back to conserve fuel, began a lazy orbit, well over everyone, and tried to make sense of the tense messages being flung back and forth. Big Six, the brigade commander, was giving unasked-for advice to the young-sounding platoon leader hidden beneath us in the trees.

"Latigo Six, this is Big Six. How many of your people have been hurt?"

"Big Six, this is Latigo Six." His voice was shaking from fatigue, excitement, or fear—maybe all three. "We've got six KIAs that I know about. We've also got another fourteen or fifteen WIAs that need dusting off real bad. I've lost almost all of my first squad, and second squad has been hit hard. We're taking heavy fire from both flanks and the front. I'm going to try to move my wounded about 500 meters to the rear, where there's an LZ. We're going to need gunships to help us get out. Over."

"Negative, Latigo Six," the colonel replied. "You hold your position. I'm going to have the remainder of your company flank the ambush and we'll have him in a pincer between them and your platoon."

He changed frequencies before the lieutenant could object, and on my other radio I picked him up giving movement instructions to the company commander of the ambushed platoon. My God, I thought, maybe this is what's wrong with the war. We've got a bird colonel trying to play platoon leader. And if he got tired of the role, the air was filled with helicopters carrying assorted military brass willing to take over. They'd all be delighted to give that kid on the ground the benefit of their experience gained at the Battle of the Bulge or on Porkchop Hill in Korea. I was sure they meant well and would have gladly changed places with the platoon leader. But, this was not their war to fight. Denied the combat position on the ground, they chafed at the rank and the middle-aged bodies they had acquired and tried to fight vicariously through that frightened twenty-five-year-old down there beneath the tree canopy. I felt sad for all of them, but especially for the beleaguered company and platoon commanders who were trying to save their people. Before this I had not believed the tales of entire units hiding from command and control helicopters flying in their area.

The drama unfolded over the next hour. Several things became apparent very quickly: The enemy troops were not disengaging but rather closing in in an effort to prevent air or artillery attacks against them. Furthermore, Charley was either feeding more troops into the fight or doing a little flanking of the company himself. The volume of fire from the enemy forces was increasing, which not only prevented the planned American flanking movement but made it impossible to get dust-off helicopters in to pick up the wounded.

By the end of the first hour and a half, the entire company had managed to get itself effectively surrounded. The amount of advice from the circling helicopters had greatly diminished now. There are considerably fewer options when you're surrounded and the people overhead can't locate you beneath the trees.

Resupply was starting to become critical, for the enemy gunners had triangulated fields of fire for their overlocking 12.7s and were now punching holes in those helicopters foolish enough to stay low. If the enemy had been smart, he would have fired only at the resupply ships, for the command and control birds seemed to be valuable allies.

I waylaid one of our FACs who had wandered over to find out what was happening and designated him to stay on station while I went back to Di An for refueling. While I was on the ground I had the armorer fill my empty rocket tubes, and I grabbed a quick sandwich. It already looked to me like it was going to be a very long day.

Back on station I found that two additional companies of U.S. troops had been inserted on one flank and were already getting their butts kicked. Charley either had no place to run or had decided he was through running for a while. Artillery was impacting along a line several klicks to the north of the engagement, not allowing the enemy to withdraw in that direction. Helicopter gunships were making firing passes into the jungle, but they simply didn't carry ordnance large enough to dig out anyone who wanted to stay.

Two smoldering helicopters lay on their sides among the trees, shot down by intense fire from the ground. The courage of the helicopter crews was magnificent, but sometimes that's not enough. As I watched, or rather listened, to the battle taking place beneath me, I felt like a substitute waiting to go into the big game. I knew I'd be called soon, for the helicopters just didn't have the punch to engage the NVA properly. And it was definitely NVA. These boys weren't local rice farmers.

Listening to the confused reports coming over the ground net and to the numerous helicopter pilots' sightings, I tried to place the friendly units as well as I could. I was very conscious that this was my first troops-in-contact (TIC), and I wished for Phil's calm guidance from the rear cockpit.

I called my control room. "Sidewinder Control, this is Sidewinder Two-one. You'd better have them get ready to launch the alert birds. It doesn't look like it's going to be long now."

"Roger, Two-one. This is Control. I've been listening in here in the TOC and I figure the army will be requesting tac air pretty quick. Do you want another FAC standing by?"

I should have thought of that. If I had to leave for any reason or got myself shot down, standard operating procedure says that another FAC should be available. "Yeah, Control. I forgot all about it. Get the next man on the duty roster over to the TOC so he can monitor what's going on and won't have to go into this thing cold, because they're spread out all over the place up here."

Switching back to the ground net, I listened carefully to see if I'd missed anything while talking to the control room. The commander of the platoon that was first ambushed sounded as if he were weeping as he requested the dust-off medevac helicopters to try again for a pickup of his wounded. One dust-off had already been lost and they were understandably reluctant to make another attempt until the LZ was a bit more secure. Right now no one could even stand erect down there, much less expect a chopper to get in.

The helicopter gunships were still madly attacking and continuing to be badly hurt. They'd lost another ship and had two more pull out of the fight—one with extensive battle damage, the other with a dead gunner. Radio discipline on the aviation nets had gone to hell and the ground net continued to be monopolized by the brigade commander and his staff. Excited requests from the ground unit blended with orders, often contradictory, from the airborne staff. Gunship pilots were trying to call out positions from which they were receiving ground fire. An artillery forward observer circled above the battle in his O-1 Birddog trying to get firing coordinates from the troops trapped on the ground. Smoke was starting to obscure the battlefield and a quick glance to the south showed that rain showers and thunderstorms would soon make our day complete. It looked like Dante's version of military hell. Or maybe a sketch by Dali.

"Sidewinder aircraft, this is Big Six." The call I'd been expecting from the CO was coming through."

"Big Six, this is Sidewinder Two-one."

"Roger, Sidewinder Two-one. It looks like we're going to need some tac air to even things up down there. If you've been monitoring, you know that we've now got three companies on the ground, almost line abreast, with their fronts facing north. In the center of the line the forward positions are farther north and there are pockets of people scattered about who don't know where they are. When you get your aircraft here we'll have the forwardmost units pop smoke and let you identify them. We'd like the bombs about one hundred meters north of the main line of resistance. Can you do that?"

"Roger, we ought to get some air here within fifteen minutes and I'll let your people know when to pop smoke. The other thing is that I'm gonna' need to have this frequency clear of everybody but me and the people on the ground. We're going to be dropping awfully close and I don't want a screwup because somebody overrides his transmission." I had already decided that if they wanted air strikes, I'd have to do it without listening to all the extraneous directions and orders now cluttering the airways. I was too new at this game to try to sort the wheat from the chaff.

Moments of silence followed, perhaps for the first time that day. Big Six was not thrilled to be told that he was not to transmit to his own troops.

"Roger, that," he finally said. "Everyone not involved with the air strike should monitor, repeat monitor, this frequency. Do not transmit unless there is an emergency. Sidewinder, let me know when you're ready for the smoke."

Not too gracious but it would do, I thought. I checked with Sidewinder Control and found that he had requested the launch of the alert birds as soon as he had heard the request from the CO. Bombing within a hundred meters of the troops is tricky. Most of the ground-pounders didn't realize the destructive radius of a 750-pound bomb. Shrapnel and concussion can produce casualties far away from the bomb's actual impact point. I would start them farther out and try to move them closer if the troops needed it.

The fighters were coming out of Bien Hoa, so it would take only a few minutes after takeoff for them to get to the rendezvous point. I turned the aircraft and headed in that direction. I was almost there when I heard the flight leader.

"Devil Flight, check in."

"Two."

"Three."

"Sidewinder, this is Devil Lead. A flight of three approaching the rendezvous point at twelve thou. Negative contact on the FAC."

"Roger, Devil Lead, this is Sidewinder Two-one. Good morning. I'm coming up to the rendezvous point in about one minute. I'll be coming from your eleven o'clock at three thousand. I'll turn my smoke on now for five seconds." I pulled the toggle switch that activated the smoker. "Smoke is on Devil Flight."

"Negative contact...no, wait. Lead thinks he has you in sight, but there's so much smoke in the background that it's hard to say for sure. Rock your wings for me. Yeah, Devil Lead has a tallyho on the FAC. Are you ready for our lineup?"

"Rog, Devil Lead, Sidewinder has you in sight now. Go ahead with your lineup."

"OK, Devil Flight is three Fox-One hundreds, each has four snake-eyes and four canisters of nape. Also, a full load of twenty mike-mike all around."

"I copy that, Devil Lead. What we have today is a troops-in-contact situation and they're awfully close to each other. It's important that you adhere closely to the run-in directions. We've got three companies of U.S friendlies on the ground and an unknown number of dinks. The green-suiters have already lost three choppers and had two others put out of action, so there's lots of ground fire about. The friendlies are fronting north along a more or less east-west line, so we'll be running parallel to them with a north break off target. There are also isolated pockets of friendlies whose location we're not sure about. But, don't worry about them; that's my job. Just drop 'em where I tell you. Target elevation is about 300 feet and the best bailout area will be anywhere to the south of the bombing line. I want you to call rolling in for each pass and off target. Call FAC and target in sight on each run. If you don't get positive clearance for each run, then go through dry. You're going to have to make each run on an east-to-west heading. Sorry 'bout that, but the way the friendlies are stretched out we can't do it any other way without overflying them. Unless you have some questions I'll lead you toward the target and have you hold high and dry until the friendlies can pop some smoke and I'm able to identify it. Then, I'll mark and we can go to work."

"No questions, Sidewinder. Let's get some!"

Devil Lead sounded ready and not particularly daunted by the reports of ground fire. It wasn't worrying me either, but I was very afraid of screwing up and hurting some GI on the ground. I led them back to the target, switching back to the ground radio frequency and telling the colonel to have his men pop smoke canisters. The different colors began to drift up through the trees, diffused but still workable. I identified each color and tried to mark the locations on my map as well as I could for reference after the bomb blasts had blown away the pretty colored smoke.

It was quickly apparent that the troops were nowhere near being in the line the colonel had suggested. Their configuration resembled instead a long "S" with the top toward the west. It was workable, but I remained concerned about those "isolated" pockets of friendly troops invisible somewhere below. The platoon commander was in contact with the survivors of one of the lost squads, but they had no idea of their location in relation to the rest of the platoon. All they knew was that they were pinned down and unable to pull back.

When I thought I pretty well had the main line of friendlies pinpointed, I told the platoon CO that I was going to put in a smoke rocket and that he should check with his lost people to see if they could either hear or see its impact. Still at 3,000 feet, I rolled the aircraft over into a forty-five-degree dive and fired my first rocket well to the north of the forwardmost troop positions.

"Latigo Six, this is Sidewinder. Did any of your people who are pinned down hear that rocket?"

"Stand by," he yelled into the microphone. I could hear the sound of rifle fire crackling in the background when he keyed the radio to transmit.

"Sidewinder, Latigo Six. My people say they heard the rocket impact about a hundred meters north of their position."

"These are the people who aren't sure of their positions, right?" I wanted to make sure that we weren't talking about his forward perimeter people.

"That's affirm, Sidewinder."

"Good enough, Latigo Six. I'm going to put the first bombs in at about that spot. Tell your lost people that when they hear the detonations to start hauling ass back toward your lines, because I'm going to gradually bring it in pretty close. Let me know if they don't get back south of your smoke or they're liable to get a snake-eye dropped on them." I switched back to the fighters, now in a holding pattern above the target area.

"Devil Lead, Sidewinder here. We'll make the first pass where you see my willie pete smoking. There are troops about a hundred meters south of there who'll be hauling back toward the line after your first pass, so I'll have to re-mark for you then. Let's go with the bombs first. I'll want 'em in singles for the first pass, then we'll switch to pairs. If you have me in sight you can start your run-in." Lord, don't let me screw up and kill any of those Americans!

"Devil Lead is in hot from the east, FAC and target in sight."

I flew directly at him until I was assured that his alignment was good and that he wouldn't be able to drop on the friendlies below, then said, "You're cleared, Devil Lead."

The bomb was good, exploding in the middle of the smoke drifting up from my marking rocket. Two trails of green tracers followed the lead ship's break off the target. I quickly changed to the army FM frequency.

"Latigo Six, this is Sidewinder. Are your people heading back now?"

"That's affirm, Sidewinder. All are heading back at this time. Stand by for one and I'll let you know when they're all back."

As I waited for the report, I overflew the target area at 3,000 feet. Then, thinking that I might catch the enemy napping, I did a quick wingover and flung the Bronco at the ground. My tricky maneuver may have fooled them for about three seconds, for that's how long it took for the tracers to begin floating my way. I let the aircraft continue its dive for the trees, leveling off just above the tops, jinking wildly. At such a low altitude I could see only the southern edge of the bomb crater, but the explosion had cleared out enough of the undergrowth to let me peer beneath the tall trees. The enemy was impossible to count in the brief seconds allowed, but there were many of them and they were moving south toward the beleaguered company. Charles was no fool. When the heavy stuff started falling, he knew that the safest place to be was snuggled as close as he could get to the American unit, effectively canceling out the friendly advantage in air and artillery. If we wanted to stop that, we were going to have to do something in a hurry.

"Sidewinder, this is Latigo Six. My people are all back inside the perimeter."

"Understand, Six. Have your northernmost element pop another smoke immediately because we're going to have to bring some stuff in real close to you. The bad guys are moving south in a hurry toward your positions. Your forward elements ought to be seeing them pretty quick. We're going to use the twenty mike-mike cannon to stop the advance. These fast movers are pretty good with them, but pass the word for everybody to get behind something and keep their heads down because we'll be dropping heavy stuff immediately after the gun runs. I'll be monitoring your freq, but don't call unless it's absolutely necessary since we'll be working awfully close to you.

Out."

"Devil Lead, this is Sidewinder back with you. Change of plans. We're going to strafe before we do any more bombs. The dinks are trying to close, moving south. We'll try to make them go to ground, then work with the bombs and nape. I'm going to put in a string of three rockets along an east-west line and I want all of you to make gun runs within fifty meters on either side of that line. Any questions?"

"Negative, Sidewinder. Watch your butt, they're shooting pretty good today."

OK, Devil Flight, Sidewinder is in for the mark. Hold dry until I can get back into position to clear you. Be careful. We're going to be working very close to the friendlies. If you have to make a mistake, make it to the safe side—north of the line. Remember about the arty going in three klicks north of here and watch out for the helicopters on pull-off; they're all over the place."

"And let's don't forget about the thunderstorms either," Lead answered with a chuckle. I had forgotten about them but could spare only a quick glance. They were still about five kilometers southwest of us but seemed to be tracking truly into the area.

I rolled the Bronco up on one wing, then let the nose slide below the horizon, blending the aileron and rudder forces to align the little aircraft along the firing axis. What a marvelously responsive thing it was, like having a well-trained horse beneath you, responding to your slightest pressure. I held the stick forward to keep the nose down, which was trying to rise with the increasing airspeed. The needle on the airspeed indicator brushed against the red line; I pulled the throttles back slightly, then abruptly shoved the nose down into a sixty-degree dive toward the dark green jungle.

At 1,000 feet I fired the first rocket, then raised the nose a few degrees, waited for a count of three, and fired again. My altimeter showed me to be at 700 feet. I leveled there momentarily, then, shoving the nose down once more and letting the aircraft stabilize in its new attitude, fired once again. Only then did I become conscious of the automatic weapons winking at me from the tree line. Shoving the throttles fully forward once more, I let the aircraft ease down until it felt as if my bottom were dragging through the treetops. I thought I could hear rounds impacting against the fuselage, highly unlikely considering the close-fitting helmet I was wearing.

Out of the area of most intense ground fire, I pulled hard back on the stick, climbing and beginning a turn back toward the run-in line. Smoke from the three rockets was filtering up from the treetops, presenting a passable line for the fighters to follow.

"Sidewinder, this is Devil Lead. We've got your smoke and I'm in from the east with guns, planning a right break off target. FAC's in sight."

I picked up the glint of his wings as he made his right turn onto base leg toward the target, accelerating in his dive. I waited until he completed his turn and was flying directly at me. I had to be sure that he was correctly aligned. If he were off only a few degrees, his cannon fire would fall into the U.S. positions. He looked good.

"OK, Lead, you're cleared in hot."

I watched the smoke burst from beneath his aircraft. The sun glinted on the brass as it fell away expended, looking like a small rain shower as it tumbled to the ground. I turned the Bronco so I could watch the explosive slugs impacting. They sawed at the trees like an insane woodsman. The fighter pilot was fishtailing his aircraft slightly to increase the swath of fire. There were also the blinking fireflies of the enemy's return fire. It didn't look so bad up here at 1,500 feet.

"Latigo Six, this is Sidewinder," I called to the platoon commander. "How did that look?"

"I think you may be too far north," he responded immediately. "My people report that they have some NVA elements in sight no more than 150 meters to our north front. They say they're not advancing though."

"Rog. I'm going to move it in closer to you. Let me know how it sounds and if I'm getting too close."

Returning quickly to the fighter frequency I told the number two aircraft to move his fire fifty meters farther south. My heart remained in my throat as I moved the attacking aircraft ever closer to the friendly units. It almost stopped beating when, on the last gun pass, the platoon CO began screaming, "Stop them, you're hitting my forward positions!"

The brigade commander was instantly on the radio: "What in hell is going on over there, Sidewinder?"

I was confused and scared. I didn't see how we could possibly be firing into the U.S. positions. I had a good fix on them and had been carefully aligning and following each firing pass by the fighters. Before I could investigate, the lieutenant came back on the radio.

"Disregard that last transmission, Sidewinder. One of the new troops got excited and thought he was being strafed when the brass from the cannon fire began to fall on him. I'm also getting reports that Charley has started moving away from us toward the north."

I breathed a sigh of relief. I explained to the fighters what was happening. They'd heard it before.

"Devil Flight, Charley is moving back toward the north so we'll have a little more room to work, but beware of artillery up that way. I'm going to mark about 150 meters north of the last gun run line. You'll have to stay on the east-west heading, but let's go to the bombs. I'll want them dropped in pairs and I'll clear you in after the new mark. We're still going to be working close to the friendlies, so be careful."

I rolled inverted and let the lighted gun sight drift down to the area I'd selected to hit. I had visually marked a large emergent tree with skeletal branches as a reference point for myself. Rain suddenly erased it from sight, along with the ground, and I found myself in the ludicrous position of diving in an inverted aircraft straight for the ground, which was invisible below me and completely enveloped. The thunderstorms had sneaked into the area and caught me completely unaware.

First things first. I brought all of my attention back inside the cockpit and concentrated on my instrument panel. Staring at the attitude horizon indicator, I used it as a reference to level my wings, then began a steady back-pull on the stick. Glancing at the accelerometer I noticed that the needle was nudging past five and was almost at the figure six. Six g's! No wonder I was having trouble focusing on the instrument panel. Releasing a little back pressure on the stick, I felt the blood start to flow to my brain again. As suddenly as I had flown into the squall I popped out into clear air once more in a nearly level flight attitude.

"Sidewinder, you really ought to find a different way to wash your airplane," Devil Lead said. "If you don't get back up here where you belong, you're gonna have a few too many drain holes in it."

"Sorry, but I just couldn't pass up the challenge," I said. "I've never been that impressed with the Thunderbirds. Let them try that in a cloud! I'm in for the mark for real this time."

I located my landmark tree once again and did another wingover toward it, this time making sure I was well away from the encroaching storms. I punched the firing button, watched over my shoulder as the rocket impacted, and made a steep, climbing turn back toward a safe altitude. I wondered why there hadn't been as much ground fire that time. I knew we couldn't have hurt the enemy that much with the cannon fire.

Maybe they weren't firing as much because they were moving fast to get out of the area. How fast could they move through the jungle? I had no idea. I decided to play the odds that they could move a hell of a lot faster than I thought.

"Devil Flight, put your bombs about 100 meters north of my last smoke. I think they've had time to move beyond my mark."

It was a guessing game now. Which way were they heading? Between bomb runs I made occasional low passes but was unable to detect any movement, nor was I fired upon. They'd probably broken up into small groups or individuals, making their way back to a predesignated assembly point. At least we had brunted the attack. I could hear the dust-off helicopters beginning their approaches into LZs to pick up the American wounded. The NVA pressure around the besieged company had disappeared. No one was taking fire. The enemy seemed to have evaporated.

I finally decided, what the hell, and directed the fighters to drop their napalm in a likely-looking area. It was as good as any other place. The army was already taking control of the area once again. Small scout helicopters, covered overhead by Cobra gunships, flitted back and forth over the cratered area like small angry wasps.

"Devil flight, this is Sidewinder Two-one. I'm going to clear you out of the area now. It looks like the army's taking over again. I'll have to pass along your BDA as soon as I can get it, but I'll give you 100 percent of your ordnance in the target area. It was damned fine bombing and shooting you did, folks, in pretty close quarters. Y'all have a good flight home now."

"Thank you, Sidewinder Two-one. It's been a pleasure working with you, and if you ever get down toward our squadron, look me up and we'll tell each other a few lies. In particular, I want to know how you learned to do aerobatics in a thunderstorm. Adios."

I watched the fighters bank, rejoin, and climb gracefully back to the south. I hung around the area for another few minutes, but it soon became obvious that they had no further need of my services, though no one actually told me to go home. I called Sidewinder Control and gave him my after-action report. We probably wouldn't need additional tac air, but I said they might send the next FAC up this way just to be sure.

I was banking hard to leave the area when I heard a voice transmit on the FM radio: "Sidewinder, this is Latigo Six. Thanks, friend. You saved our asses." The colonel was silent.

MIDDLE EAST CONFLICTS

19

The Six Day War

from ISRAEL'S BEST DEFENSE: THE FIRST FULL STORY OF THE ISRAELI AIR FORCE

by Eliezer Cohen

This is the stunning story of the execution of Operation Moked, the surprise assault by the Israeli air force on the Arab air forces at the start of what became known as the Six Day War. In it Eliezer Cohen captures the intense excitement of individual pilots' attacks even as he paints the larger picture of the planning that went into the operation.

Operation Moked drew its inspiration from the Luftwaffe's June 22, 1941, attack on the Soviet Union. Then, hundreds of Luftwaffe aircraft swarmed over the advance enemy airfields and destroyed thousands of Soviet air force planes on the ground. The Luftwaffe had used such tactics before, in the invasions of Poland and France, but its training was not dedicated to the role of airfield destruction. The Luftwaffe was focused primarily on the close support of the German army, with airfield destruction being but one task in that role.

In sharp contrast, the geographic, political, and military situation in the Middle East had, over time, forced the Israeli air force to adopt a stance foreign to its original philosophy of defending the homeland in indigenous airspace. Born in battle, the Israeli government had recognized from the start that air superiority was essential to survival and later that the destruction of enemy airfields was the key to air superiority.

Israel was surrounded by hostile Arab states, and their strength was formidable. Egypt alone possessed 50 percent more aircraft than did Israel, and its equipment was first rate. As early as 1953, the concept of a devastating preemptive strike on key enemy air bases became the keystone of Israeli air force strategy, and by 1960 the concept had expanded to the almost simultaneous neutralization of all Arab air bases.

There were enormous difficulties involved, even though Israel had developed a thoroughly well trained, well-equipped air force. Absolute security had to be maintained, and while Israeli security was excellent, it was unable to execute training missions that simulated the attack without giving the strategy away. The risks were enormous, both militarily and politically. If the attack failed, Israel would be subject to a catastrophic counterattack at the very moment in which its aggressive attack had sacrificed the sympathy and support of its friends.

Nonetheless, the Israeli high command recognized that a successful attack would require repeated sorties, and that this in turn would depend upon the discipline, skill, and adaptability of the ground crews. Intense drilling resulted in incredibly short turnaround times, and ground crews knew their aircraft so well that they could conduct essential maintenance in minutes, having prepositioned all the necessary parts and tools. It was an egalitarian approach: the pilots and the mechanics knew and respected each other.

Not unlike the British preparations for Hitler's invasion, when everything from bombed-up de Havilland Tiger Moths to awkward Handley Page Harrows were to be thrown into the breach, Israel scraped the bottom of its aeronautical barrel for the all-out attack. Its strike force of long-range Sud Ouest Vatours were counted on for the deep penetrations, while even its Fouga Magister trainers were modified to carry out attacks on front-line targets.

The key to success lay in the neutralization of airfields by bombing the runways and then serially picking off the aircraft that were thus fastened to the ground. Author Cohen admirably describes the planning, then uses individual pilots' accounts to bring home the drama and the rising, almost exultant joy they felt as they saw the plan succeeding.

The attack shook the world; shattered the Arab alliance; destroyed Arab faith in Soviet weapons, tactics, and training; and placed Israel in a commanding position for decades to come. It is a glorious story of well-conducted battle, and Cohen tells it with style and grace.

W.J.B.

Israel's Operation Moked was devised upon a model similar to that of Operation Barbarossa, the German Luftwaffe operation that, on June 22, 1941, eradicated much of the Soviet air force before it could even take off. For the first time in military history, an air force had been built and trained over many years with the goal of defeating its enemy in just such an operation. The idea that the best defense of the nation's skies and the achieving of air superiority must lie in a devastating preemptive strike on the enemy's air bases was not easy to assimilate after years of defensive thinking. Dan Tolkowsky had initiated it, and from 1953 he had also issued the operation orders, which included only the front-line bases in Sinai.

In the early 1960s, the Operations Branch commander, Rafi Har-Lev, and the top helicopter navigator, Rafi Sivron, had begun the first discussion in IAF headquarters regarding a new and broad plan for the early neutralization of all Arab air bases. The primary problem of this effort was to involve all the necessary elements of the air force in the planning and development while maintaining the secrecy necessary for the plan's ultimate success. The design was rooted in superior, comprehensive intelligence. The information they needed to assimilate included locations of aircraft, munitions, and fuel supplies, as well as data on pilots and their operational training; on air base design and defenses, including runway thickness and materials; on flight control, radar, and regional control centers; and on aircraft scrambling techniques. The answers to these and countless other questions needed to be organized in an intelligence center and dispersed to every squadron according to its function, so that the information could be used in both planning and training. This change in approach demanded a radical modification of the intelligence network's style of thinking in addition to extensive work by the reconnaissance aircraft and all branches of Israel's intelligence network.

Israel was prepared for war in 1967 with 180 bombers and attack aircraft including Ouragans, Mystères, Super Mystères, Mirages, and

Vautours. In addition, the IAF had twenty Fouga Magister training aircraft, which had been modified for limited attack operations, forty helicopters (Sikorsky 58s, Super Frelons, and Bell G-47s), and thirty transport aircraft (Nords and Dakotas). Still, the three enemy Arab air forces outnumbered Israel more than two to one. Egypt alone outnumbered Israel one and a half times with its 420 combat aircraft, which included MiGs and Sukhois, as well as some Vampires and Hawker Hunters, Tupolev Tu-16 Badger bombers, Ilyushins, and Antonovs. In addition they had forty-two helicopters (Mi-4s and Mi-6s). Syria had one hundred aircraft of the same types as Egypt's and Jordan had twenty-four (primarily Hunters). Backing up Jordan, Iraq had ninety-eight fighter and bomber aircraft.

The aircraft of the Egyptian Air Force were located at eighteen airfields, four of them in the Sinai, three along the Suez Canal, six in the Nile Delta, and five in Upper Egypt. The Syrians were using six airfields, and the Jordanians two. The first strike would have to include the seven forward airfields in the Sinai and the Suez Canal, and the six in the Nile Delta.

Plans for Operation Moked began in 1963 and were repeatedly updated over the course of the following years as intelligence information dictated. An ever greater number of squadrons were sent on reconnaissance missions whose technical efficiency was constantly improving. These included high-altitude vertical reconnaissance shots as well as low-altitude angle and panorama shots.

The general plan involved grounding enemy aircraft during the first run by bombing the runways, and then destroying the aircraft themselves in the following runs with rockets and cannons. In 1966 came the first trial use of a bomb for runway demolition. The bomb had been developed by the Israeli Military Industries according to the planners' requests. Its power of destruction was reciprocal to its light weight of 154 pounds. It would create a crater five meters wide and one and a half meters deep, much greater than the damage inflicted by the heaviest conventional bombs that could be used. Unlike conventional bombs, the runway demolition bomb would be dropped from an altitude of one hundred meters, slowed down by a parachute that would simultaneously activate a rocket that would propel it with super force through the protective layers of the runway. The explosion would occur after six seconds.

Because of the need for maximum bomb loads to be carried by a maximum number of aircraft in every wave, a greater degree of autonomy would be given to each air base in controlling the activities of its squadrons. To cope with the huge scale of the attack, every plane was scheduled for four to five sorties each day. During the first two runs, emphasis was placed on the technical readiness of the aircraft, with maintenance intervals between sorties reduced to mere minutes. The operational and technical crews would not give up. Shortening the technical break turned into a competitive sport. At first it was between the aircraft crews, but later it turned into an organized series of events between squadrons and bases, with judges measuring times to tenths of seconds presenting awards and prizes at the conclusion. During peacetime, however, they could not rehearse unforeseen technical problems or battle damage to the aircraft. Maintenance control centers were built that held files on each aircraft and the services it had undergone during its history. A communications system was developed to receive warning of problems as damaged or malfunctioning aircraft were returning to base. This ensured that the appropriate experts would be waiting for the aircraft upon its return, with the necessary tools and parts. The system covered all aspects of technical support and guaranteed that the bases' warehouses held the necessary fuel, munitions, and parts while not having more than they could hold. The aircraft sheds now became a second home for the technical crews. Beyond professional pride, they sought to prove that they were of equal value to themselves and the aircrews, able to prepare an aircraft for operations under any conditions and with top quality. This attitude was the primary achievement of all levels of the commanding ranks of the technical network during the preparations for Operation Moked.

As Ezer Weizman had planned, air superiority would be achieved within six hours of the commencement of the attack through the decimation of the majority of the enemy's aircraft while still on the ground.

In the weeks prior to June 1967, Operation Moked was updated according to current intelligence information. Under the assumption that the Syrians would not be able to respond until the completion of the first wave, almost the entire IAF would be sent to destroy the Egyptian Air Force. The attack on the thirteen Egyptian air bases was designed to cause paralysis and prevent any attempts at defense or the escape of aircraft from base to base, a maneuver that the Egyptians had rehearsed many times.

Targets were allocated according to flight range of the attacking aircraft, level of threat at each target, and the attack capabilities of each type of aircraft. Priority was given to the destruction of the MiG-21s and Tu-16s and their air bases. The bases near the Sinai Peninsula were allocated to the Ouragans, the Mystères, and the Fouga Magisters, which were slower and had a shorter range. The faster and more sophisticated Super Mystères and Mirages were assigned the bases along the Suez Canal and the Nile Delta. The Vautours were sent to the distant bases in Upper Egypt. Last-minute changes were necessitated by the discovery of MiG-21 squadrons at the nearby bases, and the original forces were reinforced by several Mirages.

During the first wave, Israeli aircraft would take off in formations of four planes each on three primary flight plans, reaching the Mediterranean together and then diverging according to target. Speed would be under Mach 1, and altitude would not exceed thirty feet, at which height the aircraft would remain undetectable to Egyptian radar. Though still in its infancy, electronic warfare would be used to confuse Egyptian communications and radar systems as well as the missile batteries and anti-aircraft guns. This would occur precisely during the seconds when the aircraft were to pull up and reach altitude prior to diving down to the targets. In actuality, only one Jordanian radar station near Amman noticed the takeoff of the first wave, but its officers attributed this to the presence of the U.S. Sixth Fleet in the region.

After a long period of studying the region of operations in Egypt, gathering meteorological data regarding the desert and the Nile Valley during the summer months, and determining the daily routines of the Egyptian aircrews and technical teams, attack times for primary targets, near and far, were calculated. At 0745 hours, all Egyptian fighter aircraft would have landed after their dawn patrols. Most of the commanders, pilots, and technicians would be on their way from home or to the dining halls, out of reach of communications and flight control. The sun would already have risen, and the morning patches of fog would have dissipated.

Even during this final period of planning, the new IAF commander, Maj. Gen. Moti Hod, was attempting to convince the IDF Upper Command of the operation's reliability. Though Prime Minister Eshkol repeatedly demanded a commitment that "not a single bomb" would fall on Tel Aviv, Hod would only promise that the city would not be damaged by "massive bombings." Never did he state directly that the entire IAF would attack during Operation Moked and that only twelve aircraft would be allocated to defending the nation's skies.

On June 5, at 0700 hours, in the underground control center, the countdown concluded. At Hod's command of "Execute Moked," the formations began to take off from the runways at Ramat David, Tel Nof, and Hatzor, one after another, according to a schedule calculated to the minute and second. A fleet of 160 aircraft, the likes of which had never been seen in this region, turned toward the Mediterranean, flying just above the waves' whitecaps. . . .

June 5, 1967, 0700 Hours: Zvi Umshweif, Hatzor. Zvi's Story: All around us, everything was tight and crowded, everything on edge and ready. We were set to take off in two minutes. Precision and order were the name of the game. Everything had been calculated, from takeoff until our turn over the target at the exact time. Though timing is always crucial, in this operation seconds were critical.

We had been trying to pretend that the tension had diminished on our side. On Saturday, two days earlier, the beaches had been packed with thousands of reservists who had received weekend vacations. A few Fouga Magisters simulated the radio transmissions of two squadrons to give the impression that the flight school was having regular exercises. The quiet in my cockpit was so intense that all I could hear was my heart pounding and the sound of my breathing in the oxygen mask. I wondered if the line of MiG-17s in Kabrit would still be waiting for me when I arrived. I knew every corner of that Egyptian base, which was our squadron's target, 280 kilometers from here on a roundabout route over the ocean. Flying time of half an hour, more or less. Every photo and every piece of data was embedded in our memory.

In the air, the G force of five hundred knots pasted me to my seat. Suddenly Kabrit was below us, clearer than any practice range I had ever seen in my life. Black strips of runway on a bright carpet. Even the MiG-17s were just as in the films. Not a single one had been moved. I could not believe that we had surprised them so completely.

We began to execute our mission with no interference. I focused on my dive—angle, speed, altitude. The runway closed in. When the precise moment arrived, I released my bombs. We rolled sharply and began a strafing run. In the midst of our turn we could hear incredible explosions. The delay detonators of the bombs that we had sunk deep into the runways had awakened on time. Every shot a wonderful bull's-eye, and the field was littered with gaping holes. It would take hours to fill them, if there remained any reason to do so. The line of MiGs, our strafing target, came into focus. At full engine power and with clean wings (no bombs, no fuel tanks, no loads), our speed was tremendous.

I was amazed at the quiet. Why had we not heard any antiaircraft fire? It was hard to believe that they had really been caught with their pants so far down. The only panic could be heard on the communication network. Above a nearby airfield, our planes were dogfighting with MiGs. Apparently not everyone was sleeping.

I placed the line of MiG-17s in my gunsights. Slightly before coming into range, I squeezed hard on the trigger. The 30-millimeter cannons roared, and their bullets plowed into the runway beneath the MiGs. The planes convulsed under the cannons and collapsed. An entire line of MiGs was wiped out before my eyes.

We turned in strongly again for a third run. This time we needed to hit only the planes that had not been struck in the previous runs. Only a few remained. A pull of the trigger, and the mosaic of destruction was complete.

"I shot down an Il-41!" I could hear our wing leader calling.

The Ilyushin had been on its way back to Kabrit from a transport mission, and everything had erupted around it. Dazed, the Ilyushin pilot did not know where to go, and flew directly into the wing leader's sights. The enemy plane continued to fly, trailing smoke. On my way to the final strafing, I contributed my own rounds. Below us, almost nothing was left. The control tower had exploded. The fuel tanks were burning. Lone figures darted across the fields. We had ruined their breakfast.

Again I heard the wing commander's voice on the radio. "We didn't down that Il-41? How can that be? I saw him hit the ground two runs ago! Oh . . . sorry. It's another one."

We all converged on it, and it escaped toward Sinai, pouring out smoke. Later that week it was found, crashed in the desert and filled with the bodies of paratroopers who had not jumped.

We had turned to cross the Sinai for the trip home when the wing leader's Number Two screamed, "MiGs in the air!" He sounded almost elated. Opening a war with a bombing and not a dogfight was not his cup of tea. This time it was a pair of MiG-21s, apparently refugees from Faid or Bir Gafgafa. Number Two wanted to add them to his record, but the wing leader denied him permission. We had achieved our goal, and with our cannons all but empty, we had precisely enough fuel to get us home. A dogfight would be nearly suicidal. Still the MiGs pressed us.

"Head east with full engines! Disconnect from them! Do not get involved!"

One of the MiGs stuck himself on my tail. I shook him off with two sharp turns, and he passed. Suddenly he appeared in front of me, too close, filling my entire windshield. I fired, and the sputtering of my cannons told me that I had finished my ammunition. To my luck, he turned west and disappeared. Lacking any ammunition and short of fuel, I cut back on the power of my engines and climbed to the minimum altitude needed for the flight home. Each of us was alone. I could see no one from my wing, and could hear no one on the radio. Later I learned that the wing leader had crashed during a sharp low turn. He was the squadron's first casualty of the war, a painful blow.

Above Hatzor, I told the controller that I had only two hundred liters of fuel remaining. He requested that I continue to circle the base. Apparently I was in better shape than most. By the time my turn to land came, I was running on empty as well. . . .

What distinguished Operation Moked was its awesome and smashing speed, along with its execution according to plan and the lessons learned from exercises leading up to the operation. The Egyptians were paralyzed. The primary achievement of the operation could be measured by the shattering of the enemy's air power, which was its spinal column, and by the prevention of their ability to organize themselves into a secondary strike response. The number of aircraft destroyed was considered secondary. The level of resistance was on a par with the level of readiness and the daring of the antiaircraft gunners and the pilots on each base. Despite the surprise, many of the air bases were not at a loss to respond, and they fought bravely even during the first wave. The IAF's loss rate on the first day—ten percent of the attacking force—was high. Nonetheless, the level of success was astounding, and it pushed aside the pain and criticism regarding the final and unplanned leg of the operation, the attack on H-3. This had been a nonessential target whose attackers were victims of the routine of the plan, sent in repeatedly on unvarying routes and methods, and falling into a well-planned and executed ambush. The heavy toll was relatively greater than the attack on any Egyptian, Jordanian, or Syrian air base attacked, and was not worth the light damage that the Iraqi Air Force sustained. If they had dared penetrate Israeli airspace after the second day, the Iraqi planes could have been dealt with in air-to-air combat.

The air superiority achieved during the first day allowed the entire power of the IAF to be turned toward assisting the ground forces and deterring the last-ditch sorties attempted by remnants of the demolished enemy air forces, which sought to disrupt the processes taking place on the three fronts. At this point, the initiative to decide where and when to attack was removed from the IAF, and it became a supportive and not always decisive force, subordinate to demands from the ground. After two days that had demanded a total effort by every pilot and plane, the IAF's ability to supply was greater than the demand. The average daily number of sorties dropped by a quarter, from four on the first day to three on the following days. Few of the ground force's commanders requested IAF support.

Three Israeli divisions penetrated the defensive Egyptian positions in the Sinai within thirty-six hours. Twelve hours later they were within range of gaining control of the Suez Canal. Hundreds of attack sorties aided in demolishing the convoys of Egyptian artillery and armored vehicles. Most of the destruction was done by the Vautours, Mystères, and Super Mystères. Preventive bombings blocked the flow of support to the forward positions and, jamming the routes of escape, shortened the battles.

20

Across the "Line of Death"

from **THE UNTOUCHABLES**
by Brian Shul and
Walter Watson Jr.

No aircraft, ancient or modern, has so captured the imagination of both flying professionals and the general public as the beautiful Lockheed SR-71 Blackbird.

With its sculptural beauty and a performance that has remained unsurpassed for more than thirty years, this aircraft inspires awe in everyone who sees it. This account by Brian Shul and Walter Watson Jr. of a reconnaissance mission supporting the April 1986 surgical strikes against Libya is all the more remarkable for the way it shows how the Blackbird's flight crews develop not only admiration, but affection, for the most advanced aircraft to date.

In many ways, the SR-71 is a fitting symbol of the towering personality who led the team who created it: the inimitable Clarence "Kelly" Johnson. Johnson was a great bear of a man, given to profanity, absolutely incapable of tolerating incompetence in anyone, not adverse to a drink or to a blast of publicity, and an inspiring leader who took the Lockheed Skunk Works, the industry's premier aircraft design shop, to the peak of aeronautical engineering. Johnson's great talent was that he inspired not only awe but also excellence in engineering. Engineers who might merely have been superb became brilliant under his tutelage.

Johnson ran the Skunk Works with an iron hand. No Lockheed executive, not even the toughest of all chairmen, the mule-skinner-tough Dan Haughton, could enter the sacred precincts without getting Kelly's approval. Johnson created a climate of inspired engineering, and he maintained control through close personal oversight. Curiously enough, as immense as Johnson's talent as an innovative engineer was, he was even more talented as a program manager. He knew so much about so many things—aerodynamics, thermodynamics, materials, engines, and so on—that he could elicit the very best performance from the team of incredibly bright engineers that he had personally selected. A single telling example is Ben Rich, who was equally brilliant as an engineer but had a totally different personal and managerial style, for while Kelly drove, Rich cajoled. Yet Kelly not only fostered Rich's career, he selected him as his personal successor, perhaps the very highest compliment he might have paid.

All of the Skunk Works' team had to be at their very best to create the brilliant series of aircraft that ran, in many variations, from the A-12 through the SR-71A. And these aircraft, perhaps particularly the SR-71, which had such a wide variety of demanding missions laid upon it, required equally brilliant crew members to fly them to their limits.

Thus it is absolutely consistent that the account of a mission in the SR-71, as told by Brian Shul, the pilot, and Walter Watson Jr., the rear-seat reconnaissance systems officer, should be written in such an engaging and readable style. Shul tells us how it is to fly from the front seat of the Blackbird on a mission over hostile territory. The SR-71 has to be coaxed to its maximum performance, in both speed and altitude, to provide a minimum measure of security, and this must take place at a time when that performance is threatened by a slight mechanical malfunction, a vibration from the inlet doors.

The crew's pride in and affection for the Blackbird are evident as they enter Libyan airspace, a target for the advanced missiles that the Soviet Union has provided Libya. Shul's moving account of how the "jet" feels as it pushes to Mach 3.31 clearly reflects both his confidence in his mount—which could actually accelerate away from a missile—and his skill. He lets the jet take us to Mach 3.5, 80,000 feet—and ultimate safety—in one of the finest accounts of flying ever written, closing with four words you know he means: "I loved that jet."

W.J.B.

WITH THE LIBYAN COAST fast approaching now, Walt asks me for the third time if I think the jet will get to the speed and altitude we want in time. I tell him yes. I know he is concerned. He is dealing with the data; that's what engineers do, and I am glad he is. But I have my hands on the stick and throttles and can feel the heart of a thoroughbred, running now with the power and perfection she was designed to possess. I also talk to her. Like the combat veteran she is, the jet senses the target area and seems to prepare herself. For the first time in two days, the inlet door closes flush and all vibration is gone. We've become so used to the constant buzzing that the jet sounds quiet now in comparison. The Mach correspondingly increases slightly and the jet is flying in that confidently smooth and steady style we have so often seen at these speeds. We reach our target altitude and speed, with five miles to spare.

Entering the target area, in response to the jet's new-found vitality, Walt says, "That's amazing..." and with my left hand pushing two throttles farther forward, I think to myself that there is much they don't teach at engineering school.

Out my left window, Libya looks like one huge sandbox. A featureless brown terrain stretches all the way to the horizon. There is no sign of any activity. Then Walt tells me that he is getting lots of electronic signals, and they are not the friendly kind.

The jet is performing perfectly now, flying better than she has in weeks. She seems to know where she is. She likes the high Mach, as we penetrate deeper into Libyan airspace. Leaving the footprint of our sonic boom across Benghazi, I sit motionless, with stilled hands on throttles and the pitch control, my eyes glued to the gauges. Only the Mach indicator is moving, steadily increasing in hundredths, in a rhythmic consistency similar to the long distance runner who has caught his second wind and picked up the pace. The jet was made for this kind of performance and she wasn't about to let an errant inlet door make her miss the show. With the power of forty locomotives, we puncture the quiet African sky and continue farther south across a bleak landscape.

Walt continues to update me with numerous reactions he sees on the DEF panel. He is receiving missile tracking signals. With each mile we traverse, every two seconds, I become more uncomfortable driving deeper into this barren and hostile land.

I am glad the DEF panel is not in the front seat. It would be a big distraction now, seeing the lights flashing. In contrast, my cockpit is "quiet" as the jet purrs and relishes her new-found strength, continuing to slowly accelerate. The spikes are full aft now, tucked twenty-six inches deep into the nacelles. With all inlet doors tightly shut, at 3.24 Mach, the J-58s are more like ramjets now, gulping 100,000 cubic feet of air per second. We are a roaring express now, and as we roll through the enemy's backyard, I hope our speed continues to defeat the missile radars below.

We are approaching a turn, and this is good. It will only make it more difficult for any launched missile to solve the solution for hitting our aircraft. I push the speed up at Walt's request. The jet does not skip a beat, nothing fluctuates, and the cameras have a rock steady platform.

Walt receives missile launch signals. Before he can say anything else, my left hand instinctively moves the throttles yet farther forward. My eyes are glued to temperature gauges now, as I know the jet will willingly go to speeds that can harm her. The temps are relatively cool and from all the warm temps we've encountered thus far, this surprises me . . . but then, it really doesn't surprise me. Mach 3.31 and Walt are quiet for the moment.

I move my gloved finger across the small silver wheel on the autopilot panel which controls the aircraft's pitch. With the deft feel known to Swiss watchmakers, surgeons, and "dinosaurs" [old-time pilots who not only fly an airplane but "feel it"] I rotate the pitch wheel somewhere between one-sixteenth and one-eighth inch, locating a position which yields the 500-foot-per-minute climb I desire. The jet raises her nose one-sixth of a degree and knows I'll push her higher as she goes faster. The Mach continues to rise, but during this segment of our route, I am in no mood to pull throttles back.

Walt's voice pierces the quiet of my cockpit with the news of more missile launch signals. The gravity of Walter's voice tells me that he believes the signals to be a more valid threat than the others. Within seconds he tells me to "push it up" and I firmly press both throttles against their stops. For the next few seconds I will let the jet go as fast as she wants.

A final turn is coming up and we both know that if we can hit that turn at this speed, we most likely will defeat any missiles. We are not there yet, though, and I'm wondering if Walt will call for a defensive turn off our course. With no words spoken, I sense Walter is thinking in concert with me about maintaining our programmed course.

To keep from worrying, I glance outside, wondering if I'll be able to visually pick up a missile aimed at us. Odd are the thoughts that wander through one's mind in times like these. I found myself recalling the words of former SR-71 pilots who were fired upon while flying missions over North Vietnam. They said the few errant missile detonations they were able to observe from the cockpit looked like implosions rather than explosions. This was due to the great speed at which the jet was hurling away from the exploding missile. I see nothing outside except the endless expanse of a steel blue sky and the broad patch of tan earth far below.

I have only had my eyes out of the cockpit for seconds, but it seems like many minutes since I have last checked the gauges inside. Returning my attention inward, I glance first at the miles counter telling me how many more to go until we can start our turn. Then I note the Mach, and passing beyond 3.45, I realize that Walter and I have attained new personal records. The Mach continues to increase. The ride is incredibly smooth.

There seems to be a confirmed trust now, between me and the jet; she will not hesitate to deliver whatever speed we need, and I can count on no problems with the inlets. Walt and I are ultimately depending on the jet now—more so than normal—and she seems to know it. The cooler outside temperatures have awakened the spirit born into her years ago, when men dedicated to excellence took the time and care to build her well. With spikes and doors as tight as they can get we are racing against the time it could take a missile to reach our altitude. It is a race this jet will not let us lose. The Mach eases to 3.5 as we crest 80,000 feet. We are a bullet now—except faster.

We hit the turn, and I feel some relief as our nose swings away from a country we have seen quite enough of. Screaming past Tripoli, our phenomenal speed continues to rise, and the screaming Sled pummels the enemy one more time, laying down a parting sonic boom.

In seconds, we can see nothing but the expansive blue of the Mediterranean. I realize that I still have my left hand full-forward and we are continuing to rocket along in maximum afterburner. The TDI now shows us Mach numbers not only new to our experience but flat out scary. Walt says the DEF panel is now quiet and I know it is time to reduce our incredible speed. I pull the throttles to the min 'burner range and the jet still doesn't want to slow down. Normally, the Mach would be affected immediately when making such a large throttle movement. But for just a few moments, old 960 just sat out there at the high Mach she seemed to love and, like the proud Sled she was, only began to slow when we were well out of danger. I loved that jet.

THE PERSIAN GULF WAR

21

Which Technologies Worked?

from GULF WAR AIR POWER SURVEY SUMMARY REPORT

by Thomas A. Keaney and Eliot A. Cohen

Iraq's Saddam Hussein had long demonstrated a single-minded temerity and a flagrant disregard for standing principles of international law by the time he embarked on his expansionist adventure into the neighboring state of Kuwait in 1990. With the territorial sovereignty of an important oil-producing nation violated, and with the real threat of a push into the even larger oil exporting kingdom of Saudi Arabia, American President George Bush drew a "line in the sand." Essentially, Iraq's brazen ruler was given an ultimatum—either withdraw from the illegally occupied land or forcible action will be taken.

Backing up the warning was a rapidly formed coalition, practically unprecedented, that consisted not only of Western powers heavily dependent on Middle East petroleum but also on many of the nations from the region offended by Iraq's unabashed takeover of a much smaller and nearly defenseless neighbor. The region's balance of power was sent into tumult by Iraq's invasion of Kuwait. The matter was all the more precarious given Saddam's demonstrated proclivity to use deadly chemical weapons against his chosen enemies.

As the leader of this newly assembled coalition, the United States would be putting to the test the hardware and concepts developed in the years succeeding the Vietnam fiasco. The American administration and the Pentagon brass sought to apply the bitter lessons of the last war to this latest crisis. To begin with, there would be no gradual buildup. Instead, a massive force would be brought to the theater of operations at the outset. Also, rather than micromanaging the war from afar, the military leadership would call the shots with substantial authority vested in the field commanders. The new American conventional weaponry, including never before deployed high-tech gadgets and systems cultivated over years of almost unreserved military spending, would be amassed in the region and concentrated against one of the world's most formidable military forces.

The Gulf War's air campaign dramatically demonstrated the imperative of establishing air superiority early on. Coalition forces, led by the United States, did so with lightning speed such that after the first several days the airspace was cleared for the coalition's aircraft to conduct air-to-ground sorties as so-called bomb trucks with impunity from enemy interceptors. For the first time on a large scale an air war was won by nontraditional means. Exercising blanket electronic control of the airspace from the start, as opposed to relying on a succession of air-to-air engagements where the outcome of each is dependent on the skills of the individual pilots, resulted in the swift and conspicuous dominance of the air.

Following the remarkably short Gulf War, which was waged largely from the air, the U.S. government sponsored a comprehensive, multivolume review of the air campaign. The resulting summary report includes a chapter exploring five particularly efficacious technologies. In considering the role of high tech in air warfare, it is important to remember that sophisticated weaponry by itself hardly assures a victorious outcome. The application of high tech seems more effective in linear war and less so in guerrilla war. Moreover, as has often been said in various ways, there is no substitute for the mettle of the warrior.

The history of war is to a large extent the evolution of weapons systems, meaning that the side fielding a more advanced system first usually obtains the advantage. One of the lessons from the Gulf War would, therefore, seem to be that the winning side should not rest on its laurels and expect to win the next war with the equipment and tactics of the last war. Rather, it should immerse itself in newer technology, leaving no stone unturned. In this regard, it is quite likely that space systems will become an increasingly important component in future warfare.

P.H.

The uniqueness of a war is partly reflected in its characteristic technologies and equipment. Gen. Dwight D. Eisenhower and his staff identified what they believed were the five most important pieces of equipment contributing to success in Africa and Europe. Eisenhower speaks of them in his memoirs:

> ... the "duck," an amphibious vehicle ... proved to be one of the most valuable pieces of equipment produced by the United States during the war.... [F]our other pieces of equipment ... [that] came to (be) regarded as among the most vital to our success ... were the bulldozer, the jeep, the 2½ ton truck and the C-47 airplane. Curiously enough, none of these is designed for combat.[1]

The uniqueness of the Gulf War can be approached in a similar way by looking at five kinds of technology—not always single pieces of equipment—that seem to best characterize the air campaign. The number five is of course arbitrary and was chosen simply to limit the discussion and, in part, to mirror the Eisenhower example. We selected five capabilities and technologies from a longer list of candidates, any one of which could arguably have been included in the top five. Space systems, logistics, and strategic and tactical airlift were just a few of the candidates. Unlike Eisenhower's list, however, the Gulf War listing focuses solely on the execution of the air campaign, not on the many worthy logistical and support elements that could have been cited. Note, too, that our selections are not intended to suggest that these technologies are the best or most important items of U.S. air power but only that they worked best in the Gulf War. The five topics chosen for discussion are Stealth/Low Observability, Laser-Guided Bombs, Aerial Refueling, the high-speed antiradiation missile (HARM), and the STU-III, a secure telephone.

Stealth/Low Observability. Stealthy, low-observable platforms were the keystones of Coalition attacks against the Iraqi air defense system, leadership, and communications targets early on the first day of the war, even in heavily defended areas. Throughout the war, they attacked with complete surprise and were nearly impervious to Iraqi air defenses.

---

[1] Dwight D. Eisenhower, *Crusade in Europe* (New York: Doubleday and Company, 1948), pp 163–64.

Stealthy platforms needed minimal support from other aircraft but were able to provide stealth to a much larger force by disabling the enemy's air defense system, thus making all Coalition aircraft harder to detect and attack.[2] Stealth thus not only restored a measure of surprise to air warfare, it provided air forces some freedom of action that otherwise would not have been attainable.

U.S. forces used three platforms during the Gulf War that were in the stealth/low-observability category: the F-117 stealth fighter[3] and two long-range cruise missiles, the Tomahawk Land Attack Missile (TLAM) and the Conventional Air-Launched Cruise Missile (CALCM). Neither cruise missiles nor the stealth fighter figured in the deployment plans envisioned in pre-Desert Shield of Operations Plan 1002-90, but they became vital parts of the strategic air campaign. The F-117, which flew only two percent of the total attack sorties, struck nearly forty percent of the strategic targets and remained the centerpiece of the strategic air campaign for the entire war. Two hundred and eighty-eight TLAMs were launched during the war, sixty-four percent in the first two days of the air war and none after 1 February. Only thirty-five CALCMs were employed, all launched from B-52s on the first day of the war.

Low observability made possible direct strikes at the heart of the Iraqi air defense system at the very outset of the war. In the past, air forces fought through elaborate defenses and accepted losses on their way to the target or rolled those defenses back. In the Gulf War, the Coalition could strike Iraqi air defenses immediately, and they never recovered from these initial, stunning blows. With the combination of stealth and accuracy possessed by the F-117 and cruise missiles, these two platforms carried out all attacks against downtown Baghdad; the F-117 operated at night, and the TLAMs during the day. Given American sensitivity to casualties—our own and Iraqi civilians—they were ideal weapon systems for attacking targets in the heart of a heavily defended,

---

[2] Low observability as a design and engineering goal involves the systematic reduction of observable signatures in various spectra, including, but not limited to, radar. The design of stealthy aircraft like the F-117 focused on reducing radar signatures because radar-based air defenses have long posed the greatest threat to air operations. Strictly speaking it is the combination of low observability and tactics that produces stealth in an operational sense. During this discussion, however, these terms will be used somewhat interchangeably.

[3] In some ways it is incorrect to call the F-117 a fighter—it is really a single-seat bomber.

heavily populated city. Moreover, the F-117 had a psychological utility that was probably shared only by the B-52. Both were aircraft of a kind that only a superpower could have, and both could deliver destruction with no advanced warning—small wonder, then, that both figured prominently in psychological operations pamphlets that were showered upon Iraqi troops.

On the other hand, the F-117 and long-range cruise missiles also had limitations: both were less flexible and considerably more expensive than most conventional systems. The F-117, a subsonic, light bomber, had to operate at night to maximize stealthiness, and nearly nineteen percent of the strikes attempted by F-117s were adversely affected by weather (misses or no drops).[4] While not as sensitive to weather conditions as the F-117, cruise missiles had a smaller payload, required a lengthy targeting process, and could not be retargeted after launch. Even without the flexibility of other aircraft, however, these were able to set the terms for air operations over Iraq and to bring the reality of the war home to the residents of Baghdad.

Laser-guided Bombs. Few scenes were as vivid on television as the picture of a guided bomb going through a ventilation shaft in an Iraqi office building. From all appearances, a new age of precision bombing had supplanted years of employing less accurate, unguided bombs. In fact, the new age had only partly arrived: laser-guided bombs (LGBs) achieved dramatic success in the war, in some measure because of the early neutralization of Iraqi air defenses, but overall, laser-guided bombs comprised only a small fraction of the munitions expended in the war.

Laser-guided bombs are simply general-purpose bombs with guidance kits added—computer control and guidance canards in the front to detect laser energy and give steering commands and a wing assembly in the rear to provide lift. Laser-guided bombs are part of a larger family of precision-guided munitions (PGMs), many of which (air-to-air missiles, for instance) have been around for over 30 years. Radio-guided bombs

---

[4] The F-117 database contained more than 400 weather-related misses or no-drops. Equivalent data were not available for other aircraft.

were used in World War II and Korea, and the Air Force dropped over 4,000 LGBs on North Vietnam during the period April 1972 to January 1973, targeted almost exclusively against bridges.[5] In the Gulf War, more than 17,000 PGMs were expended, of which 9,342 were LGBs; 5,448 were air-to-surface missiles (predominantly Mavericks); 2,039 were antiradiation missiles (predominantly HARMs, discussed later); and 333 were cruise missiles (see above). By way of comparison, approximately 210,000 unguided bombs were dropped in the Gulf War.

What, then, explains the wartime prominence of LGBs, a not-so-new weapon that comprised less than five percent of the total weapons employed? There are three reasons, one of which has been noted—the marriage of LGBs and imaging infrared target sensors with stealth in the F-117. The stealth characteristics of the F-117 made the normally high-risk tactic of directing the path of an LGB while flying in a heavily defended area a much more routine affair. Any target in Iraq became open to destruction by the F-117's GBU-27, a 2,000-pound bomb designed to penetrate hardened facilities. A second reason for the importance of LGBs was Iraq's extensive system of hardened bunkers and aircraft shelters that were vulnerable only to a precision bomb with a penetrating warhead; it was vital that these targets be destroyed, and the LGBs were the only option for doing so. And third, LGB attacks were needed to attain attrition of the heavily revetted Iraqi armor in the Kuwait theater.

Laser-guided bombs were particularly effective because their employment came as something of a surprise to the Iraqis. Their reaction is understandable, because the LGB performance also surprised the United States. The one new U.S. weapon system prepared to drop LGBs was the F-117, an aircraft whose existence had been kept secret until just a year or two before the Gulf crisis and whose capabilities were largely unknown. Its one publicized employment had been in the Just Cause operation in Panama; in that conflict, the F-117's main notoriety came from a dispute on whether its LGBs, deliberately aimed to miss a building, missed by the correct amount. The U.S. fighter bombers designed in the 1970s, the F-16 and F/A-18, could not laser designate, and the

---

[5] Headquarters, Pacific Air Forces *Summary, Air Operations Southeast Asia*, monthly reports for May 1972 through January 1973.

first squadron of F-15Es received laser-designating equipment only after deploying to the theater, as did the RAF Tornados.

Laser-guided bombs carried principally by F-117s and F-111Fs were planned for precision air attacks on nearly the entire Iraqi target structure: air defense operations centers; national leadership and military headquarters; communications nodes; nuclear, chemical, and biological weapons research and storage facilities; and bridges were the most prominent. Beyond this planned use, much of the LGB employment was unplanned, growing instead out of adaptations made in the midst of the air campaign. Originally, the Coalition intended to destroy the Iraqi Air Force when its aircraft rose to meet the Coalition attacks. When the Iraqi aircraft instead remained on the ground in hardened shelters, Coalition aircraft shifted the attacks to the nearly 600 shelters themselves. Only weapons with the accuracy of LGBs and with hardened warheads, often dropped two at a time, were able to penetrate the reinforced concrete of these shelters. The results of these attacks were the flight of much of the Iraqi Air Force to Iran and the dispersal or destruction of the rest.

In the Kuwait theater, CENTAF turned to the use of LGBs when the planned air attacks on Iraqi armor with cluster munitions or unguided bombs proved to be largely ineffective. Iraqi revetted armor was simply less vulnerable to these munitions, particularly at the bombing altitudes used by the Coalition. The use of F-111Fs, F-15Es, and A-6s carrying 500-pound LGBs against the dug-in Iraqi armor was one of the major innovations of the war and marked a major turning point in the attrition operations against the Iraqi Army. This episode was an excellent example of the flexibility of the weapon, the aircraft, and the organization in dealing with the unexpected.

Laser-guided bomb employment also had limitations. Laser designation was not possible through overcast skies, fog, or smoke. The designating aircraft also had to remain in the target area and within line of sight of the target until bomb detonation. On the one hand, LGBs opened up new targeting possibilities: without them, systematic attacks on a communications system would have been unlikely simply because the probability of disabling a telephone switch or an antenna would have been too low without an excessive number of sorties; second, targets that would have been considered lucrative and vulnerable but too costly to attack were now open to assault. On the other, LGBs were of less value against large area targets, such as supply depots or deployed forces, without a single key node to attack. Against the key Iraqi targets in this war, LGBs were as devastating to the Iraqis as they were unexpected.

Air Refueling. Air refueling between aircraft took place well before World War II and has been a part of normal U.S. air operations since the 1950s. During the Gulf crisis, it was absolutely essential both to the deployment and to the war itself. Some aircraft required as many as 17 refuelings to deploy from the United States to the Gulf region. More than 100 tankers operated the Atlantic and Pacific air refueling bridges, permitting the rapid deployment of some 1,000 fighters, bombers, and support aircraft. During the war, Air Force tankers alone flew almost 17,000 sorties, usually with multiple receiver aircraft per tanker sortie.[6]

Nearly 60 percent of the wartime sorties by aircraft capable of being refueled in the air actually required tanker support. An elaborate network of air refueling tracks and anchors extended from the Red Sea across the Arabian Peninsula and into the Persian Gulf to support these requirements. This complex arrangement produced more than 60 air refueling tracks in which 275 tanker sorties per day operated, responding to the changing demands of the receiver aircraft. Liaison officers placed onboard the E-3 airborne warning and control aircraft managed the dynamic air refueling process, changing tankers from track to track to fill gaps as plans changed or emergencies developed.

The distances between Coalition air bases and targets meant that aircraft attacking deep into Iraq frequently had to refuel at least twice— once en route to the target and again on the return to home base. In some cases, refueling was conducted over Iraqi territory, an indication of the extent to which the Coalition controlled the air. Coalition air forces also relied on refueling to help them control the skies over the battlefield and strike into the enemy heartland. A list of representative aircraft and target areas shows the extent of the dependence:

---

[6] (S) Hq SAC, Plans and Requirements (XP), "Desert Shield/Desert Storm Tanker Assessment," 23 Sep 1991, p 2–13.

Aircraft	Combat Radius	Target Distance
F-117	550 nm	to Baghdad—905 nm
F-15E	475 nm	to Western Scud areas—680 nm
F/A-18	434 nm	Red Sea Carrier to Kuwait City—695 nm
B-52G	2,177 nm	Diego Garcia to Kuwait—2,500 nm

In addition to supporting Coalition attack aircraft, aerial tankers refueled combat air patrol aircraft and an entire array of airborne warning, reconnaissance, targeting, and control aircraft that had to provide 24-hour coverage during both Desert Shield and Desert Storm. Only aircraft such as A-10s and AV-8Bs, flying from the more forward operating bases and attacking targets in the Kuwait theater, could fly back and forth without in-flight refueling.

Air operations without the extensive support of aerial tankers would have changed the character of the war; by how much can only be guessed. Initial deployments to the theater would have been delayed, making more use of en route bases and requiring considerable logistical support at these bases. Because of the ranges to the targets, all dimensions of the air campaign would have been altered: the number of sorties a day as well as operating bases used. In short, the air campaign was designed with the assumption that all necessary tanking would be available, and a change in that assumption would mean a change in the design. Aerial tankers facilitated the speed and mass of the attacks and provided a margin of safety in air operations. Moreover, against an enemy capable of attacking air bases close to the border, the ability to refuel extensively permitted operations from distant, secure bases and provided a buffer of inestimable worth.

HARM. Several air power weapons contributed to the Coalition's command of the air over Iraq and the Kuwait theater, but no single weapon was as significant as the high-speed antiradiation missile (HARM). The use of HARMs effectively neutralized both elements of Iraqi ground-based defenses—antiaircraft artillery (AAA) and surface-to-air missiles (SAMs)—by suppressing the SAMs and thereby allowing Coalition aircraft to fly above the lethal range of AAA. Other forms of countermeasures to Iraqi radars (jamming, in particular) were important, but the HARM was the chief lethal component of the effort to suppress enemy air defenses.[7] The HARM homed in on Iraqi radar emissions and destroyed the emitter, and it was launched from a variety of platforms, most notably the F-4G "Wild Weasel" aircraft. The U.S. Air Force fired some 1,067 HARMs, and the U.S. Navy and Marine Corps fired 894. Combined with the destruction of Iraqi air defense control centers and of Iraqi aircraft in the air and on the ground, overall air defense suppression resulted in an attrition rate for Coalition aircraft of less than a tenth of that incurred by the United States operating over North Vietnam during the Linebacker II campaign of 18 to 29 December 1972.[8]

Although most of the HARMs were fired during the first week of the war—200 on the first night—they continued their influence throughout the war. On the first night of the air war, an elaborately choreographed combination of stealth aircraft, specialized electronic warfare aircraft, decoys, cruise missiles, and attack aircraft delivered a sudden, paralyzing blow to the integrated air defense system from which the Iraqis never recovered. The HARM's role was to take out the Iraqi SAM radars, activated by the decoys and attack aircraft. As important as the ability of HARM to actually destroy Iraqi radars was its deterrent effect: after the first day of the war, Iraqi radar activity declined precipitously because of the unwillingness of operators to turn on their radars for anything more than brief periods of time. Iraqi operators would, in fact, turn off their radars if they knew a HARM-carrying aircraft was in the vicinity. This was a classically indirect effect of a weapon; a measure of HARM's physical destruction of enemy targets tells only part of the story. By the third day of the war, the radar threat had been so reduced by the Iraqi fear of HARMs that the Coalition could fly at altitudes of 10,000 feet or higher, where normally radar-guided SAMs would have posed an unacceptable threat.

The experience of the 35th Tactical Fighter Wing (Provisional), whose F-4G aircraft were the main employers of HARM, indicates how the dominance over SAMs came about. The 35th Wing fired 905 HARMs and recorded 254 radars destroyed, for a 28 percent success

---

[7] Other lethal missiles that homed in on Iraqi radars included the British ALARM and the older American Shrike system, of which fewer than 200 were launched.

[8] Linebacker II losses were 25 aircraft out of about 3,200 combat sorties, compared to 38 losses out of about 70,000 combat sorties in the Gulf War.

rate. More significant, however, was that the radars, if not destroyed, had virtually ceased to operate. The F-4Gs that accompanied strike packages invariably fired all their missiles during the first week of the war; later, some of these aircraft returned with all of their missiles. In the Kuwait theater, the F-4Gs began a patrol, the "Weasel Police," so that they no longer accompanied each strike package, but each element of the F-4Gs could cover thirty to forty attack formations. Later in the war, the dominance became so complete that tanker aircraft could accompany the F-4Gs further north, allowing them to remain on-station even longer. During the entire war, only five Coalition aircraft were lost to Iraqi radar-guided SAMs, and four of those five did not have F-4G support.[9]

STU-III. The Secure Telephone Unit (STU) III was an essential item of support equipment for the units that deployed to the Persian Gulf region. Over 350 STU-IIIs were used in the area of operations alone. This unit and the associated family of secure facsimile machines and field phones enabled air campaign planners and staffs to preserve operational secrecy and still establish the informal and ad hoc organizations that sprang up to conduct the campaign.[10]

Campaign planners communicated regularly with agencies in Washington and with deployed wings, frequently bypassing intermediate theater-level organizations. The STU-III and secure fax created the potential for a tremendous volume of communication between parallel groups in the theater and the United States, dealing with everything from the selection of targets to the status of various spare parts or key munitions. Traditional hierarchies and cumbersome procedures were bypassed, leading to improvisation and creativity on the one hand and confusion on the other.

Targeting and sortie production were affected in many ways. On numerous occasions, the Checkmate organization in the Pentagon

---

[9] (S) TSgt Charles L. Starr, *History of the 35th Tactical Fighter Wing (Provisional), Operations Desert Shield and Desert Storm, 2 August 1990–2 August 1991,* Volume 1 (35th Fighter Wing Special History), pp 148–50, 179–83, 190.

[10] Col Randy Witt, et al. "Air Force Tactical Communications in War: The Desert Shield/Desert Storm Comm Story," Hq CENTAF, Mar 1991, GWAPS, NA 49; Hq TAC DCS Communications-Computer System, "Desert Shield/Desert Storm After Action Report," 16 Jul 1991, GWAPS, NA 180.

worked with Washington intelligence organizations to develop prospective targets, then called or faxed the target identification, often including building or site diagrams, to the strategic planning cell in Riyadh. If the target was a high priority one, General Glosson might call a fighter unit on the same day and divert aircraft to this new target. A day later, another call from Washington could bring the first information on target damage. Significantly, the entire intelligence organization in Riyadh could be unaware of these actions until later, if at all. Similarly, adequate coordination with tanker, electronic countermeasures, and reconnaissance aircraft was at times omitted in these late targeting changes, with a resulting loss in sorties and effectiveness.

Conditions in the theater made extensive use of secure telephones a necessity. In the early days of the deployment, the STU-III tied into the local commercial telephone system was one of the few communications capabilities available. Later, premission communications by a mission commander with elements of an attack package at distant bases still took place by secure telephone; so too did subsequent coordination on changes to call signs, times, radio frequencies, and so forth.

The daily air tasking order (ATO) grew to hundreds of pages and was laboriously transmitted over the Computer Assisted Force Management System (CAFMS), but most units had already received the ATO information that pertained to them via secure telephone from Riyadh long before the ATO was sent electronically. Some units avoided CAFMS entirely by arranging for electronic transmission of the ATO from personal computer to personal computer over the voice network through STU-IIIs. The Black Hole also used this technique to transmit master attack plans to Checkmate. The down side of using STU-IIIs for data communications was the pressure put on voice circuits.

Although callers (who would have liked more secure phones and lines) often had trouble "going secure," the STU-III came to symbolize the aspects of computers and telecommunications that worked best. The great promise of these intertwined technologies was only partly realized in this war. CAFMS was by no means the only computer-communications system to prove inadequate under the demands of Desert Shield and Desert Storm. While the American military led other armed forces in its use of computers, the rapidity of technical change had left many of its systems out of date even before they were fully developed. Older mainframe systems were only beginning to acquire the hardware and software necessary for integrated databases and distributed processing.

Problems with mainframe systems, exposed immediately at the beginning of the crisis in August 1990, required even more extensive use of secure phones to overcome efficiency breakdowns. Because the Iraqi invasion came while CENTCOM was still developing an operations plan for that contingency, the Joint Operation Planning and Execution System (JOPES) did not have the necessary data to help commanders schedule the deployment. JOPES was itself undergoing hardware and software development and was not ready to manipulate rapidly changing deployment data fast enough to meet CENTCOM's demands. JOPES ran on the Worldwide Military Command and Control Systems's old Honeywell mainframe computers acquired in the 1970s; it was supposed to integrate separate databases for peacetime planning and crisis planning. JOPES' problems, however, extended beyond its transitional condition to a shortage of personnel trained to operate in this evolving system. For weeks, manual calculations, personal computers, and telephones had to work around JOPES to get American forces deployed to Southwest Asia.

Computer system after computer system followed the sorry pattern of JOPES' performance. Military Airlift Command did not have enough time to schedule missions using its Flow Generation (FLOGEN) model and resorted to personal computer spreadsheets.[11] The Combat Ammunition System was still under development, and the version used by Tactical Air Command, U.S. Air Forces in Europe, and Pacific Air Forces did not have sufficiently accurate data to be helpful. As for the larger problem of tracking supplies in general, the interim solution of having each deployed unit linked to the supply computer at its host base in the United States never worked well. The precrisis plan to deploy mainframes to the theater for supply accounting gave way eventually to linking as many deployed units as possible to Tactical Air Command's Unisys computer at Langley Air Force Base, Virginia. Achieving that arrangement, however, took the better part of Desert Shield's five months and innumerable STU-III calls.[12]

---

[11]Lt Gen Vernon J. Kondra, *Operation Desert Shield–Desert Storm: The Vernon J. Kondra Notes* (McGuire AFB, 1992). Kondra was at Hq MAC DCS Plans and later DCS Operations.

[12]Intvws, GWAPS with Col Mike Christensen, 18–20 Nov 1992; Col Van McCrea, 4–5 Apr 1992; and Frank Spruce, 22 Oct 1992, all at Langley AFB.

The STU-III, like the other four technologies featured in this chapter, hit its stride in the Gulf War. For the most part, these technologies were not really new and were available in less sophisticated forms during the Vietnam War. Thousands of laser-guided bombs were dropped on North Vietnam, together with even more numerous radar-seeking missiles; bombing missions from Thailand depended on air refueling to reach the Hanoi-Haiphong region; and the bases scattered around Thailand coordinated strike packages over the telephone. Some other technologies went through more dramatic changes after the Vietnam War. Airborne radar, for example, came into its own first with the Airborne Warning and Control System and then (just in time for the Gulf War) with the Joint Surveillance Target Attack Radar System. If Iraq's air force and army had been more active, these radar systems would have played a more central role. All of which raises the question: how revolutionary was the air campaign against Iraq?

22

Command and Control

from **AIRPOWER IN THE GULF**

by James P. Coyne

In a manner unprecedented in history, most of the world watched in awe the brilliant aerospace feats of Operation Desert Storm, when a hastily established coalition of United Nations forces utterly defeated Saddam Hussein's well-prepared, well-equipped troops.

People were able to watch because of the advanced system of satellites that transmitted images in real time from Baghdad and Washington to television sets around the world. The entire audience—civilian and military alike—was both mesmerized and dumbfounded by the sight of precision guided munitions guiding unerringly into particular windows or ventilation shafts of key targets. It was warfare as Douhet or Mitchell had never dreamed—precise, devastating, and yet oddly merciful, for the very method of execution ensured minimum collateral damage.

Curiously, the entire spectacle was a de facto sleight of hand exhibition, a series of military magician's tricks. Just as David Copperfield arranges ultra-elaborate deceptions for his onstage magic feats, so did the very brilliance of the Desert Storm attack mask the fact that an absolute revolution in warfare had taken place. This revolution was not in the results of the attack, as spectacular as they were, but rather in the methods by which the attack itself had been conducted. The revolution was simply this: Desert Storm was a seminal point in history, a cusp that marked the transition of warfare from traditional means to the age of information warfare.

James P. Coyne recounts this transition in lucid style in this excerpt, which clearly outlines the importance of what was then C³I (command, control, communications, and intelligence) and is now C⁴I (command, control, communications, computers, and intelligence).

Iraq possessed a formidable C³I system of its own, developed by French and Soviet engineers and installed with multiple redundancy. Saddam's troops were veterans of combat, and his air defense system was one of the best in the world. As such, Iraq's C³I system became the single most important target for Lieutenant General Charles "Chuck" Horner's coalition forces. To avoid the mistakes made in Korea and Vietnam, Horner was given authority over all aircraft of all nations in the theater—nothing flew without his permission.

Horner used proven aircraft systems such as the Boeing E-3B Sentry Airborne Warning and Control System (AWACS) and Lockheed EC-130E Airborne Battlefield Command and Control Center (ABCCC) aircraft. In an unprecedented move, he also called upon a prototype system, the Grumman/Boeing E-8A Joint STARS aircraft, for its amazing air-to-ground radar coverage. These aerial command posts worked with the strike aircraft and with the space-based navigation, communications, intelligence, and weather systems to dominate the air war.

Perhaps the most amazing part of the war was not its successful execution, nor even that it heralded the arrival of a new age in warfare. It lay instead in another analogy, one that Coyne makes well. The Joint STARS aircraft radar tracking system could be played backward, and the sequential blips on the screen would track back to illuminate the source of ground traffic and thus provide a target. The irony is that the information warfare that the United States currently dominates can, like the E-8A radar tracking, be reversed to be used against it. When the United States becomes so heavily dependent on space-based satellite systems, computers, and the intricate passing of encrypted information from center to center, it becomes vulnerable to being rendered impotent by some clever attacker. And unlike Desert Storm, where the attack was delivered by aircraft against ground targets, these attacks can be delivered by missiles against satellites—or by hackers against computers. The most powerful nation in the world might be maneuvering itself into a position where an electronics genius in a small country can short-circuit its C⁴I at the most critical moment.

Coyne tells us the story of brilliant battle in the Gulf—and he gives us something to think about!

W.J.B.

Before the age of electronics and aerospace technology, command and control—in the modern sense of the term—was a comparatively minor element in warfare.

Field commanders used information about the enemy when they could get it, of course, but communications and the means to exploit intelligence were limited. To win their battles, commanders relied mainly on firepower and maneuver.

By the time of the Gulf War, that had changed. Technology had given military commanders the capability to perceive the battle area quickly and in considerable detail, allowing them to adjust tactics and make decisions based on hard information. They could also direct their forces with communications of unprecedented quality.

Command and control (in extended jargon, "command, control, communications, and intelligence," or C^3I) is no longer peripheral to strategy. Information and the means to use it well are among the most effective of modern military weapons.

A military C^3 systems loop includes five elements: a sensor—often radar—to collect data, computers to sort and analyze it, communications to pass the information back and forth, a means of imagery and interpretation so that humans can use the data, and command posts or other facilities enabling them to plug into the system.

Command and control also refers to the command arrangements for using these assets and data.

Desert Storm showcased the role of C^3I in modern warfare. There were many innovations both in the systems and the process, and airborne and spaceborne sensors were employed with stunning effect.

Shortly after Saddam instigated the Gulf crisis, Lt. Gen. Chuck Horner, temporarily operating as "CINCCENT Forward," set up headquarters in Riyadh, Saudi Arabia. Among his first tasks was to get the C^3I arrangements in place.

"My job was to receive forces. Then, figure out where to put them and how we would use them if Saddam attacked," Horner said. Saddam Hussein already had an efficient, well-oiled C^3I system of his own, which had been installed by the Soviets and the French. Stripping him of it was a prime objective of the coalition.

"As Desert Storm began, our commanders emphasized again and again that targeting Saddam Hussein's command and control network is a number one priority," said Lt. Gen. Gordon E. Fornell of the Air Force's Electronic Systems Division....

Command and Control Aircraft. Horner controlled the entire air effort. He operated three types of command and control aircraft. They were central to the success of the air and ground war during Desert Storm. These were the E-3B Sentry Airborne Warning and Control System (AWACS), the E-8A Joint STARS, and the EC-130E Airborne Battlefield Command and Control Center (ABCCC).

The big AWACS birds operated out of Riyadh and flew over Saudi Arabia. As the hot war loomed, Air Force Systems Command provided special communications equipment to enable the Saudi AWACS to communicate with the U.S. fleet despite enemy jamming.

For purposes of coverage and control, Gulf war airspace was divided into three zones—east, central, and west—along the Saudi border with Iraq and Kuwait. One AWACS controlled the air battle in each zone. An additional E-3 was always airborne as a spare or to fill in when one of the primary aircraft left its orbit for inflight refueling.

The AWACS battle staff did its work well, controlling pre- and post-strike refuelings, tankers, reconnaissance aircraft, and other support aircraft as well as the air-to-air and air-to-ground fighters.

The rotating domes atop the E-3s contained not only deep-looking radar but also Identification, Friend or Foe (IFF) systems. In the early going, AWACS performed the valuable function of sorting out coalition aircraft from the Iraqi force. This task eventually vanished because the only aircraft in the sky were those flown by the coalition forces.

AWACS controlled "packages" of fighter aircraft as they entered and exited air-to-ground battle areas. The flying command post identified and contacted post-strike fighter-bombers on their way home, obtained bomb-damage assessment and other strike information, and, if necessary, coordinated additional attacks. The two Air Force E-8A Joint STARS aircraft, with their remarkably discriminating air-to-ground radar, proved adept at detecting enemy ground formations as they formed up or moved across Iraq and Kuwait. Early in the ground war, Joint STARS picked up an Iraqi armored division marshaling for a night attack and sounded the alarm. Coalition air attacks destroyed the enemy formation, so the Iraqi attack never materialized.

The E-8As frequently spotted Iraqi mobile Scud launchers as they moved into position and setup for night launches. They relayed the location coordinates to strike aircraft in orbit over known Scud launch areas. The fighters on orbit were usually F-15E Strike Eagles, equipped with LANTIRN night attack systems, and thus cued, they made short work of numerous Scuds.

The prime Joint STARS job is to report where and how enemy traffic is moving, but the flip side of this information also turned out to be extremely useful. Ground commanders, for example, said it was enormously valuable to know where the Iraqis were *not* moving.

Early in the war, Joint STARS told the coalition defenders in the border town of Khafji that the Iraqis attacking them were not backed up by reinforcements. With that information, the allies launched an immediate and successful counterattack.

In another "flip side" application, tapes from the E-8A radar tracking were played backwards—with the result that sequential blips on the screen pointed directly to the places where the enemy vehicles had begun their trips. If that point of origin turned out to be a supply dump or some other concentration of Iraqi assets, an air strike would soon be on the way.

"We will not ever again want to fight any kind of combat without a Joint STARS kind of system," Air Force Chief of Staff McPeak declared part way through Desert Storm.

EC-130E ABCCCs, less famous than their more elaborate AWACS and Joint STARS cousins, controlled the air-to-ground attacks. In the cargo hold of each EC-130E deploying to the Gulf was a new computerized module with fifteen console positions. At these, controllers and communicators scanned nineteen-inch cathode-ray tubes, calling up maps, imagery, and air tasking order information to use as they employed attack aircraft over the battle area.

Coping With Friction and Fog. All in all, C³I in the Desert Storm went far, far beyond anything seen in previous wars. The technology, the training, and the systems worked. So did the chain of command and tasking, and coalition forces found ways to overcome or work around most of the problems they encountered.

Clausewitz's *friction and fog of war* weighed heavily. Saddam's Soviet-style command and control system, dependent upon centralized direction from Baghdad, was rendered virtually useless. Allied air attacks destroyed the coordination and effectiveness in the first twenty-four hours of the war.

Individual command nodes, radar, surface-to-air missile sites, and antiaircraft batteries could not function efficiently in isolation from the command and control system.

For the coalition it was different. Talk of "battle management," Gen. Ronald W. Yates of Air Force Systems Command noted early in the campaign, "implies a kind of calm, boardroom style of warfighting. What commanders in the Gulf are really dealing with are dispersed forces in an environment where the fog and friction of war exacerbate every problem. The job of C^3 is to pierce the fog and minimize the friction."

The strength of coalition C^3I, plus the fact that Saddam's had been essentially destroyed, was important up to the end of the Gulf War.

"The allied coalition was able to covertly reposition forces immediately before the ground combat phase began because the Iraqis did not have an aerial surveillance capability," said Gen. Donald J. Kutyna of U.S. Space Command. "This move allowed General Schwarzkopf to completely surprise Iraqi ground forces and minimize allied casualties."

23

Strike Eagles to the Rescue

from **STRIKE EAGLE: FLYING THE F-15E IN THE GULF WAR**

by **William L. Smallwood**

Since its introduction into the operational U.S. Air Force inventory in 1976, the McDonnell Douglas (now Boeing) F-15 Eagle has reigned supreme as the world's premier air superiority fighter. Developed in the generation immediately preceding stealth, super-cruise, and advanced digital avionics, the F-15 represents the apex of its era and continues to hold the line until the next generation of fighters, led by the promising F-22 Raptor, can be fielded.

Conceived as strictly an air-to-air fighter, from the outset the Eagle's design emphasized a beyond-visual-range (BVR) capability, permitting the aircraft's pilot to detect, identify, track, and fire at bogeys prior to entering the ring of visual contact. At the same time, massive control surfaces and an incredible thrust-to-weight ratio confer the traditional air-to-air fighter attribute of maneuverability. The aircraft, big for a fighter, was scaled up to provide for twin-engine reliability and a fuel capacity allowing for an extended combat radius.

These air-to-air fighter virtues have application to tactical aircraft committed to the air-to-ground mission. Logically, then, the contractor considered producing an adaptation of its basic airframe as a dedicated ground attack aircraft retaining air-to-air prowess. Approximately a decade after the first F-15 entered service, the ground attack variant, designated the F-15E and called the Strike Eagle, made its maiden flight.

The complexity of this type's mission requires that there be two crew members, the pilot up front and the weapon systems officer (WSO) in the rear seat. Becoming operational in 1989, the Strike Eagle was able to take advantage of the unfolding digital revolution. The WSO has four multipurpose cathode ray tubes providing a variety of data from navigational coordinates to bogey locations to a weapons selection menu. Systems include the AN/APG-70 synthetic aperture radar. LANTIRN navigation and targeting pods allow high-speed terrain-following flight and laser designation of ground targets, respectively.

The F-15E can carry more than twelve tons of ordnance, including sophisticated precision guided munitions and "iron" bombs, as well as an array of air-to-air missiles for its own defense. In addition, the aircraft, like its air-to-air counterpart, is equipped with a 20mm cannon. Even in this new age, the aircraft remains an impressive dual-role platform. The Strike Eagle has replaced the aged F-111 tactical bomber.

Given its ability to conduct surgical strikes and to more than hold its own against air-to-air threats, the F-15E, not surprisingly, was in the forefront of the hunt to eradicate the Scud missile menace during the 1991 Persian Gulf War. The mission was frustrating because the Scuds could be constantly repositioned on mobile launchers across the vast Iraqi landscape. The missiles could be concealed from aerial view by, for example, placing them under bridges. Also, there were reports that decoys were being used to dupe the coalition's forces.

The tactics that were developed to cope with these problems involved the use of airborne infrared sensors to pick up a heat source immediately upon launch of a Scud. Yet, even this methodology had its drawbacks, since the mobile launchers would ordinarily be well on their way into hiding by the time a Strike Eagle or other ground attack aircraft could be vectored to the area. Meanwhile, Scuds were raining down on Israel, which was sitting out the war at the behest of the United States. It was feared that continued Scud attacks on Israel would pressure its leaders into striking back, which would threaten the fragile coalition. Scud hunting became a top priority.

Both British Special Air Service (SAS) and U.S. Special Operations teams were inserted surreptitiously into western Iraq to find Scuds "the old-fashioned way." As these teams roamed the desert for signs of Scud missiles, they would at times be discovered by enemy forces and become vulnerable. In such circumstances, they urgently called for air cover. This excerpt from *Strike Eagle: Flying the F-15E in the Gulf War*, by Bill Smallwood, describes a flight of Strike Eagles being diverted from a Scud combat air patrol (CAP) by an airborne controller to assist one of these covert teams that was about to be overrun by Iraqi forces.

As this excerpt demonstrates, the intricate planning of military strategists and the extensive deployment of sophisticated weaponry do not assure smooth operations in the inevitable fog of battle. Every weapon has its limitations, and with humans in the loop, confusion will always be an element of warfare. Nevertheless, in this case determination and teamwork coalesced to save the day. Rescuing comrades from death or capture is the most satisfying kind of mission for the air warrior. Strike Eagle air crewmen Captains Tim "TB" Bennett and Dan "Chewie" Bakke provide a first-person account of an inimitable episode that is sure to have a lasting place in the annals of air combat.

P.H.

BENNETT: "It was February 13, approximately 0200 and we were on a Scud CAP mission into western Iraq. We were Packard Four-One and leading the two-ship element. Capt. Greg Johnson and Lt. Karl Von Luhrte were on our wing; they were Packard Four-Two. We had been on station about forty-five minutes when AWACS gave us a call. They said there were some 'troops in contact' and they gave us coordinates where there were some Iraqi helicopters threatening our guys. AWACS couldn't see up there, but what they heard was a burst transmission—an HF [high frequency] transmission—from the guys on the ground saying that they had been discovered."

BAKKE: "When they called we were in the process of hitting an SA-3 site near Al Qaim. We were mapping the site and starting our attack when AWACS called us with 'priority targeting.' We broke off the attack and sent our wingman to high cover—they had twelve Mark-82s and we had the targeting pod with four GBU-l0s [2,000-pound smart bombs]. I plug in the coordinates AWACS gives us and they are in the middle of a no-drop zone—I read that as a zone where special forces are operating. I confirm with AWACS that these coordinates are correct and they are in a no-drop zone. She came back and said, 'Roger, those are the correct coordinates.' "

BENNETT: "Her call sign was Cougar."

BAKKE: "Yeah, so I continued the conversation with her—this isn't verbatim but close—she said, 'There are three Iraqi helicopters dismounting troops with possible friendlies in contact. Kill all helicopters.'* I reconfirmed with her, 'Kill all helicopters?' She came back and said, 'Roger, kill all helicopters.' "

BENNETT: "The reason Dan is repeating that is because it is real uncommon to get an order to kill [all helicopters]. You never hear anything like that because you always ID them."

BAKKE: "At that point, TB is starting to the coordinates and we aren't saying anything back and forth."

BENNETT: "I am talking to my wingman real quick because we were getting into a lot of weather. Since he had dumb bombs there was no reason to bring him down there with us. I wanted him to stay above the weather. Also, once we got below 10,000 feet we couldn't always talk to AWACS. I am telling him to relay whatever we say back to Cougar and we'll let him know what is going on. By now we are dropping down through the weather at mil power. We're moving pretty good when we get down below the weather. There was no doubt in our minds from the radio transmission from AWACS that we had to get there in a hurry. Normally, we would be a little cautious because we were going into the Sam's Town area, but we're in a hurry. If they were in contact up there, time was of the essence. There was a lot of stuff up there that wasn't good, but we're ramping over there in mil power going about 600 knots. Then, when we're about fifty miles out, Dan gets contacts on the radar."

BAKKE: "On two of the three [helicopters]."

BENNETT: "We talked real quick, back and forth, and it was like, well, let's just let a bomb go if we can ID them as helicopters."

BAKKE: "I called AWACS and I reconfirmed with them that we have the helicopters. Actually, what we have on radar contact is their rotor spinning."

---

*"Kill" is a directive to commit on target with clearance to fire—with no identification required.

BENNETT: "We aren't getting an air speed readout yet on them. We are pretty sure they are sitting on the ground. [Their IR image is two-dimensional.] We said, 'Okay, let's go in there.' If he [Bakke] can get them on the targeting pod, we'll let a bomb go. That way, if they take off and move, at least we will get their attention and divert it from our guys on the ground. But, if they start moving, we'll come back and shoot them with an AIM-9. Our main goal was to get something on them fast, to let them know we are there. At this time Dan is working with the radar and about the time we are deciding that we are going to drop a bomb, we are going through 10,000 feet. Finally, we break out of the weather at about 3,000 feet—it was not good weather that night. Just as soon as we break out, the triple-A starts coming up. We're about twenty miles from the contacts and then, at around fifteen miles, Dan's got them in the targeting pod."

BAKKE: "We didn't make a map; you can cue the targeting pod from the air-to-air radar. You can get a designation just using the pod. I'm looking solely through the pod now. It's infrared and the helicopters are hot and the rotors look like discs. I have two of the three and we're assuming they are on the ground. At this point, we can still hear AWACS talking but it is broken—we're expecting our wingman to pass on anything important. We go in, get a release cue, TB drops a long ball [bomb] and starts a left-hand turn so that I can track the target."

BENNETT: "I'm turning toward Syria [hands showing the banked turn]."

BAKKE: "I'm doing the laser, putting it on the white spot, waiting. We released the bomb about six miles away and it has over thirty seconds time of flight."

BENNETT: "Meanwhile, I'm looking at the radar because he is concentrating [on the image in the pod]. About ten seconds after the bomb comes off, I start seeing an air speed readout on the radar. I'm thinking, this thing is moving; go back into air-to-air and bring up an AIM-9. Meanwhile, Dan is tracking it big time, but I'm thinking, shit, this bomb is never going to make it. I'm starting to jink around—they're firing some triple A—but I can't jink too much—it's hard enough back there keeping the laser on the spot without me giving him any more problems."

BAKKE: "We jink off to the left and it appears to me that this guy is moving. What in fact happened, according to the guys on the ground, is that the helicopter was at 800 to 1,000 feet when the bomb impacted. It hit just forward of the center of the rotors, right in the cockpit. And I guess, if you've ever seen a James Bond movie where the helicopter—the model they film—just vaporizes and disappears, that is exactly what happened. At this point, we have already figured out that this guy was airborne so TB goes into a hard left-hand turn and calls up an AIM-9. Also, we tell our wingman to come down and drop six Mark-82s on that spot to stop any troops that have been let off."

BENNETT: "I called him in because he could see the fireball through his FLIR and there was no danger of hitting our guys. Also, I wanted to keep the Iraqis' heads down until we could get back in and make another pass."

BAKKE: "Right at this point, TB and I are ecstatic, although we haven't said anything to each other. [As soon as we get enough altitude] I get on the radio to AWACS and I say, 'Cougar, Packard Four-One, splash one helicopter. Engaging second [with air-to-air ordnance].' Shortly thereafter we get a call from AWACS asking us to confirm that we had ID'd this helicopter as Iraqi. Now there is no doubt in your mind, when AWACS tells you to kill something, they have basically taken away all your responsibility for identification of that aerospace vehicle. However, in our case, whatever levity was in the airplane dissipated immediately. Our spirits went right through the floorboard of that airplane. And I'll tell you, as soon as she said, 'Confirm you ID'd that helicopter is Iraqi,' I went through the roof. I told her to get off the scope and get us Hammer, who is the person on AWACS with commit authority.

"While I am talking to AWACS, TB is trying to maneuver behind these guys for the AIM-9. I mean, we have a single [helicopter] running northeast and we are just doing circles down the middle of the entire threat area trying to get confirmation on whether we should engage these guys. As it turns out, we push them as far north as we can for the known threats in the area. For our own safety and for lack of fuel, we turn around. And we don't have any friendly words for the AWACS controller at that point. There was silence in the cockpit."

BENNETT: "Hammer did get on the horn eventually. The first thing we thought, since we probably had helicopters operating out of Syria, was that we might have hit one of our own that had come over from there. However, the one we got looked like a Hind [Russian-made helicopter] to me and to Dan, too. But as soon as she asked if we had ID'd it as Iraqi, all that confidence went right out the window.

"Then Hammer gets on and says, 'Yeah, you are okay.' But when I came back around again, they put that same idiot controller back on and I'm running around in the clouds, right over triple-A alley, and I'm saying 'What are we doing?' Hammer gets on again and says, 'You are good to go on those guys,' so we ran back to the north hoping to get the one [helicopter] heading toward Sam's Town."

BAKKE: "I never did see the third one. We saw it on radar, but not in the FLIR."

BENNETT: "I think the third one sat down somewhere, but we could see this guy running toward Sam's Town on radar and we're going after him when all of a sudden, I see flashes. I think, oh, shit, I've drug us right into a SAM launch. Then I realized that those weren't SAM launches, those are bombs. That AWACS controller had vectored another flight in even though we had told Hammer that we were going down to get this last guy. She had vectored another flight in from another squadron on a different freq and told them to drop on coordinates. We had twenty-four Mark-82s raining down on us. They had no way of knowing we were down there—she didn't tell them.

"After that, I'm thinking we have exhausted about all of our lives tonight so I said, 'Let's get out of here.' We beat it, no kidding, all the way home."

BAKKE: "As soon as we got back, I called the special forces liaison up at TACC and talked with him and tried to get confirmation from him that their guys were safe. About six hours later we got a phone call from TACC saying that their guys were safe and they had witnessed the explosion [of the helicopter]. Then, after the war, I was on a briefing team that went to CENTAF, then to the Pentagon, and then to the White House. One of the guys on the briefing team, Warrant Officer Cliff Wolcott,* was a U.S. Special Forces helicopter pilot and had been out there hiding that night. He witnessed the whole thing. As it turned out, these were the guys who had originally called in for help. From what he said, I'm convinced that we, in fact, saved some casualties, if not some lives out there that night."

---

*Warrant Officer Wolcott was killed in October 1993, flying a Blackhawk in Somalia during a Special Forces operation.

THE ART AND SCIENCE OF AIR WARFARE

24

An Independent Air Force

from THE COMMAND OF THE AIR
by Giulio Douhet

Perhaps the most often cited exposition of air warfare theory, *The Command of the Air* actually had far more profound effects upon diplomacy in peacetime than it did upon aerial warfare. Its concepts were accepted as gospel by the press and by many national leaders, even if they were rejected by the military services of most countries.

The combination of Douhet's thinking, minor experience with bombing during the Great War, and the horrifying fictional representation of bombing in a number of influential works resulted in the growth of a number of myths. Among these were the great lethality of aerial bombardment, the efficacy of a limited number of relatively small aircraft, and the susceptibility of the civilian populations of the world to panic and revolt under relatively few attacks.

These myths created a mind-set among world politicians that was wonderfully exploited by Adolf Hitler and his propaganda minister, Joseph Goebbels. The two men, particularly the latter, imbued their fledgling Luftwaffe with extraordinary powers, so much so that two powerful nations, Great Britain and France, were terrified into appeasement policies right up to the invasion of Poland. Goebbels's propaganda had been enhanced by the prevailing British viewpoint, first articulated by then Prime Minister Stanley Baldwin, that "the bombers would always get through." As a result, the Germans were able to parlay a handful of pitifully ineffective Junkers Ju 52 bombers into a war-winning weapon—without ever having to commit them to battle.

The hard truth was that Germany had neither the bombers nor the bombs to mount a bombing campaign. The Ju 52s could reach England from German bases—but not if they carried bombs. When the real air war ensued in the Battle of Britain, even harder truths emerged. Both sides learned at great cost that bombs were not nearly as lethal as thought and that huge fleets of bombers were required to conduct sustained operations before they even began to be effective. Most important of all, the civilian populations of both Great Britain and Germany proved to be incredibly tough, able to take casualties and hardships in their stride without losing their morale or critically diminishing their productive capacity.

Giulio Douhet was almost forty when, in 1909, he began considering airpower as a tool of war. He had direct experience, commanding the Italian army's aviation section, and by 1915 was advocating that Italy assemble a force of 500 bombing aircraft to strike Austrian cities. As is the fate of many airpower prophets, he was court-martialed, not so much for his outspoken ideas as for his criticism of his military and political superiors for not taking his advice.

And although Douhet had no grasp of the scale of aerial warfare ultimately required and grossly underestimated the intestinal fortitude of the civilian population, he was correct in many respects. He foresaw that war would become total in the future. He advocated an Independent Air Force, always ready for action and determined to achieve air superiority by carrying the war to the enemy homeland. He even accepted that it might be necessary to absorb punishment from the enemy while inflicting even more massive destruction upon him. If he erred, it was in his failure to see securing air superiority as a first essential step in conducting a bombing campaign. He believed that air superiority would result from the bombing campaign, rather than from securing it in battle in the air and on the ground. The United States Army Air Forces and the Royal Air Force did not learn this until 1944—when it was almost too late.

It is too much to expect that the first philosophical proponent of airpower would be correct in all his ideas. Douhet actually served his greatest purpose by providing a baseline for later theorists to depart from. It is an irony of warfare that Douhet's ideas became much more valid in the nuclear age, a time he could not have fore-seen. By then the performance of aircraft, and particularly inter-continental ballistic missiles, had grown and their warheads had become so lethal that Douhet's basic principles were exactly correct.

W.J.B.

As LONG AS AERIAL FORCES remain mere auxiliaries of the army and navy, there will be no real aerial warfare in case of conflict. True, there will be air battles of major and minor proportions, but always subject to land or sea operations. Before any real aerial warfare can take place, its basic elements, such as planes, personnel, and their organization into an autonomous fighting body, must first be created and forged into an efficient fighting organization.

Under the circumstances, the first nation to arm herself with a real Independent Air Force will be in a superior military position, at least until other nations follow her example; for she will be in possession of an offensive weapon of formidable power, while the others will be dependent upon mere aerial auxiliaries. No doubt the necessity of establishing military equilibrium among the nations will induce others to follow her lead.

To study the development of aerial warfare, let us consider two cases: (1) a war between Nation A, armed with an Independent Air Force, and Nation B, without one; and (2) a war between two nations, both armed with an Independent Air Force.

An Independent Air Force must be always ready for action; otherwise 90 percent of its effectiveness is lost. Given the speed of its units, no matter how widely dispersed their bases of operation may be in time of peace, it should be able to concentrate its forces along its line of battle and be ready for action in a few hours. If civil aviation units, scattered over the country, are a part of the Air Force's organization, they must be located where their integration into the Air Force can be accomplished as quickly as possible. In short, the Independent Air Force must be organically and logistically organized so that it can go into action immediately upon the outbreak of hostilities.

Now let us examine the first case. Independent Air Force A begins its action to catch Nation B in the midst of mobilization. But let us assume that Nation B is found to have immediately mobilized all her military aviation. Only her pursuit and bombing specialties, however, could take part in the battle, because her other specialties are suitable only for integrating the action of her naval and land forces. It is clear, then, that Independent Air Force A will have freedom of action, for B's pursuit aviation certainly could not hinder it. On the contrary, assuming that Air Force A has an adequate number of combat units, it will be able to inflict losses on B's pursuit aviation. Thus Air Force A will rapidly gain command of the air by destroying the mobilization, maintenance, and production centers of Nation B's aviation.

Once the command of the air has been won, the combat units of A's Independent Air Force will naturally cease functioning solely to protect bombing units and will be used to neutralize the fire of antiaircraft batteries during bombing operations by the entire Air Force, and to bomb and machine-gun troop concentrations, supply trains, transport or marching columns, et cetera. Furthermore, if constructed to undergo the necessary conversion in equipment, these combat units can quickly be transformed into first-rate bombing planes. Therefore, with the command of the air an accomplished fact, Independent Air Force A will have won complete liberty of action to strike at will, with no risk to itself, over all the enemy's territory, and quickly bring him to his knees.

By bombing railroad junctions and depots, population centers at road junctions, military depots, and other vital objectives, Air Force A could handicap the mobilization of B's army. By bombing naval bases, arsenals, oil stores, battleships at anchor, and mercantile ports, it could prevent the efficient operation of B's navy. By bombing the most vital civilian centers it could spread terror through the nation and quickly break down B's material and moral resistance.

The reader who thinks this picture overdrawn has only to look at a map of Italy, and imagine himself the commander of an Independent Air Force belonging to any of the nations on our frontiers. Let him remember that his Air Force is capable of destroying 50 surfaces 500 meters in diameter every day; and then ask himself how many days of operation it would take to achieve the aim described above. He must also take into consideration the fact that, even in the present stage of aeronautical development, the daily operational strength of such an Independent Air Force would be, even if only half of it were used on alternate days, about a thousand machines, requiring only a few thousand men to man it. Then he may draw his own conclusions.

At this point I want to stress one aspect of the problem—namely, that the effect of such aerial offensives upon morale may well have more influence upon the conduct of the war than their material effects. For example, take the center of a large city and imagine what would happen among the civilian population during a single attack by a single bombing unit. For my part, I have no doubt that its impact upon the people would be terrible. Here is what would be likely to happen to the center of the city within a radius of about 250 meters: Within a few minutes some 20 tons of high-explosive, incendiary, and gas bombs would rain down. First would come explosions, then fires, then deadly gases floating on the surface and preventing any approach to the stricken area. As the hours passed and night advanced, the fires would spread while the poison gas paralyzed all life. By the following day the life of the city would be suspended; and if it happened to be a junction on some important artery of communication traffic would be suspended.

What could happen to a single city in a single day could also happen to ten, twenty, fifty cities. And, since news travels fast, even without telegraph, telephone, or radio, what, I ask you, would be the effect upon civilians of other cities, not yet stricken but equally subject to bombing attacks? What civil or military authority could keep order, public services functioning, and production going under such a threat? And even if a semblance of order was maintained and some work done, would not the sight of a single enemy plane be enough to stampede the population into panic? In short, normal life would be impossible in this constant nightmare of imminent death and destruction. And if on the second day another ten, twenty, or fifty cities were bombed, who could keep all those lost, panic-stricken people from fleeing to the open countryside to escape this terror from the air?

A complete breakdown of the social structure cannot but take place in a country subjected to this kind of merciless pounding from the air. The time would soon come when, to put an end to horror and suffering, the people themselves, driven by the instinct of self-preservation, would rise up and demand an end to the war—this before their army and navy had time to mobilize at all! The reader who thinks I have overcolored the picture has only to recall the panic created at Brescia when, during funeral services for the victims of an earlier bombing—a negligible one compared with the one I have pictured here—one of the mourners mistook a bird for an enemy plane.

Now to the second case, of two nations each armed with an Independent Air Force. It is easy to see that in this case, even more than in the first one, the nation who struck first would have the edge on the enemy; or, conversely, how imperative it would be to parry as well as possible the enemy's blow before it struck home. To simplify the situation, then, let us admit that both independent Air Forces could begin operations simultaneously. We have already seen that the fundamental concept governing aerial warfare is *to be resigned to the damage the enemy may inflict upon us, while utilizing every means at our disposal to inflict even heavier damage upon him.* An Independent Air Force must therefore be completely free of any preoccupation with the actions of the enemy force. Its sole concern should be to do the enemy the greatest possible amount of surface damage in the shortest possible time, which depends upon the available air forces and the choice of enemy targets. Whatever resources, of men, money, and equipment, are diverted from the strength and essential purpose of an Independent Air Force will result in slowing down the conduct of the war and delaying its final outcome.

The choice of enemy targets, as I have already pointed out, is the most delicate operation of aerial warfare, especially when both sides are armed with Independent Air Forces. In such a case the final decision depends upon the disequilibrium between the damage suffered by the enemy and his powers of recuperating from a blow which must be struck as quickly as possible, lest the enemy strike at us first. Of course, it may still be possible for one side to use its Independent Air Force to conquer the command of the air, which would ultimately win the war. But there may not be time enough for this if the other side succeeds in striking first and throwing the country into complete confusion.

The truth of the matter is that no hard and fast rules can be laid down on this aspect of aerial warfare. It is impossible even to outline general standards, because the choice of enemy targets will depend upon a number of circumstances, material, moral, and psychological, the importance of which, though real, is not easily estimated. It is just here, in grasping these imponderables, in choosing enemy targets, that future commanders of Independent Air Forces will show their ability.

Once the choice of enemy objectives and the order of their destruction have been determined, the task of the Air Force becomes very simple—to get on with their destruction in the briefest possible time, with no other preoccupation. In the case we are considering, therefore, both

Air Forces will, at least in theory, proceed simultaneously in mass from their points of concentration toward their chosen objectives, without seeking each other out on the way. Should they happen to meet in flight, an air battle is inevitable; but I repeat that their purpose is not to seek each other out and fight in the air.

I consider this phase of aerial warfare very important, and I should like to pause here to clarify it further. Let us suppose that one of the Air Forces does seek out the other; but meanwhile the latter, avoiding an encounter, goes straight to its chosen objectives. He who seeks may find; but he may also return empty-handed. If one Independent Air Force deviates from its essential purpose, wastes time and fritters away its own freedom of action by seeking out the enemy in the air, the chances are not only that it will fail to find the enemy Air Force in the air, but also that the latter is at that very moment carrying out unchallenged its operations against the home territory. The one will have accomplished its task successfully; the other will have missed its opportunity and failed. In this kind of war, in which time is a vital factor, such a failure may have grave consequences in the outcome of the war, and should at all costs be avoided.

Speaking of aerial actions, I have already mentioned the possibility of having units of an Independent Air Force operate on alternate days; but I meant it merely as an illustration of how an Air Force might achieve results of major importance even with only half her strength, or with a relatively small number of planes. But during actual operations it would be an error to employ the strength of the Air Force piecemeal; for the purpose of an Independent Air Force is to inflict upon the enemy the greatest possible damage in the shortest possible time. The potential strength of an Independent Air Force should always be used to its fullest, with no thought of economy, especially when confronted by another equally strong Air Force which could do equally heavy damage. To replace personnel and equipment with fresh reserves may be expedient; but the Air Force itself—that is, its full complement of planes—should always remain in the air battering at enemy targets. It is the total effect of these bombing operations which decides the outcome of the conflict in favor of that Air Force which succeeds in dumping the largest quantity of bombs in the shortest time.

In presenting these ideas of the general character of aerial warfare, I have attempted only to show that if aerial warfare in its broad outline looks like a simple matter, it nevertheless presents staggering problems, the solution of which is very complex. But even in this brief résumé we can catch a glimpse of the heights of atrocity to which aerial warfare may reach.

When we stop to think of the magnitude and power of aerial offensives, and realize that no really effective method of parrying them exists; and since it would be futile to divert aerial forces to defense, the phrase "to submit to whatever damage the enemy may inflict" becomes a phrase expressing actual circumstances of tragedy attending aerial warfare.

Tragic, too, to think that the decision in this kind of war must depend upon smashing the material and moral resources of a people caught up in a frightful cataclysm which haunts them everywhere without cease until the final collapse of all social organization. Mercifully the decision will be quick in this kind of war, since the decisive blows will be directed at civilians, that element of the countries at war least able to sustain them. These future wars may yet prove to be more humane than wars in the past in spite of all, because they may in the long run shed less blood. But there is no doubt that nations who find themselves unprepared to sustain them will be lost.

25

The Defense Against Aircraft

from **WINGED DEFENSE**
by William Mitchell

If Giulio Douhet was a hero to the philosophers of airpower, the far more famous Billy Mitchell was a hero not only to the men who flew and fought in the two world wars but also to those who followed as well.

Mitchell's background contrasted sharply with Douhet's in that he first learned to fly at his own expense, and then, by sheer perseverance and force of personality, worked his way into a position of command. In the process he developed his own ideas on airpower, drawing on his personal experience and on the principles espoused by the man who became the first marshal of the Royal Air Force, Hugh "Boom" Trenchard.

Unlike Douhet and most other airpower theorists, Mitchell gained firsthand experience at the front, as this excerpt from his later book, *Winged Defense,* clearly shows. His arch-rival in the American Air Service, Benjamin Foulois, violently disapproved of Mitchell's insinuation of himself into a leadership position. Foulois's view was understandable. He had fought his way up through the ranks, teaching himself to fly, and never even considered the possibility that he would have an air force to command. When that time arrived, however unexpected it was, he was dismayed to find Mitchell ready to take over.

It did not sit well, and Foulois quickly found a way to oust

Mitchell, who was everything Foulois was not—charismatic, an ardent Anglophile and Francophile, and a consummate schmoozer. As unmilitary as Foulois considered these characteristics to be, Mitchell was precisely the type of person needed to weld the infant American Air Service to both the French and British air forces, drawing upon them for knowledge, procedures, and equipment.

Perhaps out of sheer frustration, Foulois often pointed out that Mitchell was not a "regular" Army flyer because he had not gone through an Army flying school. Notwithstanding this, Mitchell flew a wide variety of aircraft at the front, including Nieuport 28s and the mulish Spad XVI. (He flew the Prince of Wales, later Edward the VIII and still later the Duke of Windsor, over the front lines in the two-seater Spad. It was a risky political business that only someone of Mitchell's sublime self-confidence would have undertaken.)

Foulois eventually recognized Mitchell's worth and, despite genuine rancor, recommended that he be made chief of the Air Service, 1st Army, American Expeditionary Forces. As a result, Mitchell personally commanded the largest aerial armada of World War I, assembled for the attack on the St. Mihiel salient. He molded 101 American, British, French, and Italian squadrons, with 1,476 airplanes and 20 balloons, into a huge striking force, one that presaged the future.

After the war, Mitchell would continue to demonstrate his piloting prowess, including setting a world's absolute speed record in a Curtiss R-6 racer. He would also demonstrate considerable showmanship in the hugely publicized sinking of German warships off the Virginia coast, as well as colossal ineptitude in public relations by managing to antagonize not only the navy but the army as well.

With his courage, piloting skill, and military ability established, it only remains to be determined how correct were his theories on airpower, and this excerpt manages to do just that. Within it one can determine that Mitchell understood the concept of air superiority; the efficacy of offensive versus defensive action; the need to develop what the Germans called a *Schwerpunkt,* a point of main effort; and the need to mass airpower for decisive encounters.

Many of Mitchell's detractors jibed that he was too articulate, too glib, and wrote too well for his own good. This excerpt shows that he was all of these, indeed, but that he was also, and foremost, what every air force needs most: a fighter.

W.J.B.

It was proved in the European war [World War I] that the only effective defense against aerial attack is to whip the enemy's air forces in air battles. In other words, seizing the initiative, forcing the enemy to the defensive in his own territory, attacking his most important ground positions, menacing his airplanes on the ground, in the hangars, on the airdromes and in the factories so that he will be forced to take the air and defend them. To sit down on one's own territory and wait for the other fellow to come, is to be whipped before an operation has even commenced.

During the Chateau-Thierry operations when our air forces first came up on the line in the last part of June and the first part of July 1918, the Germans controlled the air completely. They had concentrated the major part of their aviation against the air force assigned to the Sixth French Army and destroyed it, while their offense on the ground was so rapid that they captured the French airdromes with the planes still in them. We were ordered from our concentration area in the Toul region to reinforce the Sixth French Army that was holding the line of the Marne River. We started there on the 28th day of June 1918, arriving that night with all our planes. We were under French command and they assigned us to what is known as barrier patrol duty along the front. This consists of having a flight of five or six airplanes or maybe a squadron patrol back and forth on a front of about ten miles, which makes both ends of such a patrol sector visible from the other end. The barrier patrol was designed to keep out any hostile aircraft that might come into the area. These patrol areas were joined on each side by other patrols, and in this way the whole front was covered. If only one or two German planes attempted to break through, this system worked, but it was fallacious because the Germans, finding out the strength of the patrols, could concentrate their aviation and outnumber any one of our patrols three or four to one, jump on it, destroy it and go ahead and do whatever they wanted to.

In a few days our losses were terrific. Among the lost were Quentin Roosevelt, Allan Winslow and other valuable men. In the meantime, some of us had flown clear across the German position all the way from La Ferte Sous Jouarre across Fere-en-Tardenois to Soissons, cross cutting the whole German area. I did it alone in a Nieuport single seater, and later Major Brereton with Captain Hazlett as observer did the same thing. We had definitely located the German center of supply at Fere-en-Tardenois. The woods were full of ammunition, machine guns, cannon, fuel, gasoline and oil, motor transport, pontoons, temporary railroads, and everything that goes to make up an army's equipment.

We had found a place that would have to be protected in case it was menaced from the air, because a few bombs dropped on the ammunition dumps would blow them up, gasoline and oil would be set on fire, and the losses of material might be so great as to completely stop a forward movement. I therefore asked that bombardment aviation be called for immediately as we had none. The French air division, used as the great mass of maneuver of air operations, was attempting to cover the front of the Fourth French Army which was menaced by a strong German attack. They had been badly depleted and were very tired as they had been fighting constantly since the German attack against the Fifth British Army under General Goff, in March. They could not come to assist us. We therefore asked the British to send a brigade of their air force to help us. They despatched it immediately. It consisted of three squadrons of two-seater D.H. 9 bombardment airplanes, and two squadrons of pursuit, one of which was equipped with Sopwith Camels and the other with S. E. 5's. They arrived full of fight and ready to go.

On the following morning the British bombardment force was given directions to attack Fere-en-Tardenois at dawn. We concentrated all our pursuit aviation, four squadrons of ours and two of the British and converged on Fere-en-Tardenois from three different directions so as to arrive there at the same time that the bombardment did. About thirty-six British bombardment ships made the attack at an altitude of from five hundred to one thousand feet. It was a remarkably brave feat. They blew up several ammunition dumps and caused consternation among the Germans. The German pursuit ships, concentrated to defend Fere-en-Tardenois, shot down twelve British bombardment planes on that day. Our pursuit aviation, on the other hand, shot down more than this number of Germans with small loss to our pursuit. The tables had been completely turned on the Germans and they had to stand with their aviation and defend Fere-en-Tardenois. They no longer could keep penetrating our lines because if they did they would so weaken themselves around Fere-en-Tardenois as to become incapable of defending it. If they did not keep a large part of their aviation constantly in the air, on account of the short distance from our lines to Fere-en-Tardenois they would be too late to attack us; because, if they awaited us on the ground, they would be unable to climb up to us before we were well on our way back, after having dropped our bombs. Therefore, they could never oppose us with more than one-quarter of their total aviation, usually with not more than one-sixth, because the part that was not in the air when we arrived there was useless. If they put all their aviation in the air at once we would watch it and attack when they returned to the ground for fuel. We had seized the power of initiative by finding a spot very vulnerable to the Germans which put them on the defensive although they greatly outnumbered us. We concentrated our whole aviation and launched it in one body. Of course, the Germans might have done the same thing to us if we had had a place behind our lines that was as important to us as was Fere-en-Tardenois to them. There was no such a place, because our troops were being supplied on converging lines, while theirs were being supplied on diverging lines from Fere-en-Tardenois. The same condition lasted practically during the rest of the Chateau-Thierry operations, because the area around Fere-en-Tardenois had to be kept full of supplies for the German army.

26

Fighter Missions

from FIGHTER COMBAT: TACTICS AND MANEUVERING

by Robert L. Shaw

The concept of the fighter has been the single most engaging aspect of military aviation since the debut of the Fokker E.I in 1915. There is a romantic appeal to the idea of "clean single combat in the cerulean blue" that pervades not only literature and films but also the consciousness of almost everyone associated with aviation.

Unfortunately for all concerned, the idea of a gallant knighthood engaged in chivalrous combat is utterly absurd. The ideal air combat is a cold-blooded murder in which the attacker approaches the victim unseen, fires, and kills his opponent without any exposure to danger. This is not gallant, but it makes a great deal of sense to any pilot who wants to survive.

Granted, not all air combat takes place under these conditions, but for the execution of the mission—and for building a victory streak—this is preferred technique.

The problem implicit in such an attack is enemy vigilance, the question of relative aircraft performance and, ultimately, of relative pilot performance. Through most of aviation history, nations have been able to provide their air arms with roughly competitive equipment. Thus in the early days of World War I, the Albatros was countered by the Spad, which in turn was countered by the Fokker D VII. In World War II, the Messerschmitt Bf 109 was bested by the Spitfire, which in turn met its match in the Focke Wulf Fw 190, which was then more than matched by the North American P-51.

The same progress followed in Korea, Vietnam, and the Middle East. Only in recent years has the world situation developed to the point where one nation—the United States—is capable of manufacturing fighters like the Grumman (now Northrop Grumman) F-14, the McDonnell Douglas (now Boeing) F-15, the General Dynamics (now Lockheed Martin) F-16, the McDonnell Douglas (now Boeing) F/A-18, and the Lockheed Martin F-22, which have dominated or will dominate the world's combat arenas.

But the rules developed during the years of relative parity might still apply, and author Robert L. Shaw lays out in great detail the rules that govern fighter missions. Curiously enough, the rules are rather pedestrian, almost what one would expect. They call for the fighters to maintain all the possible advantages, to expose themselves to a minimum of risk, and to take into account such factors as enemy strength, the reliability of both enemy and friendly C^3I capability, the availability of refueling aircraft, and other such tactical factors.

As Shaw points out, the speed and mobility of a fighter aircraft lends itself to offensive action. The increasing sophistication and versatility of fighter aircraft now enable a single type of aircraft to engage in both bombing and air-to-air combat on a mission. This capability has considerably broadened the concept of a "fighter sweep." This is a tactic intended to bring enemy fighters into action in the air, or to catch them on the ground, with the intent of establishing air superiority. The ground attack, while hazardous because of the exposure to antiaircraft fire and surface-to-air missiles, is nonetheless a preferred tactic, for it offers the greatest assurance of victories.

In all wars since the first significant deployment of the airplane, it has been desirable to mass sufficient aircraft on a particular sweep against a particular target so that a numerical superiority is achieved. The number of aircraft in an attacking force can be "multiplied" by good battlefield management by airborne command and control centers. These relatively slow, but infinitely valuable, aircraft like the AWACS and the ABCCC provide real-time information that permits the fighters to be sent to the right altitude and the right position at the right time.

Shaw's excerpt deserves careful reading and thoughtful analysis, particularly in today's environment, when the very elements that can supply air superiority—modern fighters, good command and control, precision guided munitions, and spaced-based intelligence systems—are the subjects of continuous congressional scrutiny and are the targets for budget-cutting attacks. A nation that once fielded a bomber force of more than 2,300 multijet aircraft is now reduced to less than 50 Boeing B-52s, about 90 Rockwell B-1Bs, and ultimately 21 Northrop Grumman B-2s. The nation that put more than 1,000 fighters in the Gulf War has drawn down that force by 40 percent. The nation that once manufactured aircraft at the rate of 100,000 per year can find money in its budget for only two new fighters—the F-22 and the Joint Strike Fighter— and even these two are the subject of immense debate.

We are once again being penny-wise and pound-foolish. *Nothing* would be more expensive for the United States than the sacrifice of the means by which it can achieve and maintain air superiority. Once lost, these means might never be retrieved, and all of Shaw's lessons on how to conduct fighter missions might well become moot.

W.J.B.

THE PRIMARY MISSION of fighters is air superiority; that is, ensuring use by friendly aircraft of the airspace over critical surface areas, and denying use of that airspace to the enemy. Control of the high ground has always been one of the fundamentals of warfare. Airspace control allows strategic and tactical bombing, close air support of troops and armor, airborne or surface reinforcement and supply, reconnaissance, and other missions vital to the success of any military operation. Although no war so far has been won solely on the basis of air power, the advent of nuclear weapons certainly lends credence to this possibility for future conflicts.

The value of air power became evident in World War I, when airplanes were in their infancy. The airplane did not play a pivotal role in the outcome of that conflict, but by the early days of World War II it was inconceivable that any major military operation could succeed without first achieving air superiority. This evolution was brought about primarily by the quantum increases in firepower and destructive capabilities of the aircraft that were developed between the wars.

During World War II, the devastating tactical bombing and close air support by the German Luftwaffe during the blitzkrieg attacks on

Poland, the Low Countries, and France provided early evidence of the effectiveness of air power. The importance placed on air superiority is obvious in the German decision to cancel the invasion of England after the RAF could not be defeated during the Battle of Britain. The value of air superiority was shown again by the ability of the American bombers to prosecute daylight strategic bombardment of Germany and Japan late in the war. Since that conflict, air superiority has continued to play the decisive role in conventional warfare. Only guerrilla conflicts seem to be resistant to the crushing weight of air power, which may be one of the primary reasons behind the recent popularity of guerrilla strategies.

The major military attributes of the airplane, namely, speed and freedom of movement, are best suited to offensive action, as it is very difficult to defend against an attack that can come at any time, with very little warning, from essentially any direction. These same attributes, however, make the airplane one of the most effective defensive weapons against airborne attack. Paradoxically, the fighter is an offensive weapon used primarily for defensive missions. Regardless of how offensive the fighter pilot may feel when he is attacking another aircraft, his role in the final analysis is usually defensive. He is defending a target against enemy attack or defending friendly bombers from hostile fighters. Only once in a great while is he assigned the tasks of interdicting enemy airborne supply and transport aircraft not directly involved in hostile action or simply ranging over hostile territory in search of targets of opportunity. Missions such as these, however, are best suited to the military advantages of the fighter, and they are covered first in this chapter.

The Fighter Sweep. A fighter sweep is a mission flown generally over hostile or contested territory for the purpose of engaging and destroying enemy fighters or other airborne targets of opportunity. The fighter sweep is designed to establish air superiority by denying the enemy use of the airspace for his purposes, and to make the airspace safer for use by friendly forces. Thus, the fighter sweep can be carried out for either offensive or defensive purposes, but because the conduct of this mission allows the fighter pilot to seek out and attack other aircraft from a position of advantage, it is offensive in nature and is well suited to the inherent offensive character of the fighter. The sweep, therefore, is the preferred fighter mission, and fighter tacticians should employ sweep techniques whenever possible in conjunction with other missions. This concept is explored in greater depth throughout this chapter.

Scenarios. Since the usual objective of the fighter sweep is to engage enemy fighters, it is logical for such sweeps to be conducted in areas expected to have a high concentration of hostile aircraft. From World War I to the latest conflicts, the favorite target for fighter sweeps has probably been enemy fighter bases. A surprise fighter attack on an unsuspecting airfield conducting routine flight operations can be utterly devastating. Some aircraft are taking off, often in tight formations, and are climbing at low altitudes and slow speeds; others are circling to land, in dirty configuration, low on fuel and ammo, with exhausted pilots. The enemy pilots are over friendly, familiar ground, and they are generally less vigilant.

***

In addition, aircraft are quite often caught on the ground, where they are "sitting ducks," taxiing or being refueled and rearmed between missions. Undoubtedly it is best to attack an enemy aircraft when it is on the ground. Unfortunately, many modern air-to-air weapons are ineffective against surface targets. For this type of mission, therefore, even the true fighter pilot might consider hauling some token air-to-ground ordnance. (If everybody does it, it doesn't look so bad.) An alternative is to take along some fighter-bombers, which can concentrate on the surface targets but have the ability to defend themselves credibly or even to join in the air-to-air fun after unloading their other baggage. This is not the time, however, to saddle the fighters with escort duty.

Ability to attack surface targets is an essential element of a fighter sweep against an enemy airfield. Otherwise any aircraft on the ground, and those that can get there quickly, have an effective sanctuary. Recognizing their disadvantage in the air, the enemy pilots have little inducement to come out and play, but for some reason, fighter pilots seem to prefer even the short end of a one-sided air battle to eating mud with bombs falling around their ears. A single bomb on the local pub often turns the trick. The fighter pilots who survive this attack should be blinded by rage and make for easy airborne targets.

Aircraft on the ground are not always easy scores, however, as they can be dispersed, camouflaged, and stored in hardened bunkers. In addition, because of the value of airfields and the likelihood that they will be attacked, these installations are often among the most heavily defended by surface-to-air weapons. Against such defenses, fighter sweeps are best limited to one quick pass with the intent of taking out easy targets and retiring before the ground defenses have time to react. Hit-and-run attacks can be repeated often, generally with better results than are obtained by a smaller number of sustained attacks.

Another likely opportunity for a fighter sweep is over a surface battle, which is often accompanied by ground-attack aircraft that make tasty targets as they go about their revolting chores. Enemy transport, reconnaissance, and liaison aircraft can also be expected to be in this area. These are all very lucrative targets because of their vulnerability and their direct participation in a surface battle. Under such circumstances enemy fighters should be avoided as long as more favorable targets are available, unless these fighters are a menace to friendly aircraft.

Enemy fighter sweeps can be expected in these areas for the same reasons. It is usually good policy, whenever hostile fighters may be encountered, to split the friendly forces into low- and high-level elements. The majority can work at a low level, where more of the high-value targets are likely to be found. Low-altitude flight often makes these targets easier to see, as they are silhouetted against a light-colored horizon.

The duties of the high-level element in this scenario are largely defensive. These aircraft should remain in a comfortable supporting cover position, guarding against attack by enemy fighters on the low-level element or on other friendly aircraft in the area. In general, they should avoid contact with nonthreatening aircraft. A radio warning should be issued to any threatened friendly; this may suffice, and it is generally preferable to actual engagement with the hostile fighters. If it is required to leave its defensive station, the covering element should notify the low element of the situation and solicit help if necessary.

The greater altitude of the high element may allow it to serve as a radio relay from friendly GCI or command-and-control centers. This element can also usually make better use of on-board radar equipment. These advantages, plus a better overall view of the battlefield, may allow the high element to direct the low element to target opportunities.

Because of these factors, when more than one type of fighter is available, the type with the more sophisticated radar and communications equipment is normally assigned high-cover duties. This aircraft should, however, have good air combat capabilities, since it is more likely to engage hostile fighters. These two qualities may call for a mixture of fighter types to be employed on high-cover assignment.

In general in this scenario, as in many others, either very high or very low is the place to be, although the high element may be limited in altitude if it is to provide effective visual support for the low element. Low, middle, and high elements might be preferable in this case, depending on available numbers and surface defenses. Aircraft at medium altitudes are usually very easily detected and engaged by both surface-to-air and air-to-air weapons. Battlefields are notorious for heavy low-altitude air defense. Aircraft recognition has never been one of the soldier's strong suits, and low-flying aircraft are regularly fired on by both sides. It may be more practical under these conditions to keep the entire fighter force at high altitude, detaching small elements as necessary to descend for slashing attacks on low-level targets and then return to the fold.

The purpose of some fighter sweeps is simply to find and engage enemy fighters in a given airspace. Generally these missions are conducted over hostile or contested territory, so the tactics developed for the few-versus-many and many-versus-many scenarios are usually applicable. Quite often the enemy's GCI and command-and-control networks will be superior to friendly capabilities in these areas, so the unexpected attack should be guarded against. The basics include high speeds and very high or very low altitudes, depending on surface defenses, environmental conditions, and relative aircraft and weapons-system performance. Friendly fighter pilots must use every means at their disposal to achieve surprise, and they must approach an engagement with the intent of attaining the first shot opportunity. Whether engaging in sustained maneuvering or employing hit-and-run tactics is called for depends on the factors discussed in the previous chapter. "Slash-and-dash" methods are often preferable when friendlies are facing enemy forces superior in number or quality. The size of the friendly force should be tailored, when possible, to be equivalent to or larger than the expected hostile formations. Dividing the force into engaged and covering elements is usually most efficient when the enemy is greatly outnumbered in any engagement. If friendlies are forced to engage against superior numbers, loose deuce or gaggle tactics tend to even the odds.

Fuel state is often a critical factor in a fighter sweep. The aircraft are often deep into hostile airspace, and they can be very vulnerable if the pilots are unable to avoid extended engagement or if the aircraft are attacked on the way home. One effective technique used to alleviate this problem is multiple, independent sweeps in the same area, with entry into the combat zone staggered by several minutes. This ensures a supply of fresh fighters in the area to assist in the retreat of other friendlies and to take advantage of retiring enemy forces. The last flight to enter the arena in this scheme is devoted to defense. These aircraft should make one pass through the area, avoiding contact with the enemy if possible, make sure that all friendlies are headed for home, and then depart as rear guard at a high fuel state.

One notable example of the use of this tactic was the staggered (usually every five minutes) fighter sweeps by U.S. F-86s to the Yalu River area during the Korean conflict. These missions stretched the range of these aircraft to the limit, and dead-stick, flamed-out approaches were almost routine on return to base.

A possible complication with the use of this tactic arises when the friendly fighters have beyond-visual-range weapons capability. In order to make full use of this capability, and possibly to avoid allowing the enemy to achieve the first shot should they be similarly equipped, it is necessary to identify BVR targets as hostile at the maximum range of the available weapons. If targets cannot be reliably identified at such ranges, either visually or electronically, then it may be necessary to "sanitize" the combat arena of all friendly forces. This means making sure that no other friendly aircraft can be in the combat zone during the sweep, so that any target detected can be assumed to be hostile. Sanitizing can be very difficult in practice, requiring coordination not only within the friendlies' own air forces, but also, possibly, with other combatant forces and neutrals. Such coordination may be impractical from a time or a security standpoint. Even if this ideal condition can be achieved, only the first wave of attacking fighters can take advantage of it, limiting the desirability of multiple, staggered waves in a fighter sweep.

One of the most effective fighter-sweep tactics involves staging a simulated air strike against a high-value surface target. Fighters armed strictly for air-to-air engagement can imitate bombers by employing typical bomber formations, altitudes, and airspeeds while following expected attack routes toward an enemy target. The ruse can be as simple or as elaborate as necessary, even including deceptive communications, EW, and supporting aircraft. Once the enemy fighters have been confirmed (usually by a supporting source) to be airborne in defense against the false strike, the friendly forces can redeploy for more aggressive, offensive capability and spring the nasty surprise. Good electronic surveillance of the combat arena and adequate command-and-control are desirable, if not required, for this tactic, however, to avoid an equally nasty surprise by the enemy prior to redeployment.

Control of Fighter Sweeps. Command, control, and communications (C^3) are critical elements in the success of a fighter sweep. Often the combat arena is very large and contains many aircraft, both hostile and friendly. The ability of friendly fighter pilots to find, identify, and engage high-value hostile targets while avoiding potential threats, or at least engaging these threats from a position of advantage, rests in great measure on relative C^3 capabilities.

Supporting radar surveillance may be provided by surface-based GCI or airborne AIC controllers. Depending on tactical philosophy, these "controlling" agencies may have absolute authority to dictate every action of friendly fighters, including headings, altitudes, speeds, attack and firing clearances, and bugouts, or they may act merely as an advisory service, passing along real-time intelligence information and monitoring the progress of the battle. Something of a middle-ground approach seems to be more successful, depending on the relative capabilities of the controlling agency and the fighters themselves. It should be kept in mind that the "controllers" support the fighters, and not vice versa. All parties should recognize that, although the controllers often have a better grasp of the big picture, overall success and failure are decided by many small engagements. Generally the fighter crews themselves are in the best position to judge the critical factors and rapidly changing events in close proximity to the enemy.

There are essentially only two types of radar control: close and broadcast. Under close control the duty of the controller usually is to direct the pilots into a tactically advantageous position to attack or identify a target. In order to accomplish this task, the controller generally must monitor the positions of the fighters and the target. He then transmits relative range and bearing of the target to the fighters, and he may dictate or recommend (depending on philosophy) intercept headings, speeds, altitudes, etc. The primary purpose of the controller in this scenario is to position the fighters favorably so that the pilots can acquire the target, either visually or with their own self-contained sensors, facilitating identification or attack. If identification of an unknown contact is the purpose, the pilots may be required to perform either a visual identification or an electronic identification (EID), using onboard equipment. Depending on the outcome of the identification, the fighters may then be cleared by the controller (or by prearrangement) to attack a hostile target, but final attack procedures should be left to the pilots. During the close-control intercept process, the controller is also responsible for advising the pilots of any additional contacts that might pose a threat or that might be of higher attack priority than the original target.

In broadcast control the controller generally gives the position, and other relevant information as available, of any hostile or unknown targets in a given area, relative to one or more geographical or navigational fixes within that area. The reference point is known to the friendlies, as is their own position relative to that point. As the controller calls target positions and movement relative to the reference, the pilots can calculate their own position relative to the target, and they may be assigned by the controller to conduct their own intercepts based on this information. Unlike with close control, no group of fighters gets individual attention, but all pilots in the area get the same information and can react to it offensively or defensively. Specific fighter formations are generally assigned by the controller in real time to investigate a given contact, or each fighter element may be prebriefed to prosecute any contact in a given region.

Close control is usually preferable for fighter-sweep operations, since it offers the fighters the greatest offensive capability. Once the pilots have their own visual or radar contacts, the close controller should generally revert to providing an advisory service. His function then is to monitor the progress of the intercept and the ensuing engagement, warn of additional hostile or unknown contacts that may be a factor, give rejoin assistance to pilots who become separated from their wingmen, recommend egress headings, etc. During this period it is critical that only essential or requested information be passed over voice radio frequencies; the pilots must have those limited frequencies for their coordination purposes.

Regardless of its advantages, close control may not always be possible or practical. Limitations on controllers or control frequencies may lead to saturation of a close-control system with large numbers of separate enemy and friendly formations. Broadcast control may be better suited to such situations. A combination of these two systems may also be useful. For instance, broadcast control can be given over a common fighter frequency, while selected fighter formations may be switched to a separate close-control frequency during intercepts and engagements as controllers and frequencies become available.

Because of their dependence on communications, command and control are very vulnerable to comm-jamming. Aircrews and controllers should both practice communications brevity, and they should be briefed on alternate control frequencies. Data link and jam-resistant radios can be very valuable. In addition, the tactics employed must not be so dependent on external control that pilots are helpless without it. Just such a condition contributed greatly to the Syrian debacle over Lebanon's Bekaa Valley in 1982. "Spoofing," or intrusion, is another C^3 consideration. This is the tactic by which an enemy controller operates on friendly control frequencies and attempts to "steal," divert, or confuse pilots by issuing false instructions. Coded authentication procedures offer some protection against this trick, but they can be cumbersome and are not foolproof. A better defense against intrusions, when practical, is for the fighter crews to be intimately familiar with the controller's voice.

For fighter aircrews and controllers to work most effectively together as a team, each must know the tasks, problems, and limitations of the other. When this is not the case, friction is likely to develop when aircrews do not receive the information they believe is necessary and controllers believe their instructions are not properly followed. Probably the only solution to this problem is for aircrews and controllers to work, live, eat, and play together, so that they know each other well enough to work out these inevitable differences. Even better, fighter crews should be cross-trained as controllers, and each crewman should take his turn in the barrel on a periodic basis, maybe daily or weekly. Unfortunately, most fighter pilots will resist this idea, even with their last breath, whispering something about the high wing loading of a radar console! Threat of transfer to a bomber outfit will usually induce compliance, however.

27

Air Superiority—the Concept

from THE AIR CAMPAIGN: PLANNING FOR COMBAT

by John A. Warden III

Any powerful personality will eventually find himself or herself at the center of controversy. Colonel John A. Warden's book, *The Air Campaign: Planning for Combat,* has been widely hailed as the air-power bible that laid the foundation for the victory in the Persian Gulf War. This view has been contested by some of the leading participants in the Gulf War, who, while acknowledging the academic value of the game plan developed in the work say that it simply did not provide the high degree of detail needed as a war plan.

The facts lie between these points of view—and considerably nearer to that of the pro-Warden contingent than to that of his detractors. For Warden not only wrote the book (when he was a student at the National War College), he went on to work in the Checkmate Division of the Air Staff, where some twenty experts labored in a bunkerlike Pentagon office. Warden thus became perhaps the only person who first delineated an airpower philosophy and then worked in a position where he could foster its implementation.

The basic idea in Warden's book was that airpower was in many ways dependent upon the same factors that influenced ground warfare. Like Clausewitz, Warden sought to identify the enemy's "centers of gravity," those centers that it was essential to destroy in order to achieve victory.

Unlike Clausewitz, Warden did not espouse attacks against the enemy's armies in the field, but took an approach Douhet would have approved of, the destruction of the enemy's headquarters, its command and control resources, and its air defense system. Warden maintained that the first essential requirement was the establishment of total air superiority; after this was established all of the other elements of air action, from hitting key targets to strafing supply routes to close air support of ground forces, could be easily undertaken.

Warden's views are clearly depicted in this excerpt, "Air Superiority—the Concept." In it, Warden defines terms like *air supremacy* and local *air superiority* and cites historical examples of how they are established.

The examples are so cogent, and so consistent, that one wonders how the United States could have found itself so vulnerable in World War II, Korea, and Vietnam. Warden shows how successful the Germans were when they were able to establish air superiority, as in Poland in the east and France in the west. Their failure to establish air superiority in the Battle of Britain prevented them from invading and condemned them to a fatal war on two fronts. By 1942, air superiority had shifted to the Allied side, and the Germans were unable to resist the effect of airpower in North Africa, Italy, or France.

Despite these thunderous lessons, taught first by the Germans and then by the Allies, the United States repeatedly allowed its airpower to lapse into impotence. As a direct consequence, the United States was almost driven from the Korean peninsula in 1950. A rapid buildup of airpower reestablished air superiority all the way to the Yalu River, although at great cost and with much loss of life. It was this airpower, which permitted the interdiction of the overwhelming Communist ground forces, that finally induced the North Koreans to agree to an armistice.

Warden examines the pivotal nature of air superiority both in the Middle East and in Vietnam. In essence, the ground battle can be won only if air superiority is established. Without air superiority, superior ground forces are forced to settle for a stalemate. With air superiority, inferior ground forces can at least achieve a stalemate. With air superiority and adequate ground forces, a complete victory can be won.

W.J.B.

AIR SUPERIORITY IS A NECESSITY. Since the German attack on Poland in 1939, no country has won a war in the face of enemy air superiority, no major offensive has succeeded against an opponent who controlled the air, and no defense has sustained itself against an enemy who had air superiority. Conversely, no state has lost a war while it maintained air superiority, and attainment of air superiority consistently has been a prelude to military victory. It is vital that national and theater commanders, their air component commanders, and their surface component commanders be aware of these historical facts, and plan accordingly.

To be superior in the air, to have air superiority means having sufficient control of the air to make air attacks—manned or unmanned—on the enemy without serious opposition and, on the other hand, to be free from the danger of serious enemy air incursions. Within the category of air superiority, there are variations.

Air Supremacy and Operations. Air supremacy, for example, means the ability to operate air forces anywhere without opposition. Local air superiority gives basic air freedom of movement over a limited area for a finite period of time. Theater air superiority, or supremacy, means that friendly air can operate any place within the entire combat theater. Air neutrality suggests that neither side has won sufficient control of the air to operate without great danger.

The contention that air superiority is a necessity to ensure victory or avoid defeat is based on theory and on an analysis of the last half century of warfare. Theory alone would suggest that it is just not possible to succeed with surface warfare if the surface forces and their support are under constant attack by enemy air vehicles. And, indeed, the theory is supported by copious historical examples, a few of which should suffice to make the point.

Germany destroyed Poland's air force in the first days of the campaign. From then on, the Poles came under constant and merciless attack from the air whether they were in bivouac, on the march, or engaged. Because the Germans had air superiority, they were able to disrupt Polish schemes of maneuver, impose heavy casualties directly on their enemy, and simultaneously facilitate the movement of Germany forces on the ground. Nine months later, Germany did the same thing in France; the *Luftwaffe* won air superiority in two days.

A year later, the German attack on Russia was a classic example of seizing air superiority with massive violent attacks. The Germans capitalized on their air superiority by moving ground forces unprecedented distances up to the late fall, when weather and failure to follow up on the initial air victories helped bring the great offensive to a halt.

The attack on Russia had followed, and was a function of, Germany's failure to win the Battle of Britain and thereby establish the air superiority which was a prerequisite for invasion. The invasion of Russia was the last instance when Germany was able to establish air superiority over an opponent. It was the last strategic offensive Germany was to make before her own homeland lay devastated and occupied.

On the other side in World War II, the Western Allies achieved air superiority before German Field Marshal Erwin Rommel's last offensive at Alam Halfa. Rommel observed that "anyone who has to fight, even with the most modern weapons, against an enemy in complete control of air, fights like a savage against a modern European army."

Rommel subsequently made a similar comment about the situation in Sicily and in Italy. "Strength on the ground was not unfavorable to us," Rommel said. "It's simply that their superiority in the air and in ammunition is overwhelming, the same as it was in Africa."

The value of air superiority was even clearer in the Normandy invasion. Von Rundstedt, the German commander in France during the invasion, reported, "The Allied Air Force paralyzed all movement by day, and made it very difficult even by night."

In the summer of 1944, the Allies gained control over the skies above Germany. By the end of the war, the situation was so bad, because of the incessant bombing permitted by having control of the air, that the Germans had no fuel for their airplanes and only enough gas to give a tank enough for it to make one attack.

Lest it be argued that World War II is ancient history and thus no longer applicable, consider a few cases from wars since then.

In Korea, Lieutenant General Nam Il, the chief representative of the North Koreans at the armistice talks, remarked in a moment of candor,

> It is owing to your strategic air effort of indiscriminate bombing of our area, rather than to your tactical air effort of direct support to the front

lines, that your ground forces are able to maintain barely and temporarily their present position.

The "indiscriminate bombing" to which General Nam Il referred was a direct consequence of air superiority all the way to the Yalu River.

The Israelis have well illustrated the power of air superiority. In 1967, the Israelis destroyed the Egyptian and Syrian air forces on 5 June and then proceeded to lay waste the Egyptian army in the Sinai, where Israeli command of the air had made life intolerable for the Egyptian soldier.

Six years later, the victors of 1967 paid a terrible price for not gaining air superiority in the first phase of the war. Only after recognizing the need to suppress enemy missile systems—their primary barrier to air superiority—were they able to turn the tide of battle and go on to win the war.

Finally, the North Vietnamese were unable to conduct a successful conventional offensive as long as American air power was stationed in Indochina. Only after the Americans had left was the North able to mount a decisive ground offense into South Vietnam. In this case, South Vietnamese air attempted little and was easily repulsed by North Vietnamese mobile ground-based air defense systems. As air played no significant role in the invasion for either side, the ensuing action was essentially as it would have been before the era of the aircraft.

28

The Future of Air Combat Technology

from BEYOND THE HORIZON: COMBAT AIRCRAFT OF THE NEXT CENTURY
by Philip Handleman

In this stylish overview of combat aircraft of the future, Philip Handleman deftly assesses the rise of the technology of the past and contrasts it with the almost intimidating technology of the future.

It is really touching to consider that well within the life span of an ordinary citizen, aircraft have progressed from the first true fighter, the Fokker E.I of World War I, to the Lockheed Martin F-22 of today. The changes have been almost miraculous. The little Fokker monoplane was a 1,232-pound combination of steel tubing, wood, and fabric, and mounted a lethal—for the time—installation of one, two, or even three machine guns firing through the propeller. It had a top speed of 81 miles per hour, a duration of one and a half hours, and a ceiling of 10,000 feet. In vivid contrast, the F-22 is a marvel of structural integration, with advanced aluminum, titanium, and composites crafted into a stealthy supersonic package weighing about 60,000 pounds at takeoff. Its performance is remarkable, with a top speed of more than 900 miles per hour at sea level, a range of more than 2,000 miles, and a ceiling in excess of 50,000 feet.

Yet the amazing thing about this journey from Eindecker to Raptor is not the evolution in performance but the revolution in the research required in order to create both the F-22 and the amazing ancillary technology necessary to make it the dominating weapon system that it is.

In 1915, Anthony Fokker was tasked to match or better the French Morane-Saulnier with its forward-firing Hotchkiss machine gun; *in less than three months* he had Fokker E.Is, each equipped with a more technologically advanced forward-firing LMG.08 machine gun, flying at the front.

The E.I was the father of all fighters, and it required virtually no ground support beyond fuel, oil, ammunition, and routine maintenance. There were no test systems, ground servicing equipment, radios, oxygen, or anything else. The pilots—most notably Max Immelmann and Oswald Boelcke—simply got into the aircraft, flew, and fought.

In marked contrast, the Lockheed Martin F-22 Raptor stemmed from a November 1981 U.S. Air Force requirement for a fighter to replace the McDonnell Douglas (now Boeing) F-15. The first flight of the prototype, designated YF-22, was made on September 29, 1990. The fly-off competition with the Northrop YF-23 was won on April 23, 1993. The Initial Operational Capability date for the F-22 is the year 2005—twenty-four years after the requirement was announced.

The reason for this more-than-two-decade delay was not simply bureaucratic bungling; it was necessary, some would argue, to allow the time to do the research and achieve the technology necessary to meet the F-22's stiff requirements. The aircraft was not intended to merely establish air superiority; it was intended to establish air dominance in the first few hours of any war. To do this, the Raptor had to be backed by a tremendously sophisticated system of radar, test equipment, missiles, electronic countermeasures, and an integrated avionics system that tied it into both ground and airborne command posts.

Author Handleman, my friend of many years and a man of many talents, goes beyond the Raptor's achievement to analyze what will be required for even more advanced aircraft of the future. His eloquent, painstaking prose places the ever more startling engineering advances of the future in terms easily understood by the layman. Philip explains the what and why of stealth, the sine qua non of future combat aircraft, and explains exactly what will be required to achieve a successful advanced short takeoff and vertical landing (ASTOVL) fighter.

Some of the developments he predicts are almost eerie—such

as aircraft structures that "heal" themselves, sensing and measuring damage and automatically reconfiguring flight controls to redistribute loads to optimize aircraft performance. The author also examines the vital requirements of human engineering. As the aircraft and its computer systems grow ever more complex, pilots will need every bit of help they can get to master the situation.

First published in 1994, this essay was remarkably accurate in its appraisal of the unfolding development of air combat, its hardware, and its methods. Moreover, many of Philip's assertions possess an almost timeless validity. Combined with his ability to condense sophisticated subject matter into easily understood paragraphs, this excerpt represents a new standard in the literature that ought to be required reading for students and policy makers concerned with the conduct of current and future air warfare.

W.J.B.

From the beginning of powered flight, aircraft designers have been constrained by their understanding of such specialties as aerodynamics, materials, propulsion, structures, controls, manufacturing technologies, and human factors. Along the way, those broad categories were joined by others like avionics, computation, and, in the case of combat aircraft, weapons systems.

During the last nine decades, the sometimes daunting challenges did not stand in the way of an ongoing progression in aeronautical accomplishment. Invariably, the foundation underlying the advances was imagination. The designers blessed with a vision of the future who willingly incurred risk, incorporating the latest technologies in bold configurations, elevated the state-of-the-art to a new plateau, sometimes startling the world with planes like the P-38 and Me 262 that broke from the conventions of the status quo. Performance gains were the ultimate reward.

In the course of air warfare, events have formed perceptions about the direction that designers should take. For example, during the Vietnam War numerous high value targets were heavily defended making aerial attacks both perilous and inaccurate. Efforts at producing precision munitions produced rudimentary laser and electro-optically guided weapons which saw use at the war's end against objectives like Hanoi's Paul Doumer Bridge, a target celebrated for its elusiveness.

The frustration at seeing so many "dumb bombs" fall into the Red River on either side of the bridge like deadweights, only to splash innocuously as U.S. fighter-bomber pilots continually braved a relentless wall of flak, drove designers to devise and then improve air-to-ground weapons systems. The "smart bombs" successfully employed in the 1991 Persian Gulf War owe much of their creation and refinement to the bitter legacy of Vietnam.

The Yom Kippur War of 1973 saw Israel groping to establish a foothold in the air over its primary adversary, Egypt. Unlike the swift victory of just six years earlier in which the Israeli Air Force rapidly achieved a commanding presence in the skies, IAF Phantoms fell prey to newly-deployed Soviet surface-to-air missiles (SAMs). These sophisticated radar-guided weapons caused unacceptably high attrition. Some designers realized that among the counters to this menace would be aircraft with low observables or stealth.

In perhaps the greatest watershed of contemporary air combat history (again in the Middle East where military conceptualists have had their attention drawn repeatedly), the 1982 Bekaa Valley shoot-out, the IAF, pitted against the neighbouring Syrian Air Force, racked up the unprecedented kill/loss ratio of 85/0. This lopsided battle proved that technology affords the means to surmount the SAM threat and, further, that control of the electronic environment in the modern air war is the key to victory. The fruits of this doctrine materialized on a grand scale less than ten years later with the stunning success of the coalition's air campaign in the Persian Gulf War.

Achieving air superiority has long been recognized as a prime early objective in battle. Much of the responsibility for this falls on the shoulders of the fighter force. Until fairly recently, air-to-air combat remained fundamentally unchanged since the days of World War I dogfighting, where one-on-one aerial duels ensued, an aircraft chasing another in the wild manœuvring above a seemingly detached battlefield. Success hinged on a plethora of factors including the pilot's eyesight, reflexes, experience, training, and airmanship. A less easily defined factor, termed situational awareness, also has continued to play a major role in determining the outcome of air fighting.

Naturally, the aircraft and its weapons systems can greatly tilt the balance. Speed, climb performance, and, perhaps most importantly, agility, were the characteristics sought by fighter pilots. Being able to out-turn or out-run an enemy made the difference between life and death in what was evolving from a chivalrous endeavour into a bloody business.

Protective shielding was an attractive feature though virtually non-existent in the early days. Intelligently designed camouflage paint schemes provided a measure of cover. Devices for escape like parachutes were at first scoffed at by the hierarchy of some air forces as inherently cowardly. Having forward-firing synchronized machine-guns offered Germany a significant advantage until the other side could match this technology. Sheer quantity was another factor; attaining higher production rates and fielding the growing fleets of aircraft could swamp the enemy.

The main goal of today's fighter aircraft designers is to devise a plane that can counter the threat from afar, obviating the need to engage in old-style dogfighting while at the same time not diminishing, perhaps even enhancing, the traditional values just in case. This means developing aircraft that on the one hand are invisible to the enemy but on the other hand that can ideally strike the threat at beyond visual range (BVR).

Lowering an aircraft's observables is most important in the radar spectrum since, of all sensors, radar's range is the greatest. Additionally, the infrared (IR), visual, and acoustic signatures must be reduced. The first full-fledged stealth aircraft, the F-117A, using early-generation stealth technology was comprised of a faceted structure. Current generation stealth technology is going into the B-2, which is a flying wing devoid of customary tail surfaces and possessing smooth, curving shapes. Radar-absorbing materials (RAMs) like carbon fibreglass are part of the structure.

The future fighter will be stealthy, avoiding detection by both air and ground threats. Engines will be blended into the fuselage. Air inlets may be specially treated or inset and the exhaust stream will be shielded in some fashion. There will be no smoke or contrails. Sound will be muffled unless, of course, still in the atmosphere the aircraft exceeds Mach 1, at which point the unavoidable sonic boom occurs. All fuel and weapons carriage will be internal or conformal so as not to contribute to radar reflectivity. Refuelling probes will be retractable or receptacles will be covered.

Carrying packages of sophisticated sensors, the future fighter should be able to detect enemy fighters at BVR. An electronically-scanned antenna will replace the traditional movable antenna. IR sensors will be mounted internally rather than located in a pod affixed to a wing or fuse-lage stores station. These IR sensors will have greatly improved range and provide vastly enhanced imagery. Laser technology will be employed as part of the targeting system. Connected by two-way data link to airborne and ground stations, the fighter will be able to receive valuable input about enemy targets from deployed forces.

As the threat aircraft attempts to locate the future fighter, active jamming may be undertaken using onboard systems to intercept and purposefully deflect the enemy's incoming radar signals. In this way, the future fighter is not dependent upon dedicated electronic countermeasures (ECM) aircraft. The future fighter has a full bag of tricks before it is relegated to dispensing chaff or flares to survive.

In any full-blown combat scenario, air bases will have been struck and runways most likely will be damaged, dramatically limiting usable length. To address this concern, the future fighter must have thrust vectoring nozzles that give it short take-off and landing (STOL) capability.

An exciting variation is the advanced short take-off and vertical landing (ASTOVL) fighter. Loaded with fuel and ordnance it will be too heavy to take-off vertically, but with an advanced propulsion system could take-off in an extremely short roll. Landing could easily be accomplished vertically. The ASTOVL ought to be able to approximate the speed and manœuvrability of its conventional counterparts. Another challenge is to preserve acceptable fuel and weapons payloads given the necessary extra weight and volume for the vectoring apparatus.

The future fighter at first may have two-dimensional thrust vectoring nozzles. Testing is now being done on axisymmetric thrust vectoring nozzles that will enhance yaw and pitch manœuvrability. Not only will there be short take-off capability because of these engine nozzles, but air combat manœuvring capability will be expanded.

The future fighter will be able to achieve higher angles of attack (AOA) as a result of vectoring engine thrust. During close-in air-to-air combat this provides an immense advantage. Being able to vector thrust through a wide envelope effectively transforms engine nozzles into steering devices. This development could lead to tail-less aircraft configurations that enjoy an intrinsic stealthiness.

Adding still more to the future fighter's high AOA capabilities could be small nose-mounted thrusters able to push the aircraft beyond its normal stall departure point and continue to provide reasonable control at those high alpha attitudes. Flight testing of this concept was successfully accomplished on the X-29 forward-swept wing research aircraft.

Flying at supersonic speeds without the use of afterburner, known as supercruise, will give the future fighter better fuel economy, greater range, and a lower IR signature. Afterburner will be available for times of need when, for example, rapid acceleration is dictated. Greater thrust-to-weight ratios will improve performance. Full authority digital electronic controls (FADEC) can provide unprecedented responsiveness. Continuous health monitoring will pinpoint engine problems before they become critical.

Materials in the construction of aircraft structures have increasingly moved from customary metal alloys to composites like carbon fibre. Quite simply, composites tend to offer more strength while weighing less. Their toughness means they are ballistics tolerant. Moreover, composites are more corrosion resistant. This is a critical consideration as corrosion is a leading cause of maintenance difficulties. Combat aircraft, by the very nature of their missions, are exposed to inhospitable surroundings. Composites can contribute to a longer service life with lower maintenance requirements.

The weight savings permit more onboard fuel which translates into increased range or endurance. More payload can be devoted to weaponry and mission-related gear. Being lighter, the aircraft should be more manœuvrable.

Rather than attaching or incorporating essential equipment on or in the shell of the airframe as is traditional, the equipment may become an integral part of the aircraft structure. For example, an integrated antenna might be embedded into the contour of the fuselage, in effect, making it a "smart structure."

Smart structures and smart skins have wide-ranging utility. Examples include a sensor-laden wing that could report battle damage or even age-related fatigue. Engineers are investigating the practicality of producing structures with electro-rheological fluids injected as a constant monitoring agent that would automatically sense, measure, and signal the extent and location of structural changes occurring in flight. Aware of combat-incurred difficulties, the smart structures would automatically reconfigure flight controls and redistribute loads to optimize aircraft performance until major repairs could be made.

The crew station will have a glass cockpit. Data from the complex systems will funnel through microprocessors and be presented on three or four flat panel multifunction displays (MFDs). The presentation will take the form of easily comprehended graphics. So as not to overload the pilot, at any point during the flight only relevant data or data specifically called up by the pilot would be presented. Sensor data will be fused and presented on the few displays in an overlapping format.

Simple push button mode switches will configure the displays for the current flight regime, for example, take-off, cruise, combat, and landing. If any system malfunction occurs, a warning feature automatically engages, alerting the pilot. A suggested course of action may accompany the annunciator read-out.

Complementing or possibly replacing the holographic head-up display (HUD), which projects vital data and allows the pilot to literally keep his head up, looking out through the windscreen, will be a lightweight helmet-mounted display (HMD) incorporating its own HUD-like device. No matter which direction the pilot turns, the same crucial flight and combat data will travel with his helmet visor, never leaving his sight.

The "in-helmet" symbology will be standardized with the MFD symbology. Certain presentations may even have a three-dimensional appearance, enhancing situational awareness. The HMD will also be compatible with night vision systems.

When sensors detect an enemy plane, a data card describing the actual threat aircraft may be called up from the future fighter's data base. The display may be accompanied by stereoscopic three-dimensional warning tones originating from the direction of the threat. This kind of acoustic cuing enhances situational awareness.

As the future fighter manoeuvres into position, a new anti-G suit will inflate giving the pilot added tolerance. The hand grip on the control stick will contain many carefully-designed buttons and switches whose functions will be readily comprehensible. Just by feel, the pilot will know what system he is activating with his fingertips.

Nevertheless, as G-forces build, pilot hand movements become increasingly laborious. In the future cockpit, the pilot need only announce his command verbally. A cockpit computer will have been pre-programmed with the pilot's "voice footprint." With a voice command like "fire" or "launch," the pilot would activate his weapons.

Pictorials such as recently-taken reconnaissance photographs may be displayed with overlapping moving maps and highlighted rings depicting ranges. An onboard computer may quickly generate life-like images of the proposed ground target from assembled data. The picture may be presented from various angles. Simulated bomb runs with projected enemy air defenses will be displayed as well, with an onboard system, reliant upon artificial intelligence, calculating the least hazardous and most effective flight profile.

Since the entry of the F-16 into service there has been the expectation that future fighters will, like the Falcon, have redundant fly-by-wire (FBW) flight control systems (FCSs). The pilot manipulates the control stick and computers read the input, transferring a measured force to an actuator that moves the appropriate control surface just the right amount to achieve the desired effect. These systems are lighter weight and less prone to battle damage. They can be programmed to prevent the aircraft from entering unrecoverable flight attitudes.

Avionics advances over the last 40 years have probably outpaced progress in other aviation-related technologies. From vacuum tubes to transistors to microchips, the modern fighting plane can process and integrate large inputs of data. The current focus is on very high speed integrated circuit (VHSIC) technology. Computers based on VHSIC technology are faster, smaller, lighter, and more reliable.

Silicon, the well-known computer chip material, may give way to gallium arsenide, which offers even more improved performance. But the real revolution around the corner is in fibre optics, also known as photonics. Eventually, much electronic hardware will be replaced by photonic devices, which, using lasers, will directly transmit huge volumes of data at the speed of light. With optical signal processing, no longer will there be the intermediate steps of breaking down sensor-gathered data into digital code and then reassembling the pieces in comprehensible form for transmission.

Photonics technology promises to foster fly-by-light (FBL) flight control systems. These will weigh less and consume less energy than FBW systems. A major advantage of photonic devices is that they are immune to electronic jamming as well as radiation and the electromagnetic effects in the aftermath of a nuclear explosion.

Any future fighter, no matter how sophisticated in itself, will not gain a net advantage in the air battle unless its weaponry has kept pace with the plane's technology. Having a stealthy, super-cruising, thrust-vectoring fighter whose pilot is relegated to using short range or unreliable air-to-air missiles, requiring visual contact with the threat aircraft, negates much of the benefits from the advances incorporated in the airframe.

Not long ago, the AIM-120 AMRAAM (advanced medium range air-to-air missile) was introduced into the operational inventory and was used to enforce "no-fly zones" over portions of Iraq. This is a radar-guided missile intended to replace the sometimes controversial old standby, the AIM-7 Sparrow.

In part, because of AMRAAM's microminiaturized solid state electronics, it weighs approximately one-third less than the Sparrow. In live-fire tests of 128 missiles, AMRAAM proved more reliable than its predecessor.

Capable of engaging the enemy at BVR day or night, in any weather, AMRAAM uses its own guidance system, updated before launch by systems aboard the fighter, to midcourse. At this juncture, the missile can be further updated from the fighter's radar via data link. Then the missile's nose-mounted radar seeker alone provides guidance to the target. The solid rocket motor propels AMRAAM supersonically, but produces only a minimal smoke plume so as not to visually alert the opponent.

AMRAAM may be fired at multiple targets in rapid succession. It is also better protected against ECM. This kind of weapon, operating in a consistently reliable manner in the real-world environment, is absolutely imperative for the other technologies of the future fighter to be meaningful.

Ongoing goals include development of air-to-air weapons that are exceedingly accurate with even longer ranges and that have true "fire and forget" capability. Multiple lock-ons with simultaneous firing is important as well since the future fighter may find itself confronted by many bogeys at once. Trying to maximize kills per pass is the overriding objective. Chances of retaliatory launches are thereby diminished.

For all the high-tech gadgetry going into new fighters, there is, of course, the possibility that the perimeter of sophistication will be pierced. In such a scenario, the encounter will quickly degenerate into an old-fashioned dogfight. Therefore, more prosaic weapons like close-in heat-seeking air-to-air missiles (for example, the Sidewinder) and internally-mounted guns have an important backup role. The fighter pilot must retain the type of air combat manœuvring skills first demonstrated during World War I. It would be a mistake at any time in the near future to remove from the fighter pilot curriculum the training associated with this kind of flying.

For cost and safety reasons a greater percentage of training will occur in advanced motion simulators where, utilizing virtual reality, computer generated images will present an amazingly accurate portrayal of the real-world environment. Only the press of G-forces will be absent in these realistic simulators.

Air-to-ground ordnance has a way to go in continuation of the revolution that has dramatically increased point accuracy. Precision munitions, often called smart bombs, are being developed that will require fewer sorties per target. Advances in IR, millimetre wave, and laser radar technologies will improve detection, identification, tracking, and guidance. For example, the future attack aircraft's pilot, during the attack, will not have to hold on target directing laser energy until impact. Immediately following launch, the weapon will streak to the target under a completely autonomous guidance system. To prevent intercept, the weapon itself will have a stealthy design.

Such weapons will have greatly expanded range so as to keep the attacking aircraft and its crew out of harm's way. Warhead-free very high velocity missiles launched from high altitude where antiaircraft artillery is unable to reach, will rely completely on their energy for destructive force. Hardened targets would not be safe. The extreme speed of these missiles will make them troublesome to intercept.

A new class of weapon is being developed. Known as non-destructive weapons, they would disable vital segments of a warring power's infrastructure without causing permanent or irreversible damage. For example, electrical facilities might be crippled temporarily by interfering with electromagnetic fields. Runways would not be destroyed, but put out of service for the war's duration by spreading super slippery or adhesive agents to their surfaces.

———

Because of harsh economic realities, military planners are having to confront, with heightened intensity, the age-old issue of quantity versus quality. It would be possible, for example, to buy several F-16s off the production line for the price of a single F-22. While the issue does not always require an "either/or" decision, consideration must be given to the changing geopolitical outlook, the kinds of battles that may crop up, and the prospective sophistication of the future threat.

With the defense budgets of the major industrial powers being scaled back there is increasing pressure on the design community to create airframes with multirole capabilities rather than airframes for a lone dedicated mission. Historically, more than a few attempts to design several tasks into a particular plane, making it a "jack of all missions," resulted in an aircraft that performed none of its assignments in an exemplary manner.

Current scarce funding leaves little alternative but to "double up" capabilities. As an example, the F-22 had its original design purpose expanded from solely air-to-air combat to both air-to-air combat and ground attack. Designers, therefore, face a stiff challenge, looking for ways to squeeze more versatility out of their necessarily better performing aircraft.

Another probable impact of declining defense spending is more emphasis on retrofitting and upgrade programs. Aircraft that were constrained to good weather and daytime missions, can perform more effectively in an expanded window of opportunity with the addition of systems developed after the aircraft were designed, like F-16s fitted with LANTIRN (Low Altitude Navigation and Targeting Infrared for Night) systems. The flight envelope of older designs, again like F-16s, can be significantly enhanced through installation of thrust vectoring nozzles on their existing engines. These kinds of modifications to planes already in the inventory help modernize an ageing fleet at relatively low costs.

Development and production costs have risen dramatically and have become prohibitive. Whereas in years past military planes were built for a short service life, future combat aircraft will have to last for periods of up to 50 years. To be useful for such a long time, the design will have to allow for technological growth.

Because relatively small numbers of these aircraft can be afforded, they must meet stringent reliability standards. Attrition rates of yesteryear are unacceptable. During World War II, the Allies operated tens of thousands of heavy bombers, but in the emerging environment with, for example, a total U.S. long-range heavy bomber force of just over 100 aircraft, the loss of even a single plane represents a substantial percentage reduction in the force and a "dent" that is felt.

The often espoused concept of jointness now has come of age. The funding environment requires that the services meld their programs, resulting wherever feasible in the same aircraft for navy and air force. It is no coincidence that the Rafale is going to both the Armée de l'Air and the Aéronautique Navale. If inter-service rivalries can be suppressed, this change will produce positive results.

In the private sector, there is already an industry-wide march toward joint venturing. Because the stakes are so high and developmental costs so great, many companies have decided to share the risks associated with new aircraft programs.

Competitions for lucrative contracts have already become, by and large, contests among teams of the remaining handful of large airframe manufacturers. In the sometimes convoluted world of the aerospace business, team members can actually compete against themselves. As an example, Lockheed at one point belonged to four of the five teams bidding for the ill-fated A/F-X.

Teaming arrangements have even spanned national borders. Eurofighter 2000 is evolving from a four-nation consortium. The X-31 Enhanced Fighter Manœuvrability program is a joint effort of Rockwell in the U.S. and Germany's Deutsche Aerospace. Even the design bureau of the former Soviet Union, at the moment reportedly strapped for cash, have let it be known that they will entertain joint ventures with their Western counterparts. With the longstanding danger of the two traditional superpowers colliding in a nuclear conflagration now consigned to memory, the focus of coming joint ventures, including those between East and West, will be on designs for conventional as opposed to nuclear warfare.

The increasing corporate amalgamation occurring in the face of an ever-diminishing number of new aircraft programs has fostered a shift from design with a highly individualistic imprint to design by committee. Bureaucracy is noted for stifling creativity, so enlightened corporate managers will have to guard against this phenomenon. Perhaps periodic reminders of the success of the Lockheed Skunk Works, a semi-independent think-tank/workshop with a lean staff possessed of a can-do attitude and led by an insightful, decisive executive imbued with uncommon authority, would serve the industry well.

An inescapable problem resulting from the current state of affairs is that the centres of creativity are inexorably dwindling. Companies like Martin, Curtiss, and Fairchild, to name a few, that produced unforgettable combat aircraft, no longer design and build whole aircraft. Some of the remaining airframe manufacturers have gone on acquisition binges, gobbling up competitors, such that precious few sources for new combat aircraft are left. The multitude of sources from the vibrant industry of the past virtually assured that the right plane would emerge at the right time. Now and in the future there will be no margin for error.

In a paradoxical twist, lead times have grown geometrically. Half a century ago it was possible to take a promising idea like the P-80 from letter of intent to first flight in little more than six months. By contrast, the development of the F-22 has taken the better part of a decade from configuration concept to maiden flight of the demonstrators. This future fighter will start entering service in the latter half of the 1990s at the earliest.

Incredible design and manufacturing technologies have been developed without which future combat aircraft would simply not be buildable. Yet for all the advances such as computer-aided design/computer-aided manufacturing (CAD/CAM) and computational fluid dynamics (CFD), lead times are far longer. It is ironic that with the tools of modern technology, current lead times for combat aircraft development drastically exceed the lead times from the days of drafting tables and slide rules.

Of course, there are differences between then and now. The military today expects its planes to have much longer service lives than used to be the case. Tolerances must be much greater. For example, the B-2 Stealth bomber's 172-foot wing span is accurate to within a quarter of an inch, a tolerance unattainable at any prior time. Combat aircraft are being called upon to do more: supercruise stealthily or fly like a plane/land like a helicopter. The high price tags make popular support and the corresponding governmental support erratic. Efforts to hide details of known programs under the cloak of national security generally exacerbate the problem.

In the final analysis, lead times are a function of user need. When a nation is desperate, its industries throw out the book of accepted practices and exhibit ingenuity. Under such circumstances, people are motivated and jobs get done in unprecedented time with a higher level of quality. During World War II, despite the relentless battering sustained by German factories, aircraft production continued. It was the depletion of fuel that fatally handicapped the Luftwaffe.

The latent spirit that can cut lead times is still alive. During the Persian Gulf War, standard protocol was abandoned in a number of instances. An obscure but promising electronic warfare system still undergoing testing was pressed into service. Thus, the E-8 Joint/STARS (Joint Surveillance and Target Attack Radar System) proved an invaluable asset in the prosecution of the air campaign, providing a level of intelligence about enemy ground movements never before available to military commanders. Similarly, the U.S. Air Force rapidly responded to the need for an oversize smart bomb. Disregarding normal development channels, two 4,700 lb laser-guided GBU-28 weapons were successfully deployed as bunker busters. Iraq accepted ceasefire terms the next day.

There seems to be universal agreement that the future battlefield, in all its dimensions, will be increasingly lethal. Effectively commanding forces in such an environment will require real-time and near real-time intelligence disseminated directly to end users. There must also be improvements in the pace and accuracy of bomb damage assessment (BDA). These burdens will fall to a disproportionate degree on specialized reconnaissance aircraft.

Increasing reliance for real-time and near real-time intelligence has been placed on unmanned aerial vehicles (UAVs). The success of early generation remotely piloted vehicles (RPVs) in the 1982 Bekaa Valley battle, in which the IAF deftly employed their drones as decoys to lure hostile SAM batteries to give away their positions, encouraged other countries to pursue UAV technology with renewed vigour.

The effective utilization of UAVs has rekindled debate over whether or not manned aircraft will be necessary or prudent in the years to come. Indeed, moves away from man-in-the-cockpit have already occurred. The Tomahawk land attack missile, in a sense a more sophisticated version of the V1 and V2 weapons of World War II, is a pre-programmed cruise missile that once launched guides itself to the target. The Patriot missile intercepts aerial targets.

UAVs definitely have some advantages over manned aircraft. The most obvious is that they remove the pilot from exposure to possible hazard. They can usually loiter for longer durations than piloted aircraft. Being smaller, they are less expensive. Also, they are less complex and easier to maintain.

Yet, those who forecast the phase-out of manned fighters many years ago were premature. Even now, with enormous strides in technology, most missions require an onboard pilot or pilots. Further, even if the pilot were removed from the cockpit, he would still have to fly the aircraft during battle from a remote station. There would at least be man-in-the-loop, though at some distance.

By being so far removed from the action, the pilot would suffer from the narrow confines of the tactical situation relayed by the plane's sensors. Only by being on the scene may the pilot react to correct problems using his unmatched reasoning powers. Until technology can address the limitations of UAVs, man-in-the-cockpit seems destined to remain an integral aspect of combat flying.

It was perhaps to be expected that as air combat became more sophisticated with speeds and altitudes climbing in a kind of upward spiral, a push into space would occur. When man started to venture into this last frontier, many hoped that space would somehow retain its purity. While it still may not be too late, there are, in addition to spy satellites already in orbit, inklings of exotic planes flying so high and so fast that no SAM can touch them or for that matter even detect them.

In pondering the dazzling advances that have occurred in aerospace technologies and how these may find application in future combat aircraft it is easy to get, no pun intended, carried away. It is important to remember that all the high-tech gadgetry in the world will not replace the heart of the dedicated military pilot. Assuming the requisites of experience, training, and flying skill, the combat pilot who believes in his cause and is motivated gives added dimension to his sophisticated aircraft. High-tech, after all, is only as good as the people manipulating it.

Index

About the Editors

Walter J. Boyne is a retired U.S. Air Force colonel and former director of the Smithsonian Institution's National Air and Space Museum. He is one of the few authors to have had both fiction and nonfiction books on *The New York Times* best-seller list. His thirty books include *The Smithsonian Book of Flight, Eagles at War,* and *Beyond the Wild Blue: A History of the United States Air Force 1947–1997.* Currently, he serves as chairman of Wingspan, an international cable television channel devoted to air and space subjects. He has more than 5,000 hours of flying time in a score of different aircraft ranging from a Piper J-3 to a B-1B bomber. He lives in Ashburn, Virginia, with his wife of forty-five years, the former Jeanne Quigley. They have four children and four grandchildren.

Philip Handleman is a prolific aviation author and photographer. His thirteen books include *Aviation: A History Through Art, The Book of Air Shows,* and *Beyond the Horizon: Combat Aircraft of the Next Century.* His photograph of the Thunderbirds air demonstration team was featured on the U.S. postage stamp commemorating the fiftieth anniversary of the U.S. Air Force. He is president of Handleman Filmworks, a company whose highly acclaimed programs have aired on the Public Broadcasting Service. He has been an active pilot for twenty-seven years, and currently owns and flies two restored aircraft of military lineage, including an open-cockpit Stearman biplane. He and his wife, Mary, divide their time between their home in Birmingham, Michigan, and a private airstrip in the nearby countryside.